RHONDA:
THE WOMAN IN ME
A Journey Through Gender Transition

RHONDA:
THE WOMAN IN ME
A Journey Through Gender Transition

by
Rhonda D. Hoyman
An Autobiography

Editor
Suzanne Gibson

PEARCE PUBLISHERS, INC.
Timonium, Maryland, USA
1-800-662-2354
1999

RHONDA: THE WOMAN IN ME
A Journey Through Gender Transition
by Rhonda D. Hoyman
Edited by Suzanne Gibson

Disclaimer
To respect the privacy of persons mentioned in this book who do not wish their real names revealed, the author has used a substitute name upon their request. However, none of the facts or events regarding her interaction or relationship with them have been altered.

PEARCE PUBLISHERS, INC.
Timonium Maryland, USA
1-800 662-2354
1999

Dinah Tellent Courtney, Literary Consultant
Typesetting by Jeffrey Young & Associates
Cover by Artemis Productions & Publications International, Inc.
Printed in the United States of America.

Publisher's Cataloging-in-Publication
(Provided by Quality Books, Inc.)

Hoyman, Rhonda Dale.
      Rhonda; the women in me: a journey through gender
      transition / Rhonda Dale Hoyman ; editor : Suzanne
      Gibson.—1st ed.
      p. cm.
      ISBN 1-883122-14-7

      1. Hoyman, Rhonda Dale. 2. Transsexuals—United
      States—Biography. 3. Sex change—United States—
      Biography. 4. Gender identity.   I Gibson, Suzanne.
      II. Title.

HQ77.8.H69A3 1998   305.9'066
                            QB198-1415

Library of Congress Catalog Card Number 98-068166

TABLE OF CONTENTS

Dedication

I would like to dedicate this book to my mother and father, Doris and Ray Hoyman, who are the unsung heroes. Just like many parents, they worked hard and sacrificed to make a better life for their children. While my dad did not understand or could not accept my feminine life, he toiled tirelessly to build a better family environment and instill within me a work ethic and moral value system that has helped me be successful in my career and work life, for which I know he was proud.

From my mother I learned a caring and patient spirit, to love God, to take pride in everything I do, to do it to the best of my ability. Through her example I learned to make everyone feel special and loved, just as she did to each of her own five children, always trying to meet their needs when there never was enough time or financial resources to go around. She taught us to enjoy and appreciate the simple things in life, for they are what matters most; to find meaning, a purpose in life, and to strive for my dreams which have now come true.

My mother always did what she thought was best for me and I would never have asked for more either as her son, Ron, or now as her daughter, Rhonda. She has always been and always will be the one person who has been my source of strength and inspiration. In facing my battles in life she is the one who deserves the purple heart for heroism and valor, above and beyond life's call of duty. I love you Mom.

Rhonda

Mother's Thoughts....

I am so glad Rhonda had the perseverance to follow her dreams and finally be a happy person. There is no one more deserving of reaching this goal. Years ago when he tried to explain this to his Dad and I, or even mention the subject, his Dad wanted no parts of even thinking it could be possible. But Ron never showed any anger — just kept on being a good person. I now feel I should have somehow helped Rhonda earlier in life. Since there were 4 other children, it seems I just took it a day at a time — hoping the years would change these ideas.

Doris Stout (Hoyman)

Dad, Mother and Ron

Preface

For 48 years, I had no sense of self worth; I felt life was meaningless. Since age 5, I had a clear understanding that I was really a female trapped in a male body, being forced to conform to the expectations and role I was supposed to live in life. This inner conflict and sense of helplessness was too painful to bear consciously. In order to survive, I suppressed my femininity and suffered in silence. A part of me yearned to experience joy and happiness, but this was not possible. Instead, I projected my own unmet needs onto others and brought joy to their lives. In living to please others, I would lose myself and get lost in taking care of the needs of others, thus creating a purpose to live, to make life meaningful. I became dependent on my need to please others and gain their approval. If people judged me or disapproved, I felt worthless. I had surrendered my personal power and sense of identity to others. Doing became a reason to live.

As I became more aware of the growing sense of emptiness, I knew change was inevitable if I were ever to find true happiness. I was desperate to be me and I wasn't clear how to do that, to become a real and whole person. The pain of being trapped in the "wrong body" created a deep psychological struggle for me. To gain professional help, I chose transsexual life adjustment with Dr. Gregory Lehne, a licensed psychologist and experienced counselor on transsexual life issues, who mentored my social adjustment. For psychotherapy and clinical mindfulness training in Mind/Body Medicine, I was fortunate to work with Patty F. Cummings, M.S.W., L.C.S.W.,-C. This provided me a more holistic approach to my healing. I had never learned or allowed myself to live in the present, to feel my feelings, to know myself or to express true happiness and the joy present at each moment. As I began to regularly practice mindfulness (present moment awareness), this allowed me to deal with the repressed pain and free myself to be my true self. Gradually, I gained a sense of balance in my life. I let go of the need to rationalize my existence. I was able to concentrate on the present and let go of the need to be controlled by the expectations of family, friends, religion, and society. This awareness empowered me to finally gain a greater sense of control of my life.

The challenge of transsexual life adjustment requires a strong sense of purpose and self confidence in order to cope with the unknown, with the physical and emotional pain, and to deal with the daily grind of life. To overcome any sense of fear that would creep in to create self doubt, I learned to do a daily "gut check." This would allow me to choose more consciously how I wanted to respond, as opposed to mindlessly reacting out of fear of what others might think.

My life's experiences can be compared to a raw piece of iron which normally could be heated by the hot fires and then hammered by the blacksmith to conform to the desired shape. But, in this case, no matter how many times Ron tried to yield to the heat and mold the life he was asked to live, in facing the trials of life, the shape of life as a man could never maintain its form. It was not until the body image everyone knew and loved as Ron was allowed to be skillfully reshaped by surgeons, that the bonding of body, mind and spirit finally formed Rhonda and the total person she was always meant to be. God allowed the horseshoe everyone thought they saw to be molded into a beautiful, ornamental rose.

Being mindful has allowed me to live in the present, to feel all that life offers and to gain a greater sense of personal acceptance in my heart. Each day I have a greater love for life and for myself. I am now free to be the me I've come into this world to be.

As I continue to remain present to life as it unfolds moment by moment, I feel my wholeness. I am complete and fulfilled beyond my wildest expectations.

When you have finished with my story, I hope you will be able to see that not only was it never too late for me, that it also is never to late for your life to be all that you want it to be.

If for any reason you would like to send your thoughts, feedback or correspondence to me, please use this special address below.

Rhonda Hoyman
P.O. Box 536
Riderwood, MD 21139-0536

Introduction

When Rhonda first came to my office as Ron in 1994, she seemed like an unlikely candidate to accomplish her stated goal to live her life as a woman. She had recently married for the third time, so her decision to start the process of sex reassignment at nearly age 50 seemed belated. She was successful as a male. It was hard to imagine a female living in Ron's body.

But my job is not to judge or make decisions for people. Instead, I try to help them find what works for them, to make their lives work better. While Rhonda seems to recall that I told her she was a "classic transsexual", my memory is different. I believe that I told her what I tell all individuals seeking sex reassignment:

> You are the one who has to live your life. I hear that you are unhappy with yourself as a male. You do not like living as a male; you think living as a woman would be better for you. I don't know what will work best for you, and I don't think you know with 100% certainty yet either. I am willing to work with you in a process that will help you decide whether living as a woman is right for you. I will try to help you make the fewest number of mistakes as possible, to avoid the changes that are hardest to reverse should you change your mind. I know that you don't think you will do that, but some people start this process and find that it is not the right thing for them, it is not what they expected, and so they stop it. There is no success or failure here — our goal is not to remain a man or to become a woman, but to become fully functional and satisfied with who you are and how you live your life. As we go through the process, I want you to know for yourself that you gave it your best attempt — if it is the right decision, you will go on living as a woman. But if it is not right for you, I hope that you will be able to go back living as a man with a better feeling that this is the right decision for you.

Rhonda was not interested in therapy as it is traditionally conceived. She was not interested in reflecting upon her motivations or experiences or history that led her to the point where she was dissatisfied with herself as a male and desired to transform herself into a female. She was not interested in trying to see if anything could be done which might make her happy living her life as a male. But she is the type of person who wants to do things exactly the right way. For sex reassignment, she knew that this meant following the Standards of Care of the Harry Benjamin International Gender Dysphoria Association, which guided our professional relationship. Involvement with a mental health professional experienced in the evaluation and treatment of individuals with gender dysphoria is part of the process in order to be recommended for hormonal sex reassignment and ultimately surgical sex reassignment.

Diagnostic criteria for gender identity disorders are straightforward. Basically the person reports strong desire to be the other sex and expresses persistent discomfort with his or her sex, and sex organs or characteristics. These criteria reflect self-diagnosis, and are often expressed by the individual cross dressing and seeking out sex reassignment procedures. The professional who sees an individual claiming to be a transsexual may initially have only that person's word and presentation as evidence for his or her underlying feelings of discomfort or desire to be the other sex. What if these feelings are only transitory, true at some times in a person's life but not at other times? What if the person does not accurately represent his or her status to the professional? Sex reassignment should not be a permanent, irreversible solution to a temporary problem.

The way professionals deal with this dilemma is to require that the candidate for sex reassignment procedures go through the "real life experience." We want to know, independently of the person's word, that they have consistently desired to live as the other sex for at least one to two years. This usually requires that some professional has been following the person for this length of time. Then we expect the person to be in psychotherapy with us and/or to live full-time in the desired sex role for at least three months before we make a recommendation for hormonal sex reassignment. We require one year of living full-time in the desired sex role for a recommendation for surgical sex reassignment. The real life experience requires major rehabilitation in the desired sex role, which can be very difficult as Rhonda's experience shows. Feedback experiences from others is more effective than feedback from therapists, because the general public is not as kind and tolerant as therapists strive to be. Being able to face the potential rejection and humiliation from others is a powerful test. Going through the physical procedures can also be very painful. The real life experience literally separates the men from the women — and they learn from their own experience, not from professionals telling them.

Rhonda approached the process of sex reassignment as if she were doing a major renovation on a house, a type of work she was familiar with. I felt that I was more in the role of a helpful housing inspector. In my helpful role, I made suggestions for how to do things to be in compliance with code. She did not necessarily take my suggestions, or seek my advice in advance, which is her right. There is not always a right or wrong way to do things, so I can only offer examples from my clinical experience of what has or has not worked for others in similar situations. At other times I was more in the role of the inspector, ultimately verifying for the sex reassignment surgeon that the work was done according to code. I provide documentation as needed to verify for others what Rhonda is doing. I act as a intermediary in helping a person deal with employers or others, explaining her situation and making suggestions for how she can be accommodated. Rhonda did not require much of this, partly because she is so organized and articulate in presenting herself.

Rhonda's rehabilitation as a woman focused very much on using professional procedures to physically alter her body: electrolysis, hormones, cosmetic surgeries. At a basic level, transsexualism is a body image disorder. It is not just about clothes, or make-up or the public presentation necessary to pass the scrutiny of others. It is about altering the physical body to more closely correspond to a mental body image. As she has described in detail, Rhonda underwent numerous plastic surgeries at great expense and personal pain and suffering. These were not essential to passing in social settings as a woman. Even the genital sex reassignment surgery which Rhonda had was not necessary for social passing—the results will ultimately be seen only by few, if any, when Rhonda engages in intimate sexual relations. The transformation of the body was something which Rhonda did for her own mental satisfaction. Her body is her own, she lives there, and she designed it for her comfort. It never ceases to humble me that it should be so much easier to alter the body for these individuals than it is to change their way of thinking about themselves. You cannot talk an individual with a gender-identity body image disorder out of the way they ultimately think about their body. Body image disorders are rampant in our culture, where "normal" appearing people are preoccupied with being too fat or not muscular or too flabby or want different noses or breasts or hair color or want to look like a different age than they are. One of the wonders of modern technology is that individuals can alter their bodies to reflect more closely their idealized (and at times unrealistic) images of themselves.

You see the results in this book. Rhonda has fashioned her body into a beautiful house reflecting her concept of herself. She seems to be very comfortable living there, much happier than when I first met her. She has achieved her goals. Her story is but one story, her house is but one house. You might not choose to live there, your house might look much different, but her experience has shown her that it is right for her.

Rhonda's story shows the difficulty of dealing with gender dysphoria — and shows that the decision to go through the process of sex reassignment is not a casual decision, but a long hard process which only the most committed would endure. No one is going to be influenced to run out and start the process of sex reassignment as a result of reading Rhonda's story, unless they can relate to her experience and are not deterred by all the pain and suffering she went through in the process. But by sharing her story, she hopes that you will understand that what she did was right for her.

Gregory K. Lehne, Ph.D.
Licensed Psychologist
Assistant Professor, Medical Psychology
Johns Hopkins University School of Medicine

Dr. Lehne Congratulates Rhonda
on Her Successful Transition

Chapter 1

Reflections on the Early Years

As one of the first generations of baby boomers, some would say I've experienced the best years of my life, the formative, fun-loving, carefree days that society associates with youth. Yet for me, at 51 years of age, I am physically upon the anniversary of the first year of my life and only two-years-old in my life experiences as a woman. Is the glass half empty or half full? Will the second 50 years be as good or better than the first 50? While I cannot answer that question for anyone but myself, I hope in some way my story will prove to be an inspiration.

I am Rhonda Dale Hoyman, and this is the first year in three years that I'm not recovering from major surgery. Finally, my body, mind, and spirit are healed and in accord with each other. In the fall of 1995, I took charge of my life deciding finally to take that one total and irreversible step. For 48 years, I was known as Ron, a hard-working, conservative, Christian, Republican, and vocational educator, but in reality, I was a woman trapped hopelessly in a male body.

There comes a time in every person's life when there is no alternative but change in order to find peace within. If you are to be truly happy, to live each day to the fullest, to have choices (versus being controlled by conditions and expectations of society, work, friends, and family), there is no alternative but to change. While I wish I could have found the guts, the support, the resources, and the inner strength to overcome my fear and make this change earlier in my life,

I have learned it is never too late to do what your heart is telling you. I hope in some small way my story will enable you to take that first step, to tackle the small or large issue which keeps you from being your true self. It was only in finding true inner peace and love for myself that I could then love others.

I can honestly say that the physical, emotional, mental, and financial sacrifices and the pain I have endured the last two years has been more than compensated for by the total feeling of peace and inner joy I now experience each and every day. Even if I die tomorrow, it will all have been worth it. To have one moment in time to be all that you want to be, is worth whatever it takes to get there. If I can do it, you can, too; for "I can't" is not in my vocabulary, and it never will be again.

I was not born with a silver spoon in my mouth, but my parents gave me the love, care, and values, which have enabled me to always strive to be the best I can. In a crowded Wilkinsburg, Pennsylvania hospital (just outside Pittsburgh), Doris and Ray Hoyman had a baby boy, weighing in at 5 lbs. 6 + oz. and measuring 19 + in. Mother said I was just big enough not to be an incubator baby, as babies of that size were called in 1947. As was typical for World War II Baby Boomers, my mother and I spent time in a converted sun porch of the overcrowded hospital during the first few days of my life that May. I was the first carrot red-haired baby in the Baker/Hoyman clan in three generations; I was told people couldn't believe I was my mother and father's child.

My mother breast fed me for the first three and one half months. We lived in the upstairs apartment of a cold and cramped, wood-framed duplex home on Westminister Avenue in Greensburg, Pennsylvania. Always fighting off illness as a baby (I had colic, whooping cough, and diphtheria

Mother and Ron

all in the first few months of my life), my mother proved a real trooper — staying up with me most nights, rocking me to keep me from crying. She'd sit in an old, oak rocking chair my father rescued from a fire. I still cherish that rocker today; it's refinished and is in my family room. With my dad working long hours and two to three jobs to make ends meet, my mother got creative; and, at night, would take me on long trolley rides to keep me from crying and to put me to sleep. It took a lot of love to pull me through that first year of life. I'll never be able to repay my loving mother.

Some early memories from the first years of my life showed Ron's toys and gifts were a little rubber squeaky,

Ron, Age 2

press-me toy, a little pipe my dad gave me, just like his, a red wagon, metal tricycle, rubber tool set, truck, and a cowboy outfit.

To have a back yard and play area, my Grandfather Baker moved to Greensburg, Pennsylvania, buying a large, wooden-frame duplex home on Seminary Avenue. There was a sidewalk to ride my bike, other neighbor kids to play with, and a common door for me to visit my grandparents anytime.

My third year was when I began to interact with life. I first learned to manage money when my grandfather took me to the bank and gave me a penny to put in my new account. Instead of putting the penny in the bank, I asked the clerk for a penny, which she kindly gave me. The wonders of television were beginning to sweep the country at this time, and my dad worked extra hard so we could get our first small picture (9"-10" screen), black and white television set. I was fascinated by this modern, magical box, with my favorite show being "Howdy-Doody," a freckle-faced, red-head puppet. There was Clarabell the Clown, Dilly-Dally, the little boy with big ears, and their leader, Buffalo Bob. With my carrot-top red hair, freckles, and plaid shirt, I was even referred to by some neighbors as a little "Howdy Doody." Westerns were also popular at that time; my hero was Hopalong Cassidy, with his black hat and white horse.

My new baby sister, Mary, came along when I was only a year and a half. She was my best friend as we grew up, playing toy soldiers, Lincoln Logs, blocks, Cowboys and Indians, and doctor together. Having a sister allowed me to play house and dolls, yet I was not really supposed to do these things. I wanted my own baby doll, but I was not allowed to have one.

At almost three years old, my father's interest and experience on the farm resulted in my receiving three baby chicks, five ducks and Skippy, my very first puppy. This little square-nosed terrier quickly found his way into my heart, and I loved playing with him in our fenced back yard. On my third birthday, I received a two-piece suit, a big tool set, a Mickey Mouse car, and a new coloring book. As a child I loved to draw and color, taking pride at an early age to stay inside the lines. Living in a new house, right next door to my grandparents, had a big influence on my skills as a carpenter and overall handyman. I used to spend many hours following my Grandfather Baker, handing him tools and being his little helper.

Childhood was enjoyable. I helped my mother with chores, spent time with my animals, and just had fun being a kid. With no other boys living on my street, I played with Mary, the next door neighbor, Patty, and the other three girls down the street. Often we would play house; I always volunteered to be the mother or one of the girls in the pretend family. It wasn't until years later that I realized my early play must have been an indication of my true feelings and identity.

A year later, when I was five, I was playing dress up at home with my sister and some of her friends. I put on a white party dress, white socks and shoes, a ribbon in my hair, and some of my mom's lipstick. That is the first time I can remember really longing to be a little girl, not just in playing dress up or house. The memory is still so vivid, because my father came home early that evening. The fear of God rushed into me, for I knew he would not approve of his son looking like a little girl. Quickly, I darted behind the old living room couch, as he came through the front door. I kneeled down on the floor, careful not to make a sound. As he passed through the dining room and onto the kitchen to see what was for supper, I ran up the stairs, my heart pounding. I hurriedly washed my face in the upstairs bathroom and changed back into my own play clothes. Mary and my friends chuckled, but, thankfully, they didn't let on what had happened.

While I was raised mostly around my mother, and spent more time playing with little girls than little boys, I also had many boy toys, and I was expected to act like a boy. I did have the more traditional male experiences while working around my grandfather and playing with my male cousins when the families got together. My mother loved me, but she never babied me or encouraged me to be like a little

Ron with Traditional Toys for Boys

girl. On my fifth birthday, I received a suit, a tent, a little baseball, and a toy gun.

That September I started kindergarten in the red-brick, three-story elementary school, five blocks away. This half-day experience went wonderfully, as I enjoyed coloring, learning my ABC's, taking naps with my blanket, meeting new friends, and getting to play on the playground. My marks were noted as "passing," with one "outstanding." My mother said I adored my teacher, Mrs. Griffith.

Yes, I was fortunate to have the love and support of a caring mother, father, grandparents, and relatives, who allowed me to be a kid and enjoy life. I was expected to grow up a healthy boy and value society's expectations: family, honor, respect, and fear of authority. I was expected to make the most of life as the first born in a family struggling to make ends meet. It was a simple life, better I think than the environment many children are raised in today. My upbringing and the outside influences in my life did not create, nor could they alter my desire to be a female.

Chapter 2

The Bunny Bread Years

Little Ronnie eventually became just plain Ron. I explored the world around me, and I was a little boy everyone seemed to like. Yet, I almost feel (as was the case throughout the first 48 years of my life) that I was a spectator. I was never allowed to be a girl and certainly was not the woman I've come to know, love, and be today.

My world was beginning to open up to me, as it expanded from a six to eight block radius, beyond the houses, friends, and sidewalks of Seminary Avenue. I began walking with my friends the five blocks to school. I had graduated from my tricycle and scooter (which knew every crack and bump in the slate and cement sidewalk) to a red 20" bicycle with white stripes on the fenders, a horn, and training wheels bolted securely to the rear axle. To a six-year-old, this was the big time and the best present a little guy (or girl) could ever want. I'd even say it compared in many ways with the freedom and thrill of my first car.

I still continued to play with Mary and our girlfriends on Seminary Avenue. We went on to such activities as playing dress up (I loved exploring the world of make-up) and camping out overnight in the back yard. After a lot of practice, safety lessons, a sticker on my bike from the city, validating I was a good bike rider, and my mother and grandmother's warnings to look all ways, I was ready to ride five to ten minutes from home.

Home on Seminary Avenue

Life was not fun and games, as I had difficulty entering first grade. I was required to go to a special school for a remedial reading program after my regular classes. The extra work paid off; and, by the end of the first grade, I had caught up with my class, although reading and language arts have never been my strong points (that's why I'm writing this book).

I do remember having a very strict first grade teacher; and if you did something wrong or talked during class, she would call you up to the front of the room, make you hold out your hands, and then hit them with her yardstick in front of everyone. While a severe punishment by today's discipline standards, it was a lesson you never wanted to repeat after the first offense. The expectation to respect authority, follow the rules, and respect your elders went without question at home. If you did not listen, Mom would point out the errors of your ways, and Dad would reinforce that with his special paddle. Needless to say, I was a good boy 99% of the time - - "Mother's good little boy." In reality it was this strict discipline code, along with my desire to please others (even at this early age) and the repulsiveness of violence and fighting (more of my little girl coming out), that I was, throughout my entire childhood, a model of obedience, or as others might say, a goody two-shoes.

Walking to school introduced me to a new playmate named Charles, who lived on the next street below me. We became easy friends, and I was encouraged to play with him more than with my girlfriends on Seminary Avenue. Thus, with the freedom of "wheels" in the summer of the seventh, eighth, and ninth years of my life, Charles and I rode all around the neighborhood. We usually rode the quiet, tree-lined city street toward the north and west of home. The south and east brought you closer to the actual town of Greensburg, which was no place for a novice bike rider. There was Murphy's Five and Dime General Store with the soda fountain — a big thrill for me when I had a few pennies (hard to come by in those days). I'd survey all three of the penny candy stores and neighborhood convenience stores (no such thing as a 7-11 store) before making my decision. I worked very hard as a child, being mother's little helper and performing a lot of chores for a nickel allowance every two weeks, so I made my selections wisely. Sometimes I'd only buy one or two pieces at a time, instead of blowing my whole nickel in one shop. The day of two pieces of candy for a penny are history, but they did teach me, from an early age, the value of money. No one gave me anything in life; I have always worked hard for what I have.

Even though my father did not have the time or personal interest to go to church with us, my mother instilled within me a strong sense of religious values and love for the Lord. I went to Bible school each summer as a child and Sunday school most Sundays. In Greensburg, we could walk about six blocks to the large orange-bricked Presbyterian church on the corner. Even though I was young, I went to the regular

The Little Man—Dressed for Church

Sunday service. My mother usually sat on the left side of the sanctuary, facing the pastor. She'd sit near one of the wooden pillars, so my sister and I would not disturb the service if we made a sound. I learned early on not to make a peep in church, no matter what. My mother helped by bringing crayons to color with and giving me Saltine crackers on Communion Sunday. I never could figure out why I couldn't have one of the little glasses of Welch's grape juice.

Seriously, this respect, love, and faith in God has proved so meaningful in my life — a cornerstone, which has enabled me to handle many of the trials and tribulations I have faced in life. I'm now a new member of a beautiful church family at Towson Presbyterian Church.

When a new baby sister, Cheryl, arrived, I was needed more than ever to help set the table, feed the animals (my pal Skippy was never without a fresh drink of water), dust the furniture, and help babysit when mom was busy. Going to the grocery store was a big event each Thursday or Friday at the local A & P Supermarket; it was one of the few times each week we got out or had a chance to ride in the car. There were no McDonald's in town at that time, but a new local restaurant, Big Chef Hamburger Drive-in, did open up. Eating a store-made hamburger and fries was a real big treat.

Second grade was an improvement over first, because I had a real nice, red-haired teacher (Wonder why I liked her?), and at Christmas we got to bring big cardboard boxes to class and paint them to look like a real train. With manual and artistic skills as my strengths, I enjoyed and excelled in this environment.

The winters in western Pennsylvania were always cold and snowy, and I had the opportunity of making a few pennies by being a helper for my grandfather, who was now an elementary school custodian. I would go with him when school was out to shovel coal in the furnace, keep the boiler running, and help an elderly lady a few houses up the street with her furnace. There were coal chute windows in the front of each home that went to the basement, and even though I was little, I went every day to Mrs. Whample's to shovel coal in her furnace and clear the ashes into metal garbage cans. The ashes and cinders were then used on the icy streets in the winter. There always seemed to be something for little Ron to do.

Now that we were older, Mary and I were allowed to look through the Sears, Penney's, and Montgomery Ward's catalogs to pick out (up to twenty dollars worth) the toys we wanted from Santa. I knew I could not pick girl toys, so I selected my Red Ryder sled and Lionel train set (which I still have). I shared my toys with my sisters, so I could play with their dollhouses.

The one big event each month was when I got to go out on a Saturday night with my grandparents. I'd go with them on their weekend shopping trips to towns such as McKeesport, Irwin, and Monroeville. We would head out in the early afternoon, always stopping at a five and dime store, and then eat out at Islay's Ice Cream Store or Eat and Park Family Style Diner. We'd end up at the auction house where we'd sometimes stay until midnight. The auction house was an old barn with no heat, so in the winter we'd sit with a blanket over our legs, donning hats, gloves, and mittens, as we heard the loud call of the auctioneer above the sounds of the horses below clattering against the plank board flooring. As a treat, I was always allowed to purchase a quarter grab bag filled with a little toy, some candy, and maybe even a toothbrush. I'll never forget one night as a nine-year-old, I received a small mirror and lady's powder compact in my grab bag. My grandmother said she would buy me another, but I said, "That's okay, Nanny. I can give this one to my sisters." In truth, I was very happy with the compact, a prized possession I hid in the back of my dresser drawer for many years after that. The little girl in me finally had something of her own.

During that period in my life, advertisements began to have a big influence in sales. None was more impressionable on me than Bunny Bread. Bunny Bread was the store-bought white bread, which had a special bunny sticker on each loaf. I collected as many as possible. My mother bought Bunny Bread just to keep me happy. Besides, my grandmother said, "If you eat the crust of the bread, it'll put hair on your chest. It will make a little man of you." I, of course, could care less about the crust (or the hair); but went along with the idea just to get the sticker.

Even though my two sisters and I got along well sharing our one small bedroom, it was getting close to my 10th birthday and time for me to have my own room — so my father insisted. In reality, we were really living as three sisters in a room. Dad also wanted to live in the country. However, with three children and working at the post office annex moving mail (postal workers in those days did not make as competitive a wage as they do today), he had to work extra hard to get ahead in making this dream a reality. So, he worked a second job with a buddy of his, putting up aluminum awnings in the evenings for Sears and Roebuck. Finally, his big break came when he announced he had made a deal with Uncle Harvey (on the Hoyman's side of the family) to purchase three acres on the sloping side of a hill about five miles southwest of Greensburg.

While I was happy for the family, this meant my whole life, my friends, and my security system was about to change. At the same time, my dominant, feminine feelings loomed. I felt trapped in a boy's body, doomed to a boy's lifestyle. I had no idea what was going on inside of me. I remember one day we were riding out to take a look at the new house. I was feeling that life was quite meaningless; in fact, I wanted to open the car door of my dad's blue and white, four-door Chevy, and jump out, ending what seemed to me at the time a very unhappy life, with no hope of self-expression. Being raised with a high sense of morals and values, I did not act on my emotions, but the temptation to end my life at that time was stronger than anyone ever knew.

I rounded out the end of my ninth year of life with the chicken pox in December, 1956, and the mumps in early May, 1957. That may not seem like such a big deal in today's era of modern medicine, but at that time, I had to be quarantined and fight my illnesses alone. I was beginning to question life, and the struggles ahead of me—this trapped, little girl, was emerging. There seemed no way out.

Chapter 3

The Country Boy: Puberty

The big move came faster than I anticipated; my father worked tirelessly over the summer of my tenth year to put in a foundation, with some of his friends' help. We helped on weekends, cleaning up the work area. The big excitement came when we were allowed to select the color for our rooms. I, of course, picked green, my favorite color.

Late that fall, we moved into a skeleton of a house: plywood floors, an unfinished basement, one bathroom, no curtains, a reddog-shale driveway, and mud up to our ankles when it rained. To the Hoyman family, it felt like a mansion.

I started fourth grade at St. Clair Elementary School, four miles from our new home. Third grade at my old school seemed so uneventful compared to this modern, one-floor elementary school, with its long hallway and a class for each grade (one through six) on each side of the school. I was lucky enough to get Mrs. Wofford as my fourth grade teacher. Not only was she a nice lady, but my mother said she was a real good teacher. Mrs. Wofford became a positive influence on our family; she taught my other three sisters and brother, as well.

This was also my first experience at riding a school bus. The road down the long hill was dusty when it was dry and muddy when it rained, but Mary and our new neighbor friend, Denise, caught the bus on that road each morning. We wore rubbers on our shoes and buckle boots in the winter, as we sloshed our way to the bus stop in bad weather. It

The Last One Picked

wasn't a ten-mile hike in the snow to a one-room school-house, but it was no picnic either — no soccer-moms with their minivans. We had one car, which my dad used for work, and there was no other transportation until he came home.

There were three boys living at the bottom of the hill. I tried to fit in, but it was a futile effort. I had little time to play, since I was the oldest and my father worked two jobs. I was forced at an early age to take on a lot of man/boy responsibilities around the house. This included outside chores, such as picking up rocks and taking care of the garden, and helping with housecleaning chores, plus watching after my two sisters. I was also small and skinny for my age and did not fit the rough and tumble boy image. For example, I joined the Little League baseball team, and games were played on a ballfield two miles away in Young-wood. I had to ride my bike to get there on back country roads. When I did arrive, I was always the last one picked and only played right field in the last innings (when we were usually well ahead). The neighbor boys were much better than I — the stars of the team. They were nice to me, but I could not keep up with them. In reality, I was the little girl on the boys' team.

At Halloween, the neighbor boys would play tricks, like hide in the woods and throw tomatoes at cars. I had no interest in this type of activity, especially considering what would happen if my dad ever caught me doing such a thing.

I had more fun, when I did have play time with Mary. Often, we would hike over the hill to the city landfill close to our home to salvage other peoples' still usable junk. We were dirt poor, so I would make a bookshelf or stand for my closet out of old crates and recycled wood. I would also make play stoves, refrigerators, and sinks for my sisters to play with, painting them to look like the store-bought items we could not afford.

Fifth grade at school seemed rather uneventful, but I do remember getting swung around like a rag mop by many of the larger girls in class during square dance training. I still have never learned to dance. Now, at least I can learn the right way—to follow and not lead.

I tried to overcome my shyness and be accepted as Ron by my classmates, yet by sixth grade, I was dying to be one of the girls. I became the class clown instead. I've always felt more comfortable interacting with girls and women, although this was not an acceptable or socially correct role for me at age twelve. I attempted to make fun of things, to crack jokes when I could — even at myself. Mr. Mosser, my first male teacher, called me his juvenile Red Skelton, the famous slapstick comedian at the time. One day, he even made me come up and sit on his lap and tell a joke in front of the entire class to try and teach me the error of my ways. He had crippling leg injuries himself and had to get around on crutches all of the time. While he did not know, and I could not tell him, what was eating away at me on the inside, as I look back on it, I think he knew something was hurting

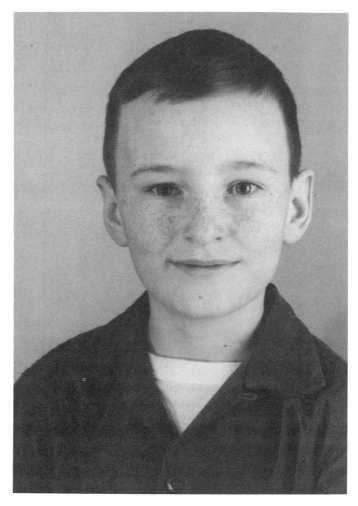

The Bruiser

me. Being small in stature, the other kids, especially the boys, gave me the nickname "Bruiser" — a resemblance which could not have been further from the truth. Thus, I joked and faked my way to social acceptance.

I learned early on in life not to feel, for to feel was to experience rejection and ridicule in life. My body, that of a pint-sized country boy, was merely an outward shell for an increasingly jealous, very feminine, little girl. I had to deny feelings, for to feel was to suffer mental pain, rejection, and anxiety at unbearable levels. After 48 years of not feeling, one of the things I have to do is learn how to feel, how to have fun — to let my hair down, so to speak. I truly love myself, but still have a long way to go in learning to really feel and enjoy the life and little girl, young woman, and woman I suppressed for all those years.

In many ways, I lived my life through others, losing myself in wholesome family shows of the time , like *Leave it to Beaver, The Donna Reed Show,* and *Father Knows Best.* Maybe that is why I am a traditional, old-fashioned values type of woman — somewhat like June Cleaver and Donna Reed, the role models I loved to watch. My favorite role model and actress, the one I most wanted to be like because of her beauty, style, and classy, romantic personality was (and still is) Ann Margaret. That is meant to be a compliment to her as much as she was an inspiration to the little girl and young woman who lived within my heart and soul.

Being one of the oldest grandchildren on the Hoyman side, and a boy (lucky me), I was also expected to take my turn on Grandfather Clair and Step-Grandmother Emmy Hoyman's dairy farm, where my dad was raised with his two other brothers and five sisters. I began my annual summer visits to Grandpa Hoyman's farm, about 15 miles away from the Youngwood area, near Delmont, Pennsylvania. He had forty acres of a hillside farm and just as many dairy cattle (black and white Holsteins) to milk twice a day. I found it odd to go to bed at 8 o'clock each night before the sun went down, sleeping on the living room couch, and then getting up at 4 am to perform the morning milking. I never wanted to get up, but when I walked out into the crisp, morning air, wet dew brushing my boots, I picked up real fast.

The first few years, we didn't even have automatic milkers, which made milking a hand-combat experience. I had a variety of jobs, from milking, to feeding straw to the cows, to cleaning out cow manure with a pitch fork. Finally, around 7:30 in the morning, we would finish milking and sit down to a hearty breakfast, officially starting the day. We would have eggs, toast, bacon, ham, fruit, vegetables, fried potatoes, and about anything else you could fit on the table. Grandpa Hoyman was a stocky man; he must have weighted over 250 pounds. He could eat an entire ham by himself for breakfast, and he used to look at puny me and say, "Son, you eat like a piss-ant."

After breakfast, we would feed the chickens and pigs, plow fields, repair fences, tend the garden, go to town, and any number of other chores before the afternoon milking, finally supper, then right to bed to start all over again the next morning. It was a hard life, and I learned something different each summer for the next five years before going into the military service.

I gained an appreciation for my grandfather, farm life, and the simple style of living — an insight to my own father's background that I wouldn't trade for the world. I value that experience now more than I did then. My grandfather knew it was tough for me to keep up with my bigger male cousins, but he never knew I was really a girl, trying to fill a boy's shoes.

Chapter 4

Coping with Adolescence

At twelve, I was not a large boy, but I was building up my stamina, and my parents began relying on me more to help our family keep ahead. My third sister, Darlene, was by now almost a year old, and mother was pregnant with, Bill, my only brother. Since I had little interest in being a boy, I found value in life by putting the needs of others ahead of my own — a survival technique I would use for years to come.

For the next three years of junior high school, I spent little effort on my schoolwork and so-called social life. Traveling now in the other direction on the school bus, I rode to the center of a small town called Youngwood, Pennsylvania, famous for its hometown hero, pro football player, George Blanda. The school was then called Youngwood Senior High, an older, but sturdy three-story red brick building. I did my homework at lunchtime, tuning noise and others out. After all, I was definitely not interested in girls or the social scene, and I was not going to be in any in-crowd. Most days after school I'd go right to my room, completing my homework during the hour before supper. My father expected supper on the table at four-thirty each evening. He was now a rural mail carrier and started his day twelve hours earlier, when we were all still asleep. My mother was a terrific cook, who spoiled all of us with great home-cooking on a shoe-string budget. Meat and potatoes were a staple, and twice a year my dad would bring home half a steer, from Grandfather Hoyman's, to stock up our large freezer. We would work long

Ron and Grandfather Hoyman

into the night, cutting and wrapping meat with white freezer paper. Being diligent with my homework helped me earn average grades even though I had little interest in school (except for the Industrial Arts shop class). In shop, I continued to build and refine the tool skills I'd already learned at home.

My nickname from sixth grade, "Bruiser," followed me through junior high; some of my old friends were in my homeroom. I rolled with the punches and kept cracking jokes as my year book shows: "To the roughest kid in school, Rick;" "Bruiser, a real nice boy. Good luck, Georgina;" and "Good luck to a boy who was the funniest kid in the school, Bob."

Things got out of hand in ninth grade. Knowing I had no interest in going to a school dance, much less girls or a social life, my ninth grade homeroom voted me Homecoming King as a joke. This meant I had to go to the dance with Georgina, one of the prettiest and most popular girls in the school. I went to the big dance, even though in my heart I wanted to be the class queen, not the king. Georgina knew exactly what was going on as far as my being her date, but she was nice enough to show up with me. After introductions, I slipped into the background, as she joined her real boy-friend, also a classroom king and school sports star. I believe they eventually won the ninth grade king and queen, and I was happy for them. Not in my element at all, I milled around, drinking punch, not dancing, and felt relieved when the night was over. I was a teenage girl trapped in a boy's body.

With the birth of my third sister, our three-bedroom house had gotten too crowded, so I volunteered to move my bed and modest belongings to the corner of the basement across from the furnace to have some privacy and stay warm in the winter. While it took a few years before I had walls for my new bedroom, an old carpet kept my feet warm, and I was happy there. Keeping my feminine feelings to myself, I at least could still hide my compact in my dresser drawer with an old pair of my mother's high heels. I cherished and wore the heels secretly, when I knew everyone had gone to sleep. I kept the high heels from a leftover Halloween outing, the only time I would get dressed up as a girl, which was considered acceptable. It was funny to others, when in reality, it was the only evening of the year I did not feel funny.

As I continued to mature, I had increasingly strong dreams of being dressed up as, or being a real girl. One morning, I had a strong dream, my first wet dream. It scared me, and I told my mother about this experience and also how I'd dreamed of being a girl.

"What's going on with me?" I asked her. "What am I to do? Am I being bad or punished for my thoughts?"

My mother was surprised by the depths of my feminine feelings, but very understanding and pleased that I had enough confidence in her to tell her. Even though she wanted to help me, she needed some time to think before giving me any answers. The one thing she said not to do was to tell my father; it was our secret. At that time, near 1960, there was no common knowledge of the term transsexualism. John Money's gender identity clinic was not established (at least to our knowledge), and we had no understanding of the reality of my feelings, personhood, or needs.

A short time later, mother asked me to come into one of the bedrooms and listen to a recorded explanation of sexuality. This was informative, but I learned a lot more listening to the boys talk at the bus stop. My interest was in being a female, living like a female, and having sex as a female. My sexual urges were not like the drives a man or teenage boy would have. I have never considered my sexual identity as homosexuality. I am strictly a heterosexual female. Mother made an appointment for me to speak with our pastor, a rather young Presbyterian, married and in his late twenties. I remember going into his office one evening when it was dark outside, feeling scared, not knowing what I should say. He greeted me nicely and asked what I would like to talk about, even though my mother had already confided in him about "the problem."

Slowly, I began to tell him everything I had told my mother, explaining that I really felt like a girl, even though I had to act like and be treated like a boy. His main response to me was that it was probably a phase I would eventually grow out of and that in a few years, when I had started dating girls, my feelings and interests would probably change. In other words, he didn't have a clue as to what to tell me. This was my first experience with poor counseling. I left feeling misunderstood; feminine interests bottled inside.

Mother and I talked at times, but she didn't know what else to do, and couldn't afford a counselor, even if she did know of a good one. We lived paycheck to paycheck, and she had the daily care of my other brothers and sisters to worry about. Since my full transition to a female, my mother has continued to be very supportive. When I told her that I was beginning my life change three years ago, her only regret was that she wished she could have helped me reach my dream and womanhood earlier in my life. My response was, "Mom, I want you to know that there was no help available at that time. You did the best you could and there is a time and place for everything. This is my time and I have learned that it's never too late." The love, care, and life skills my mother and father taught me gave me the solid foundation and ability to be the person and the total woman I am today.

To deal with my inner frustrations and suppressed identity, I did quietly and secretly raid the bathroom hamper, dressing for a few minutes each week in girl's/women's clothing. I would find a bra, pair of panties, blouse, and skirt or dress which I could wear to experience a few fleeting moments of pleasure — a surge of adrenaline. Concerned about taking too long in the bathroom, I would get scared after a few minutes, and not only take off the female attire, but also try and put them back in the hamper in a mixed-up order, so my mother would not know the clothes had been disturbed. This was like the pressure cooker being allowed to blow off a little steam, a frustrating start of my teenage years.

Survival, now more than ever in my young life, meant denial of my feelings and myself, thus I took extra chores and family duties gladly. I was now old enough to mow our three acres every other weekend during the warm months with a push power mower (we could not afford a riding one). In the winter I took care of the steep, long, shale and stone driveway, constant rock maintenance of the ditches, and shoveling it free from large snow drifts. I also worked outside, weeding, and tending two large gardens. Most Sundays, I mixed cement and carried thousands of red bricks over the four years it took us to completely brick the house and garage. My father, at one time, went to bricklaying school and was a good mason in his own right. Every evening, no matter how cold, I gave my new dog, Timmy, a loving black and white HEINZ 57, fresh water and food. My first dog, Skippy, died before I left Greensburg. My calico-colored cat, Thomas (we didn't know she was a girl — the two of us had a lot in common), was great friends with Timmy, and he would take care of her kittens in his dog box when she went out to roam. With no garbage service, I also took out and burned garbage in a big 55-gallon oil drum, three to four times a week, often smelling like a smokehouse when I came in from burning.

To help my mother, I dusted on Saturday, carried out the wash to the clothes lines, washed or dried dishes (Mary and I took turns), set and cleared the table, cleaned my room each week, swept the floors (no carpet to vacuum until I was 17), and spent many hours playing with and baby-sitting my sisters and brother. Cheryl, Darlene, and Bill still comment on the many hours I would wheel them around the house in dad's big wheel barrow; three customers kept me busy!

I say all of this not to brag or complain, because I did get a little raise in my allowance to twenty-five cents every two weeks, but to show how I took charge of my life, not only to be a valued family member, pulling his weight as a good son and growing young man, but to turn a negative into a positive — taking a meaningless existence (and that is what I was doing, struggling to exist then and most of my life) and finding value in life and a purpose for living. Although totally out of balance, I received as many blessings and lessons in life as I gave. Little Ron had found his reason to live; he was needed, and that was the best I could have hoped for at that time in my life.

We certainly appreciated everything we received in those days, and we did not have to get everything we wanted. Materially, I wanted a little motor scooter, but never got it. I had to wait a few years (after they came out) just to receive my first real, General Electric transistor radio — an olive green one in a tan leather case — for my fourteenth birthday. One thing is for sure, I learned a strong work ethic and the meaning of the word responsibility. I guess that is why one of my favorite stories is William Drake's modern adaption of the fable, "Little Red Hen."

Once upon a time, there was a little red hen who scratched about the barnyard until she uncovered some grains of wheat. She called her neighbors and said, "If we plant this wheat, we shall have bread to eat. Who will help me plant it?"

"Not I," said the cow.

"Not I," said the duck.

"Not I," said the pig.

"Not I," said the goose.

"Then I will," said the little red hen. And she did. The wheat grew tall and ripened into golden grain. "Who will help me reap my wheat?" asked the little red hen.

"Not I," said the duck.

"Out of my classification," said the pig.

"I'd lose my seniority,"said the cow.

"I'd lose my unemployment compensation," said the goose.

"Then I will," said the little red hen. And she did.

At last it came time to bake the bread. "Who will help me bake the bread?" asked the little red hen.

"That would be overtime for me," said the cow.

"I'd lose my welfare benefits," said the duck.

"I'm a dropout and never learned how," said the pig.

"If I'm to be the only helper, that's's discrimination," said the goose.

"Then I will," said the little red hen.

She baked five loaves and held them up for her neighbors to see.

They all wanted some, and in fact, demanded a share. But the little red hen said, "No, I can eat the five loaves myself."

"Excess profits!" cried the cow.

"Capitalist leech!" screamed the duck.

"I demand equal rights!" yelled the goose.

And the pig just grunted. And they painted "unfair" picket signs and marched round and round the little red hen shouting obscenities.

When a government agent came, he said to the little red hen, "You must not be greedy."

"But I earned the bread," said the little red hen.

"Exactly," said the agent. "That is the wonderful free enterprise system. Anyone in the barnyard can earn as much as he wants, but under our modern government regulations, the productive workers must divide their product with the idle."

And they lived happily ever after, including the little red hen, who smiled and clucked, "I am grateful. I am grateful."

But her neighbors wondered why she never again baked any more bread.

Chapter 5

Surviving High School

Being the last stop on a crowded high school bus made for a very uncomfortable ride; each day I hung on to the edge of my seat — a good analogy for my life at the time. To make the most of my high school experience, I struggled to survive the social pressures of being a teenager, and continue to try and find a purpose for life as a frustrated girl in a boy's body. Suppressing my feminine identity became even more difficult; the girls were not allowed to wear slacks, and their nylons and poodle skirts were torture for me. I never even considered going to the senior prom. What was the point? I couldn't have my hair done, pick out a special prom dress, or wear high heels. It was more than I could mentally bear.

To keep my cover and make my father proud of me, I tried out for the 10th grade wrestling team. I practiced for a few weeks before realizing that even though I was strong for my size, I couldn't make the team with a senior starter at 103 pounds, getting my already bare-bones body down to a 97 pound weight class was unrealistic. Dad was proud that I tried to live up to his sports expectations, so we settled for Friday night high school football games. In our community, this was a big event, and often averaged 10,000 fans at one game. What my father didn't know, although my mother did, was that I wore a bra under my sweatshirt and nylons under my pants and socks. I did fear having a car accident and being found out, but the pleasure outweighed the risk.

Hempfield area had a large high school with over 2,100 students in grades 10-12, and 759 senior graduates in my class alone; it was a mixture of rural, suburban, and small city students. Because my father encouraged me to learn a job skill, I chose to be, as they called them in those days, a vocational program student (I never thought I'd attend college). We were not allowed to mix with the business education or college preparatory classes. This supposedly was done because we spent half our school day at Hempfield and the other half at neighboring Jeanette High School for Hempfield shop/trade classes.

I liked working with wood and details, so I chose the patternmaking program. In patternmaking, students completed a drawing of a specific pattern, which was carved full-scale into a drafting board. Students then had to build the pattern, putting a slight angle on every surface (called cope and drag), so when the pattern was pulled from a sand mold, the sand would keep its shape. The hot metal or plastic was poured into the mold to produce products such as car parts or a hammer head. While it usually took one month to do a complete pattern, I did so well that I had two patterns two months ahead of the rest of the class, making straight A's by the end of the year. The following year all of the local high schools merged to make eight school districts (Central-Westmoreland Area Vocational School), so in my eleventh grade year, there was no patternmaking program. Given a choice for a new trade, I chose carpentry.

Our class started in an old, industrial manufacturing building and we spent most of our two years actually remodeling the school as part of our real life training. While I did not know it at the time, this program would have a major impact on my life. Mr. Randof, our teacher, quickly selected leaders or foremen for the projects, and because I could already read blueprints, handle small hand and power tools, and do calculations (like figure lengths and cuts of roof rafters on the carpenter's framing square), I rose to the top of the class quickly. Even though I was one of the smallest guys in the class, I was usually the crew foreman, which some of the larger guys resented. I was small, but I developed a tough exterior in order to survive this environment — just as a girl would have to do in today's construction programs. In reality, I was a girl in an all boys' class. I just couldn't show it.

I graduated from the class a straight A student. I was also the first vocational center student on the Hempfield Area High School Honor Roll and member of Hempfield's National Honor Society, with a solid 3.6 GPA, rating in the top five percent of my class. I was one of two students in the class who never missed a day of high school; the other student was the class valedictorian.

Another example of not letting circumstances control your accomplishments is when I took driver's education. As a vocational, half-time student at two schools; I had no time for electives in my schedule, not even to take the driver's education class, a requirement for getting a license. Like all teenagers, driving was important to me, but we only had one car, a new Chevy stationwagon, that my dad needed to deliver mail each day. Eager to get behind the wheel, if only on a limited basis, I scheduled Driver's Ed for the summer after my 10th grade year. We lived four miles from the high school (if you took the back roads), so I rode my bicycle the eight mile round trip each morning. I passed the test on my first try. I was a little embarrassed to arrive at school on a bike when all of the other students were showing up in cars, driving with their parents on learner permits, but I was really in shape that summer.

The flat top was the cool haircut for boys, so since I couldn't be myself, I went with the culture and also wore a

High School Graduation

flat top throughout high school. My social life consisted of my monthly weekend trips to the auction house with my grandparents (sometimes my grandfather let me drive). Because we couldn't afford an accident and since my dad needed the car for work, I didn't go out much — didn't really care to. In fact, I only had two dates all through high school: one, a set-up by the minister who knew I wanted to be a girl, and two, a neighbor girl. Both dates failed to change my feelings or went anywhere, but I tried.

I continued to wear my mother and sisters' clothing when I could, in the privacy of my bedroom, which now had walls, a door, and ceiling. I used my new carpentry skills to build my own bedroom. I even built a fake removable ceiling in my closet to hide my high heels, cheap- long-haired wig (sand blonde), and drug store make-up. I was able to acquire these additional female items from a deal I had with one of the girls in my Problems of Democracy class at school. Needing someone to talk to, I confided with a nice girl, Cindy, in my class about my feminine feelings. She was very understanding and over time became my first girlfriend, as in girlfriend to girlfriend. Cindy confided in me that she was having trouble corresponding with her boyfriend; her parents didn't approve of him, so, I helped her out by calling her house and his house, leaving coded messages this way. In return, Cindy helped me out by buying the cheap wig, lipstick, and other make-up items for me. I was ashamed and embarrassed to buy these items myself. I would tell her what I wanted, give her money, and she would bring them to me at school in a brown lunch bag, which I could carry easily and without suspicion. To me, Cindy was a lifesaver, and, although it was sneaky, I appreciated her assistance and real girlfriend friendship more than she could ever know.

While I was a dud socially and emotionally in high school, I was proud of my accomplishments. I tried to make the most of what were to me very frustrating years. I learned to survive in a world in which I felt completely out of place. My parents were also pleased with my efforts and help at home and at school; for graduation, they bought me an old '55 Chevy for $75. It'd been sitting in a field near one of my dad's friend's house. The body was in pretty good shape, but it had a faded two-tone green exterior and blew smoke like a chimney when it ran. My father pulled the car into the garage and overhauled the six-cylinder engine (a lot simpler in those days) with the help of another one of his mechanical friends. I paid $29.95 for one of the famous Earl Schives quick-paint jobs, giving the car a new maroon exterior, complete with shiny new baby moon hubcaps, so it wouldn't look like an old-fogey four-door sedan. Since my parents still had a tight budget and four other children to raise, the only way I could now drive my car was to take all of my life savings and pay $250 for a six-month insurance policy, almost four times what the car cost. They really socked it to young male drivers. Had they known I was really a girl, it would've cost half the amount. I certainly wasn't the drag-race type.

Now, I was ready to get my first job. I had my own transportation and was ready to enter the adult world, determined to be a success in society's eyes, even though I was personally very unhappy.

Chapter 6

Facing the Real World

I graduated in May of 1965 with no interest in going to college like many of my classmates; I was the only student from my National Honor Society group that did not go straight to college after graduation. Instead, I continued to build on my vocational skills, applying for the Pittsburgh Regional AFL CIO Union Apprenticeship Program, a very political and competitive organization which only selected 50 of over 200 applicants each year. Over the summer, I worked for a local residential contractor, building wood-framed houses while taking various tests (GATB or General Aptitude Test Battery and eye-hand coordination tests) and completing the personal interviews necessary to qualify for the union apprenticeship program. My former training and efforts paid off, as I was selected into this elite carpentry apprenticeship program for the local Greensburg chapter. This meant not only the opportunity to become a journey-man carpenter (should be journey person) in the mainly commercial construction field, but that I would be making $3.25 an hour (50% of the journeyman's wage) and almost twice as much as the $1.75 an hour carpentry job I had. Now that I was a full time wage earner, I could help out more at home. Since I still lived in my basement bedroom, I paid 25% of my salary to my parents for room and board, and helped my overworked mother; I used a lot of earnings to buy her a new turquoise refrigerator with an ice maker and her first dishwasher (a chore I had now graduated from).

Since I didn't care about myself, I was pleased I could help my family enjoy life.

Most commercial construction was in the Pittsburgh area, and I had apprenticeship training at the Connelly Vocational School in Pittsburgh two nights a week (45 miles from home), so I needed more dependable transportation. That winter, I traded my '55 Chevy sedan on a demonstrator model 1965 Corvair with automatic transmission, black exterior, and white interior. My dad asked why I didn't want a 1965 Mustang, which was the rage at the time, but I liked the new, bullet-style Corvair, the rear engine for traction (I could go in the snow when no one else could). To me, the white interior really fit my feminine personality, but I couldn't tell him that.

My first apprenticeship was in downtown Pittsburgh. I helped to remodel the Hughes and Hatcher Men's Clothing Store. The job was like working in a coal mine, tearing out the old plaster walls and ceilings. I got the dirty work as the new kid and I went home every day with black dust all over me. I had to wear carpenter overalls on the job — the smallest Sears Roebuck & Company made; they still hung on me. My toolbox weighed almost as much as I did. I looked like a boy in a man's job. In many ways I felt inferior, at least physically; truthfully, I was a girl in a man's job. In order to get to downtown Pittsburgh each day, I had to be on the road by six am, beating rush hour traffic through the Squirrel Hill tunnels. Just above the new Civic Arena Sports Center, there was free parking only a mile's walk to the heart of the city for my eight o'clock starting time. Being an apprentice, I could not afford downtown parking garage fees, and the two nights I stayed late for my apprenticeship class. I would cut meal costs by going to Murphy's Five and Dime Store and buying a giant Baby Ruth or Butterfinger for a nickel, making that my supper. Including the drive home, I had 12 - 16 hour days, my first taste of the real world of work.

There was no hope of being a girl; finally, I began dating them instead. Working all the time or just staying in my room was getting old, and I was past going to the auction on weekends with my grandparents. A friend of mine named Denise had a younger sister. Since Denise had no interest in dating me herself, I starting seeing her sister, Shirley. Shirley was a few years younger and still in high school, so there were strict guidelines about staying out too late. Most of our dates were spent sitting in her folks' living room watching television or going to an occasional movie on the weekend. I had no emotional or physical interest in dating women. To me, just being cared about by someone, maybe an occasional kiss, was enough. Shirley was young — to her, dating a graduate was exciting. I think she really did care for me, and I tried my best to share her attitude over the six months or so we spent together.

Just as I was settling into the real world of work and dating, another reality hit home. I received a notice to report to the military draft board for a physical. By the winter of 1965, the Vietnam War was going strong; men were being called to serve their country. I had no interest in fighting or joining the military. Early one morning in December, 1965, I arrived at the local draft board, got on a train (with most of my high school senior classmates), and took the hour ride to the Pittsburgh Military Testing Headquarters for an all day mental and physical ability draft classification test. A week later, I received notification from Uncle Sam, congratulating me for my 1A classification; I had passed with flying colors.

If I did not join the Air Force or Navy, I would've been drafted into the Army or Marines within the next six months and on my way to the jungles of Vietnam as an infantry soldier. This scenario may have been appealing to a red-blooded American male, but not for a girl trapped in a skinny male body. I weighed 115 pounds. At 110, I would've been underweight for my height and not 1A status. Life had other plans. It seemed unfair that puny me had passed the physical, while many of my high school classmates, football players mostly, flunked because of knee injuries. The college prep students received a deferment from the draft as long as they stayed in school. But I knew life wasn't always fair; I faced that every day. With my grandfather having been enlisted in the Army during World War I and my father in World War II, I had some idea of how things worked. Both were in the infantry — my dad awarded a Purple Heart for his efforts in the D-Day invasion. I knew I wasn't the infantry type. With my father and grandfather's guidance, I applied for and joined the Air Force, where there was less chance of physical fighting. In those days, you didn't get to pick your Air Force classification (AFC) or training assignment. I wanted to be a photo mapper, but on April 13, 1966, I was officially sworn into the Air Force. I boarded a chartered Braniff Airplane (my first flight) and headed to San Antonio, Texas, and the Air Force bootcamp.

Early that next morning, as the bus drove into Lackland Air Force Base, I said to myself, "What are these guys doing marching around in green fatigues?" I though the Air Force wore blue uniforms. That's how naive I was. Again, welcome to the real world.

We got off the bus and marched, if you could call it that, to the barber's for our buzz haircut (down to the scalp). Next, we were issued our fatigues, khakis (short-sleeved, tan, summer uniforms), dress blues, coats, and two pairs of black boots; the last kind of wardrobe I craved. Fortunately, our barracks was a series of rooms (four men to a room) and not one big, open barracks. After changing into fatigues, we were off to the chow hall where we got our first dose of hurry-up-and-wait — the lines were long — and two pink salt pills. Later that day we got in some marching practice. We marched through a series of open doors in our tee shirts. As we made our way through one of the doorways, a needle gun pressed our arms — surprise immunizations.

Inspections were rigorous: the bed had to be so tight that the sergeant could bounce a quarter off of it (I had a top bunk), underwear had to be folded a certain way, the neck of the toothpaste tube had to be cleaned each time it was used, shoes were to be kept spit-shined at all times. This was all done to break individuals down to a meaningless level. Soldiers had to be under complete control, reprogrammed to the military discipline code. For me, the last straw was what happened when we unpacked. I had taken with me some chewing gum and Lifesavers. "Sissy stuff" they called it. Other soldiers were allowed to keep cigarettes or chewing tobacco — a real man's pleasure (just the culture I was looking for). I went to bed at night, a mass of confusion, a girl determined to be a boy.

Basic training at that time was 30 days instead of 60. Training time was cut in half to accommodate the need for more troops, dead soldiers had to be replaced. We were called 30-day wonders. The first ten days were the roughest. My peers were living it up, drinking beer and smoking — relaxation the military encouraged. I went to the PX for soda pop and a candy bar. I was the perfect social misfit (So what's new?).

Every day we got up at 4 am to "fall out" into the cold morning air. The hot Texas sun came out during our marching, exercising, and specialized training exercises. I did qualify at the target range on the M-16 rifle, but we did not have to carry one as part of our routine. Finally, the big day came when we had completed our 29th day of training,

Airman Hoyman—May 14, 1966

nearly a month of hell. (The only time I'd felt at ease during those 29 days was during Sunday morning chapel service.)

We marched to a big Quonset hut to receive our future duty assignments. They put my social security number in the computer and I was given an assignment from the Air Force "need only" list. That day, they needed air police, mess hall cooks, and supply workers. Fortunately, my number came up supply worker, the best of the three options in my opinion. I was going to the Jacksonville Air Force (SAC Strategic Air Command) Base, support services for B-58 bombers, 50 miles outside Little Rock, Arkansas, to work as a supply/warehouse man. It was almost impossible to get an Air Force training school assignment. My training was to be an on- the-job training assignment, 12 hours a day, six to seven days a week. Scheduling was so well- organized that I finished my 30 days on May 13th and I was home on May 14, my nineteenth birthday. I had a week's leave before heading for Little Rock, Arkansas, with everything I could take stuffed in a military duffel bag.

When I arrived at Little Rock Air Force Base, I was a one-stripe airman: restricted to a male-dominated environment, no transportation, a $59 monthly paycheck, and little free time. I was quartered in a two-man room with another nice young airman, a redhead named Ralph from Missouri. We both missed our privacy, Ralph missed his girlfriend, and he didn't like having to share radio time. I liked Top 40 music. He liked Country. I missed not being able to express my pent up feminine desires. I did not drink alcohol or participate in the constant beer parties, so I used my free time to write a letter home each day to my mother, grandmother, or Shirley. I'd have a candy bar and a Dr. Pepper or Arkansas Red Pop (a strawberry soda with an Arkansas Razorback on the label). This was my enjoyment. Everything in Arkansas seemed to have some association with the Arkansas Razorback football team. "Sue Pig" was the rally cry, and the northern guys used to joke that this was the

Letters Home

only place you could call a person a pig, and they would think you were paying them a compliment. It didn't take long for my correspondence list to dwindle. "Out of sight, out of mind," Ralph and I received our Dear John letters.

On Sunday mornings I would go to early service at the base chapel then stop by the Airman's Club on the walk back for free donuts and the "Rocky and Bullwinkle" cartoon show. The base supply warehouse, my job location, was a good mile hike over the hill from where I lived, so I got plenty of exercise.

A month after I started my supply job assignment, the sergeant asked if anyone could do carpentry work to help get ready for the big base inspection. They wanted someone to put a new drywall exterior on the main office. I seized the moment. Finally, I could use my vocational training. Truthfully, I had only hung 4' x 8' sheets of drywall and had never mastered spackling putty over the joints. But with some common sense and practice I was sure I could do it. The job went well; the colonel assigned me to a permanent base supply carpentry position. This meant I could develop my skills, work fewer hours (eight) per day and get credit for my work, even as a one-stripe airman. The colonel's job always came first, then the senior master sergeant's job, and then whoever was nice to me. I had set up my own work area in the warehouse next to the crate packing department, so I could use their power tools. When I did a job, I planned it, ordered the material, built it, painted it, and cleaned up after myself. I was a trend setter. When I cut a door in half and put a shelf on it, so it could be used half-open or fully-open (called a Dutch door), then every office wanted one. I especially liked finish work, so when the colonel asked me to build a 16 foot long, four foot wide, Formica conference table, I had to build it on site. The only problem was when I spread a gallon of contact cement in an enclosed room on a hot day, I would stagger out like the town drunk. The fumes were ghastly. My work was so successful that the warehouse went from number fifteen to number two in one year during the base inspection. Consequently, I was chosen base supply "Pride Man of the Month" in April, 1967. When the yearly promotion time came, my name was placed on the list, and I was given the opportunity to build and run the warehouse coffee shop for some extra money. I sold hundreds of cups of coffee a day.

With no real social life, I volunteered to run the base woodworking hobby shop, which I did on weekends and in the evenings. I came up with a headboard shelf design which could be easily fastened to the metal, army-style bed frame. Over a six-month period, I made and sold over 200 headboards at $10 each, using old storage crates for the wood.

On a base salary of still less than $100 a month, I made and saved almost $3,000 in one year from all of my extra efforts.

After nearly 18 months of 16 to 18 hour days, I was burning out. I wanted a personal life. I wanted to be a girl. Desperate and lonely, I volunteered for a weekend retreat that fall at a country lodge. The guys from the Air Force Base chapel service group and the girls from the Little Rock Baptist Medical Center LPN training program were to meet. It was nice to just get away from the base and back into a country setting; I didn't care about meeting someone I would never see again.

On Saturday afternoon at the retreat, we were goofing around, wading in our bare feet in a small stream at the center of a drain pond. Suddenly, I felt a sharp pain and looked down to see blood pouring in the water. The nurses made me hop to the side of the bank, and quickly they applied pressure to a large gash near the heel of my foot. I was the center of attention. After the excitement died down, everyone went back to their activities except this one attractive, blond- haired nurse, Martha. For whatever reason, she took pity on my situation and was nice enough to stay around and talk. We were both lonely people, unhappy in our current lives. I was the over- worked, social nerd on a military base, a thousand miles from home, and she a preachers's kid, from Fort Smith, Arkansas, 150 miles from home. She was having great difficulty in her nursing studies and feeling very much alone and a failure. We spent time together that weekend and left with intentions to see each other again.

I purchased an old, four-cylinder, Pontiac LeMans. For the first time, I had a reason to leave the base and explore what the real world had to offer. With Martha coming from a strict Nazarene Church and a small-town background, we spent many of our dates going to the Little Rock Nazarene

Church, which had an active, young adult ministry. During that time, I found Jesus Christ as my personal Savior, and Martha and I began to fall in love. We became engaged that Christmas. That was as close as I would ever be to feeling like a normal man. I felt loved for the first time in my life, and I tried to return that love the best way I could. Still, I had little sexual drive, and I continued fantasizing about being a girl. Without any hope for even a breath of an authentic life, I tried my best, believed I could learn to be happy as a man and a good Christian husband.

Martha knew of my feminine characteristics. Soon after we met, I bought an old plaid dress, some makeup, and another cheap wig, which I wore to the nursing center Halloween party. My roommate, Ralph, went with us that night and eventually married one of the nursing students. Everyone joked about my looking like a girl. It felt good. That was all I thought I would ever be able to do with my femininity — laugh it off. I worked hard at accepting the male body life had so cruelly given me. Martha and I continued to date and planned a wedding, believing my newly found faith in God, Martha's love, and my determination would bring us happiness and fulfillment. My parents drove down from Pennsylvania to our simple wedding on April 23, 1967, in the Little Rock Nazarene church. We drove down to Hot Springs, Arkansas, for a short honeymoon, and we were both virgins on our first night together. I had never been physically close to a woman before. I could not maintain an erection unless I fantasized about being a woman. I learned I had to fake it, as I have my whole life, to have an orgasm. The most sexually sensitive part of my body were my breasts, my penis had no sensual feelings — an unwanted body part.

Martha and I continued to build a good friendship, as well as a marriage, and things went well for a few months. Then

Leaving for Okinawa—Dad's Farewell.

I received notice. I was going to Kadena Air Force Base in Okinawa January 1, 1968. Our plans to buy an inexpensive trailer were put on hold, and we enjoyed each other's company until I left for 18 months of overseas duty. We'd been married only seven months. Martha's clothes, makeup, and jewelry were a great temptation. I was jealous of my own wife; she could express her femininity, and I couldn't. I didn't say anything at that time, because I didn't want to make her feel bad or unhappy. She was counting on me, so I didn't want to let her down.

When I arrived in Okinawa, I was assigned to the supply line delivery team. We were responsible for delivering all materials from the huge supply warehouse to the flight line maintenance and repair shops. Since Kadena was the Vietnam War repair site for the B-52 bombers, KC-135 fuel tanker planes, a squadron of F-14 and F-16 escort fighters, and the SR-71 Blackbird spy plane, there was plenty to do. I was assigned to the on-line delivery team, consisting of a sergeant, two airmen, and three local Okinawan workers. By this time I had just received my third stripe and was an airman first class, the number two person in charge of our team. The job consisted of back loading (putting the last thing on first) supply orders to over 200 different delivery stops per day on a Chevy, stake-side and canvas top, two and a half ton truck. We would deliver everything from small transistors to 55-gallon or 400 pound drums. The key was to load properly and not stop for anything.

When I first arrived, we were working 12 hours a day, seven days a week for the first three months. This left little free time. The sergeant of our on-line delivery crew completed his tour and was sent home, and I was put in charge. By then, I learned the basics of what had to be done, so I figured out a new plan of loading and delivery. We worked faster and cut our hours down to eight hours a day, five days a week, with half day on Saturday. We did not take breaks anymore, and the only lazy Okinawan, who used to hide out in the bathroom, had to pull his weight for a change. Consequently, when the next promotions came, I was made staff sergeant, an accomplishment at that time and in less than three years.

It seemed I was adapting pretty well to the real world of military work, but on the inside I was falling apart. I rented a small, three-room house near the seawall (better living quarters than the base barracks), and Martha flew over to join me in April, right after I made staff sergeant. I bought a little Datsun for $75, and I joined the local Nazarene Missionary Church. The entire congregation was between 20-40 years of age, and we really became a family. But with the demanding pressure, my facade began to crack. My dominant female personality was beginning to surface. At times, I was doubled over in pain from such severe stomachaches. The base hospital physician said I was developing ulcers. I couldn't tell them the real reason for my stress, and certainly couldn't seek counseling. A feminine identity problem would be grounds for dishonorable discharge. I blamed it all on the job, drank lots of Pepto Bismol, and chewed antacid tablets. The inner struggle was so intense, I finally quit covering up for Martha and told her the truth — not exactly the kind of thing a bride wants to hear. But she was really understanding and asked if she could do anything to help. At that time, I didn't know the answer and had never heard of a medical condition called transsexualism. Cross dressing was the only method for relieving my tension. Martha and I agreed that, on a limited basis, she would go visit one of her new girlfriends, and I would have a few hours once a week to express my feminine identity in the privacy of our little home. She didn't exactly want to watch her husband walking around in a dress, nylons, lipstick, and high heels. I appreciated her understanding and it did provide some relief from the stress. But, we both knew that this was just a temporary fix. During that year we made the best of a strained marriage and spent a lot of our free time together with other young adults from the church. I also continued to avoid myself by keeping busy, making childrens' Sunday school chairs for the new church and doing a paint-by-number oil replica of "The Last Supper," which still hangs in my dining room.

In December, 1968, we returned to the states four months early. I was discharged from the Air Force. Martha and I returned to Greensburg, Pennsylvania. I was 22 without a job, a home, or money. All the strength I had was being used to suppress my feminine identity.

Chapter 7

Learning the Lessons of Manhood

The reality was that I had to rebuild all aspects of my life: marriage and career. My strong work ethic had to kick in just to keep my head above water. Having survived the military environment, mastered new carpentry and sergeant leadership skills, and found a loving wife, I was determined to be successful in spite of my constant desire to express my feminine identity.

In December of 1969, Martha and I had no other option but to move into the upstairs spare bedroom of my grandparents' duplex home on Seminary Avenue in Greensburg, Pennsylvania — the same home in which I had spent those developmental years of my early childhood. While it was nice of them to provide for us, Martha and I soon realized the lack of privacy and the cramped space was not going to help a struggling marriage or relieve my stress. That winter I became a security guard on the midnight shift to help us save a few dollars. That spring we rented a small apartment, and soon I quit the security job and resumed my carpentry apprenticeship from four years earlier. My goal was to complete the four year apprenticeship program, become a journeyman carpenter, and live life happily ever after. However, this plan did not work out as I'd hoped. The economy was weak, the Vietnam War was coming to an end, and work in the commercial/union-based construction field was limited. Over the next year and a half, I moved from job to job, unemployed about half the time. Since I was not related to

Ron & Grandmother Baker

the union business agent (political connections) or part of the minority quota needed to fill government contracts, I was fighting a losing battle to stay employed.

On the homefront, Martha and I found the closest Nazarene Church in Irwin, Pennsylvania, a social life and some new friends. We even found a little 10' x 50' mobile home and about an acre of land in Hermine, Pennsylvania, that spring of 1970. I worked side jobs to help make ends meet.

While this hard try to get established in life seemed to be working on the outside, I was again struggling very hard to suppress my female identity. To seek help, my mother and Martha encouraged me to get counseling at the Westmoreland County Mental Health Clinic, the only counseling we could afford at the time. Looking for some answers and relief, I gladly scheduled an appointment. I interviewed with the orientation counselor, took some written tests, and explained the problem as best as I could before being assigned to a counselor to start my therapy.

I was pleased to have a female counselor, Ms. Sharon. I felt she could understand my female identity issues, and in general, felt more comfortable with another woman I considered like myself. She began to question me in depth as to why I felt the way I did. She asked about my childhood and life experiences, as all counselors do, and attempted to explain to me how life would be if indeed I could live as a woman. Ms. Sharon was very supportive and tried to do her best; however, she soon realized she did not really know how to help me. "Just what would you say to other women, or how could you relate to them, when they ask you about your monthly female period experiences?" she asked. Of course, I could never experience that same feeling, being born with male genital features. Ms. Sharon did encourage me to read a new book by Dr.'s Harry Benjamin, Money, and Green, called *The Transsexual Phenomenon*. After reading this book, I felt, for the first time, there were medical professionals who understood my dilemma. Perhaps I was not the only person who felt like a female trapped in a male body. Maybe there was a valid medical definition and explanation for my condition. I was a transsexual. With few real solutions, even after a year of counseling, Ms. Sharon suggested I go to Johns Hopkins, in Baltimore to be evaluated by Dr. Money in the Gender Identity Clinic. But there was my wife to consider, the family, and our pastor, all of whom said I should not take such a drastic step, get my hopes up for a life change which would never happen. I declined — a decision I would later regret. Slowly I stopped going to counseling with Ms. Sharon. She felt there was no other help she could provide me, and so I yielded my own needs and feelings to those of family, religion, and society. I would live up to the expectations of manhood. I went back to cross-dressing, secretly. I pleased everyone in life but myself. After all, I was very good at that.

Reluctantly, I gave up my goal of being a union journeyman carpenter as well, and resigned in the spring of 1971. The apprenticeship program was not living up to their commitment of my employment and training. This time, I wanted a stable work environment. The Murrysville School System offered me a job as a full-time maintenance worker. The pay was lower than the union, but they promised that if I proved myself and worked hard, I would be promoted in a few years to lead a maintenance crew chief position — my first public school job. To earn extra money, I did my carpentry maintenance duties during the day and often worked a double shift (taking over for custodians and cleaning schools at night when they became sick). Martha appreciated all the hard work I was doing to pay the bills and get ahead, but we had limited personal time together, and she knew I continued to have great inner conflict — a conflict which could only be controlled by cross-dressing. We also tried counseling with the church pastor and his wife, the Turners, but that also seemed fruitless. Yet again, I was expected to meet the Christian man and husband ideals and deny my feminine identity — a sin and merely the cross I was expected to bear in life. No matter how much I prayed and tried to be the man I was supposed to be, my true feelings were those of a woman. It all came to a head one evening in the early spring of 1972 when I returned home after work to find Martha had packed up her clothes and left. There was a note saying not to worry, a friend from church had helped her start a new life, far away. While I can say I tried to understand her feelings, I was also very surprised, crushed, and depressed over her sudden departure. I had my inner struggles, but I was making every effort to deny them, doing what I was asked to do by everyone: Martha, the pastor, and my family. I called Reverend Turner and expressed my shock, sadness, and feelings of betrayal and helplessness. He told me he knew where Martha had gone and that he would not tell me the location unless I planned to be a strong Christian, prove my manhood, and live by faith that things would work out.

I did not fully understand why this had to happen, but agreed to follow his advice, not wanting to lose everything I had worked so hard for the previous three years. The only way I could handle the grief and mental anguish (I had thoughts of suicide) was to bury myself in work. I continued to work overtime at the school, and I added a carport and kept fixing the trailer. I broke a lot of rock with the sledge-hammer that spring. I helped with maintenance repairs at church and attended services faithfully. By September, roughly six months after Martha left, Reverend Turner called me into his office and told me that I had demonstrated my faith and trust in God, in him, and in my attempts to live up to the responsibilities as a husband. He shared with me that Martha had been living in Lakeland, Florida, with the grandparents of one of her close church friends; she was working as a dental assistant. Martha was mixed up as to what was really best for her future. Reverend Turner said I could go visit her, but she didn't really want me to.

Through all this time, I continued to suppress my feminine identity. I tried so hard to do the right thing and live up to the world's expectations of my manhood. I still felt I could make her happy and be a good husband, even though I did not have natural male feelings. I was a lonely person in all aspects of life. I had to try and make things right with Martha, so I took a week-long vacation and drove to Lakeland, Florida.

The territory was unfamiliar and unfriendly. I found the address and went to the home in which Martha was staying. Nervous and trying to build up my courage, I walked up to the door and introduced myself to a family I'd never met, and asked if I could see Martha. They were surprised to see me and kindly, although reluctantly, led me into the living room. I explained the purpose of my visit, and after about a half hour, they let me talk to Martha, who was hiding in her bedroom. After a short conversation, Martha told me to go home. By now, I was very upset, choking back my tears, but I agreed to leave.

Rejected, I cried and drove around Lakeland like a blind man, not knowing which street I was on or where to go next. It was good that it was late in the evening, and God, or someone, was watching out for me, because my mind and my driving were all over the place. Finally, I pulled into a shopping center parking lot and just sat, trying to figure out what the next hour, day, or month would be like for me. I decided the only thing I could do was not force the issue; so with a broken heart, I began the trip home, finally stopping to sleep that night at a rest stop. I made it back to Pennsylvania safely and continued to regroup, not knowing what life really meant anymore. I continued to keep the faith and counsel with Pastor Turner for many months before returning to Lakeland one more time early in the winter of 1972. Upon returning to Lakeland, I went to see the pastor of the Pentecostal Church where Martha was attending. After patiently counseling with him for a week, he agreed to set up a meeting with Martha; we would attend a service together on Sunday morning.

At this time, I was also in touch with Martha's parents by phone. They were concerned about her being alone in Florida, worried about our marriage (even though they knew about my identity struggles) and upset over Martha's involvement in a Pentecostal Church. Martha met me at a large Florida church, its mission charismatic, members spoke in tongues throughout the service, a practice I did not fully understand. After the service, we went to lunch to talk about the final direction our lives and broken marriage would take. She said she needed more time to think, so I patiently stayed a few more days, agreeing to see her again at Wednesday night's church service. I even passed time by helping with some minor maintenance work at the church. Wednesday night, we talked some more, and I could sense Martha's confusion over what to do, I knew if I left then without her, our marriage would be over. I agreed to stay until the next Sunday service, so she could search her heart for a final answer and trust in me or God's purpose for our marriage.

Finally, Sunday morning came, and I could sense that she was looking for a sign from God. When I did not understand the speaking of tongues during the Pentecostal service, in an attempt to be a part of this style of worship, I prayed out loud, saying words I did not understand — if you call that speaking in tongues, then I did. After the service, Martha smiled, she was more at ease with me. She said she'd been looking for a sign from God. She said that when I'd prayed out loud in tongues a few minutes before, she interpreted that as God's sign. She would return to Pennsylvania with me and try to make things work.

We returned to our trailer, and for the next few years, we tried to rebuild the marriage and continue improving our mobile home. We added a full size 15' x 20' living room on one side. We attended the Nazarene Church faithfully. It was a simple life in many respects; we continued to get by on limited resources, and I continued to suppress my feminine identity and live the male life I was expected to live. It was not easy, but life went on.

By the spring of 1974, I had now worked for the Murrysville School System for over two years. I began to question whether or not I would receive the maintenance crew foreman promotion. I made an appointment with Mr. Johnson, the assistant superintendent and administrator in charge of the maintenance system. Knowing the budget was being finalized for approval, I asked him about my promotion opportunities. He acknowledged all of my efforts and said I was doing a good job, but that I could not be given a promotion because it would not look good to some of the older men (even though I had outperformed them). Disappointed, I left feeling betrayed again by false promises. I realized that if I were ever going to get ahead career wise, I would have to take charge of my life, and as Mr. Johnson said, I'd have to become a professional. A piece of paper meant more than a skill, but where would I go? What would I do?

Relying on my strengths, I called a person I admired, Mr. Hatch, the Director of the Central Westmoreland Vocational Technical Center I'd attended back in high school. Being the school's first honor student, he encouraged me to combine my good carpentry skills with my honor society school record and go to Penn State's Industrial Vocational Education Training Department to become a carpentry instructor. From a career perspective, that was probably the most important phone call I'd ever made. Checking out his recommmendation further, I learned that because I was a Vietnam veteran, I could receive GI Bill benefits and go to college for four years. Also, Penn State was a state-sponsored school for veterans. If I maintained a satisfactory grade point average throughout college, I didn't have to pay tuition. I decided this was my time to become a professional. I talked it over with Martha, and she agreed. While she didn't want to move, the opportunity was too good to pass up. I should go to college. A few months after my discussion with Mr. Johnson, he was surprised to see I meant business with my career goals. I revisited his office and resigned from my maintenance job; I was off to be a professional.

I visited Penn State to see about the requirements in the spring of 1974. Martha and I, not wanting to give up everything we'd worked for, decided to rent out the mobile home we owned.

It had been a trying, turbulent four and a half years: re-entry into civilian life, adult life, marriage, happiness, and life as a man. We headed for the hills of Penn State and Mt. Nittany, determined to make life a success.

Chapter 8

The Penn State Years: The Price of Becoming a Professional

I blew out the candles on my 27th birthday and began college that summer at the main University Park Campus of Penn State. I was a hands-on carpentry student, who never took a college preparatory or keyboarding class (wasn't allowed to in high school) and now I found myself attending one of the most prestigious colleges in the country. Martha and I had no housing, little money. To top it off, I had to be admitted as an adjunct student (I had to prove myself before being enrolled as a regular freshman) and take English Composition and Rhetoric, Basic Philosophy, Psychology, and Sociology my first semester.

Cheap apartments were hard to find, so Martha and I spent the entire summer semester living out of the back of our 1970 Chevy truck with a cap over our heads each night for protection against the elements and took showers each morning at the camp ground facilities. This temporary housing made everyday living and certainly college, a challenging experience. I quickly made the Pattie Library my main headquarters, as I began to hit the books like never before. I also learned early on that college professors liked different stories and papers for class reports versus the standard kind. I received a D+ on my first English essay, an essay I had thought was pretty good. On my next 500 word essay, I wrote a paper entitled "The Perfect Wedding Gift: A Claw Hammer" and received a B+ for my ingenuity. The bottom line was that I had to struggle and work very hard for a C average in every class and a 2.0 grade point average for the term. Under the circumstances, I was pleased with my first semester.

With winter always coming early in Happy Valley, we were lucky enough to find a one-room (half a basement) apartment in an English professor's large, stately, stone house about a mile from the campus. Martha and I were glad to finally live in a real house again and have a bathroom and electricity; unfortunately, this meant extension cords dropped down from the first floor, a small toaster oven, two burner hot plates, and space heaters. The bathroom was upstairs. It would not be until the next summer that we actually moved into a real apartment, with modern conveniences and privacy.

With my first semester under my belt, I scheduled 12 credits in the fall (10 week quarter system) and brought my grades up to a respectable 3.4 GPA. It was only then that I felt I was learning to fit into college life. Maybe I could be successful. I almost dropped out after the tough summer semester; but instead, I was accepted into the Vocational Industrial Education Teacher Training Program as a regular student — no more adjunct business. During the fall term, I also qualified (5 years proven work experience in a trade area) to take the National Occupational Competency Testing Institute's (NOCTI) carpentry performance and written examination. So, one fall Saturday, I drove to a vocational school in Harrisburg, Pennsylvania, and took the eight hour (four hour performance and four hour written) examination to meet the NOCTI Carpentry Trade Competency Standards. I passed the test required for vocational teachers to teach in Pennsylvania the first time, which meant I could have quit Penn State, started teaching, and picked up the remaining 60 college credits for my professional certification at night. I felt it was better to stay at Penn State, finish my degree, and hopefully have more career options in education. This turned out to be a wise choice.

We continued to live on $297 a month (GI bill benefits) for the next two years, while the state of Pennsylvania paid my tuition because I was a veteran. Martha was supportive, working as a receptionist in various offices part time at minimum wage, but money was always tight. We lived on Arby's roast beef sandwiches, tomato soup, and popcorn most of the time.

By the time I started my third term, I was into major vocational/industrial education classes, as well as the required courses for my B.S. degree — what I called "non-essential courses," since they didn't seem to relate to my future work duties. I now averaged 14 to 16 credits every quarter and would finish my degree in two years (counting 24 transfer credits from the California State Teachers College, California, Pennsylvania). With more confidence, my hard-work philosophy, attendance at every class, studying every night until 10:00 (usually at Pattie Library), and concentrating on what the professors wanted, I made the Dean's List every quarter in 1975 and eventually finished my B.S. with a respectable 3.29 overall GPA and a 3.8 GPA in my vocational industrial education courses.

Finally, I had figured out a way to succeed in college life and prepare for a new career as a carpentry instructor, but I continued to be a failure in my home and personal life. The stress of college, combined with no outlet for my feminine feelings, led me to more counseling offered at the University Student Mental Health Clinic. I can still remember being afraid of having my secret found out on campus. I made an

Penn State Graduation

appointment and got more poor counseling with three different counselors. The first counselor listened to my concerns and wanted to know my life history and personal struggles, which I shared in the first few months of counseling. His main conclusion was that my hard childhood and lack of a father figure led me to my feminine desires. He said that if I got rid of this suppression and rejection, I could learn to enjoy life as a man. Realizing he didn't have a clue as to my struggles and real identity conflict, I stopped working with him, more frustrated than when I began.

Martha wanted me to counsel with the Nazarene minister where we attended church regularly. Reverend Daniels was a nice man and tried to help me through individual and joint marriage counseling, but his basic premise was that my feminine identity was a sin and through prayer and faith in God, I could overcome these feelings. I tried to follow this philosophy and reject my femininity, but the more I rejected my femininity, the more I rejected myself. Martha could sense this, and after returning from a Christian women's seminar one weekend, she made the ultimate sacrifice to help me. The seminar's message was to love your mate unconditionally, to accept them for who they are. Knowing nothing else was working, she said she would help me explore my feminine feelings and see if she could learn to be a friend to Debbie, my female alter ego. I asked her if she was sure, and she said yes. Not being the same dress size, and with money still tight, we went to the fabric store one day, soon after our discussion and bought some floral print material to sew a dress. After the dress was finished, I bought some cheap white flats and a blondish wig to complete my wardrobe.

Then, one Saturday afternoon, to test out her trial acceptance of Debbie, we discretely slipped our of the apartment and drove to the shopping center area of Altoona, about 50 miles away, so no one would recognize us. Martha was nervous about being with Debbie, and I was nervous about being out in public as a woman for the first time. We went into a dress store and shoe store, browsing, not really buying anything. In the safety of darkness, we returned that night. While I enjoyed myself, I saw how nervous it made Martha and felt guilty for upsetting her. We both agreed that while I still needed to deal with my feminine identity, it was unreasonable to expect Martha to accept me as a husband and a girlfriend; we discontinued the experiment.

Knowing how far Martha had gone to try to help me, I agreed to go back to the mental health clinic to seek counseling with a new counselor. After meeting and explaining (again) my struggles with another male counselor, his analysis was that I had to deal with my childhood conflicts. A childhood environment with mostly sisters and my mother had led to my femininity. He said if I accepted that reasoning, I could resolve my conflict with more counseling. There was no reason to believe that this was or ever would be a reason for my identity conflict; that ended counseling experience number two.

Just when I thought I would never find anyone to understand or help me, I scheduled an Abnormal Psychology class in the winter term of 1976. I learned information which helped me understand issues I had never even heard of before. My feminine feelings were okay and that I should not be ashamed about the person I was. I also learned that the term transsexualism was the true definition for my life struggles and that transvestite or homosexual were not part of my identity conflict. Feeling that I finally found someone who understood my feelings, I went up to Ms. Fitch, the professor, and briefly explained my situation and asked if she would help me. She was polite, but said she was sorry, she didn't have any time to counsel or help me in her busy schedule and referred me back to the University Mental Health Clinic for personal counseling. I felt so dejected. I left the room and cried.

Needing help more than ever, I reluctantly went back to the mental health clinic and set up an appointment with a third counselor. After three or four sessions of sharing my struggles and history once again, I asked the male counselor what he thought and if he felt he could help me. I'll never forget that afternoon. He said my whole identity conflict centered around a deep hatred for my mother. I felt so mad and misunderstood. I told him nothing could be further from the truth. I loved and admired my mother and suggested maybe he should reexamine his counseling skills. I walked out of the clinic, never to return.

Having no one to turn to, I buried myself in my classwork and tried to accept manhood, be a good husband, and get a good start on my new career. I graduated in May, 1976, with my Bachelor of Science degree as a Certified Carpentry Instructor and Cooperative Education Coordinator in Vocational Industrial Education. Everyone was proud of me, especially my parents, for I was one of the first grandchildren on the Hoyman or Baker side to graduate from college.

Considering all job options and trying to make the marriage work, I interviewed for and accepted my first teaching position as the building trades instructor at the Jonesboro Area Vocational Technical Center in Jonesboro, Arkansas. One of the first comprehensive high schools in Arkansas to also house a vocational wing of eight trade areas, it served students from all surrounding school systems. I felt an Arkansas environment would be friendly to Martha, which would allow monthly weekend visits to her parents' home 200 miles away at the other end of the state. I had a chance to build a new program from scratch; this would be a good start for both of us.

Ironically, I had also interviewed with a junior college in Richmond, Indiana, and was offered a job also. I didn't select it, because their work schedule did not allow summers free (I wanted to work on my master's degree). During the interview the school director couldn't keep his daughter quiet. I was visiting their home. She kept talking about how she wanted to be a boy. The parents admitted they did not know how to deal with this child's concern. They were embarrassed by it. I didn't think my prospective boss could handle another gender identity crisis so I offered no discussion. Guess I'll never know how that one turned out.

Martha and I packed everything we owned in our new, red Chevy Monza (which Martha loved) and a used van (I bought it cheaper than I could have rented a moving van) to go from State College, Pennsylvania, to Jonesboro, Arkansas. In late June, 1976, the system had hired all of the vocational teachers a month early. We were to select and write material purchase orders, organize shop equipment, and develop curriculum for the new programs. Martha and I moved into a little, two-bedroom apartment on the other side from town; it looked like we'd made the right choice.

Two weeks after I signed the contract, the director said that they'd run out of money, and they would have to delay setting up our programs; at least with the proper materials and equipment. Things were so bad that when school started, I had to have my building trade students tear apart the crates that the large equipment came in for wood. Our first woodworking activity was to make the food service program cabinets. We used birch finished veneer plywood and made a counter top from Formica, this was usually a senior level project. The final blow came when the Teachers' Union agreed to a half of one percent pay wage increase for the next school year. My future would go nowhere in Arkansas.

I had to buy some new dress pants and shirts for my professional image, even though I had little money. Shortly after school started, there was a special sale at a popular Arkansas discount store. I spent almost $100 that day, updating my wardrobe, which easily pleased my weak-spirited male image. (Quite a contrast to my current wardrobe — forty plus suits at $100 each). Martha was pleased to be close enough to her parents; we usually made the 200 mile trip once or twice a month to a little community, a few miles outside of Ozark, Arkansas. The red clay soil in that area was so sweet you could smell it in the air each time you drove along the new interstate highway.

The woman locked inside still raged to get out. So many questions still needed to be answered. I was still secretly cross dressing, a Band-Aid on a gushing wound. I sought out a counselor at the Jonesboro Mental Health Clinic to gain some professional insight. The counselor assigned to me was a female. She was a lot more understanding and open to my needs than the last three so-called counselors from the Penn State clinic. Ms. Jones went through the history of my life routine and tried to deal with my pain and the frustrations of living a male life, while trying to understand my feminine side. I even went to see her as Debbie at times, even though I wasn't really confident in my appearance. I'd change from Ron to Debbie inside my van at the medical center parking lot. This was risky, and I was nervous, afraid of being found out, as I switched back and forth during broad daylight. But the joy and significance of counseling woman to woman was worth the accelerated heartbeats and the drama of being a quick change artist.

But Ms. Jones was not an expert in transsexualism. She strongly encouraged me to take the 1000 mile trip to Johns Hopkins Gender Identity Clinic in Baltimore, Maryland. Ms. Jones helped me find the clinic phone number and scheduled me for a Friday appointment, right before our Christmas vacation in December. Martha was concerned about the results of such a major journey and a specialist's opinion, but she also wanted a resolution to the other woman problem. I took two sick days off to make the Friday appointment, and we packed the Chevy Monza and headed out early Wednesday morning for the big city of Baltimore, a place I would later call home.

There was a sense of adventure and the unknown around every twist and turn in the highway. We took the southern route, all the way across Tennessee and up through Virginia. I'll never forget the beautiful scenes of the many tree and fence lines which bordered the horse farms and rolling pastures. We arrived in Baltimore late that Thursday evening, looking for an inexpensive motel on the outskirts of the city. We finally settled on a motel made of little cottages called Brown's Motel on Route 40, just east of Ellicott City. Tired and road weary, the night's rest was sorely needed and went quite fast.

I rose early to do my best to look passable as Debbie, and Martha and I left the little hotel. Nervously, we repacked the car in the crisp morning air, which felt great against my legs, because I could now wear a dress and nylons. We slipped unnoticed out of the hotel and headed straight down Route 40 to the heart of Baltimore. Finally, we found the impressive medical center and parked across the street. I felt as if I had arrived.

With butterflies in my stomach, we walked across the street and up the long, granite steps into the medical building. After notifying the receptionist of our arrival, we sat in the small waiting room for the most important medical check up of my life. Martha had been a real trooper and words cannot describe the love and admiration I had for her. She was asked to stay in the waiting room, while I nervously entered the clinical area and was escorted to a private room to wait a few more minutes (seemed like hours), and the doctor entered the room. He was a middle-aged gentleman with the traditional white lab coat and a little mustache. He greeted me warmly and started asking a number of questions. He gave me a psychological test to complete and asked me to take off my clothes for a physical examination. After the examination, he asked a few more questions before leaving. I dressed and then completed the psychological test. After this examination process, I went back out to the waiting room to sit with Martha.

About an hour later, we were called back into a large, impressive looking office where Dr. Money explained the initial findings. He said I had characteristics of a transsexual identity conflict, but he could not help me further unless I continued to work with them over a long period of time. He also said I would have to make a full time commitment to living as a woman. I thanked him but said that would be difficult at this time, considering my current job, marriage, and location. We left the clinic with little direction and many questions. Back at the car, Debbie changed into Ron. I did not find the resolution I was looking for and now realized there was no clear or easy way to resolve the identity crisis, a crisis which continued to eat at the very fibers of my existence.

How could I afford the financial cost of moving closer to Baltimore or life as Debbie? How could I walk away from my obligations and commitment to Martha? How could I give up on a teaching career I had just started or let down my family and friends who were so proud of me for finishing college and getting a fresh start on life? The answer I wanted and the direction my soul cried out for was once again drowned by logic and common sense. We headed for Christmas vacation in Greensburg, Pennsylvania, 200 miles away.

After the holiday vacation with the traditional presents and visits to relatives (we didn't even tell them of the Baltimore trip to Hopkins), we returned home, determined to still work on our marriage, my career, and Ron's feelings of self-worth — what little there was. To add insult to my already shattered feelings, we returned home to find that our cat had gotten out, been struck by a car, and had died in the bushes near the apartment. I took it a few miles out of town to some woods for burial. There were poison ivy roots in the ground where I buried him, and I got a terrible case of poison ivy blisters on my fingers and hands in the middle of winter.

I reported back to Ms. Jones describing the Hopkins trip, and we continued to counsel for a while, but found few workable answers. Grin and bear it. We ended our counseling sessions. A transsexual identity conflict is black and white, male or female; counseling cannot solve or resolve the problems. My life was proof of that.

Martha wanted to gain better job skills, so she started dental assistant training at Cottonbowl Vocational Technical Center, an adult training facility about 40 miles east of Jonesboro. The government announced that Vietnam veterans could use any remaining credit on the GI bill college fund toward masters degree training. Since I finished my B.S. degree in two years, I could now go back to college full time for my masters degree. In early Spring, 1977, I responded to an offer to return to the Penn State Vocational Industrial Education Department as a half-time graduate assistant. I could earn $6,000 for the year plus free tuition for working twenty hours per week for the department. This incentive program, along with the GI bill changes, made this offer too good to pass up. I resigned my building maintenance instructional position at Jonesboro, and scheduled the start of my masters program for June.

The stress of my identity conflict continued to make it difficult for Martha to meet my needs, or more importantly, my ability to meet her needs. We agreed something had to be done.

Martha wanted to complete the last quarter of her dental assistant program, so we separated again. While not what I had planned, I knew in my heart this separation would give Martha the room she needed. With a supportive group of friends and a short driving distance from her family, I left Martha in Jonesboro with the red Monza. I packed the van with my personal belongings and returned back to Penn State. I left knowing this would be a permanent separation.

Chapter 9

Trying to Make Sense of it All

Returning to Penn State to complete my Master's degree in June, 1977, was easier than I thought. It had only been a year since I'd finished my B.S. degree, and I'd gained a valuable year teaching experience, during which time I'd started a new vocational program from scratch. My first order of business was to find a place to live, and I was fortunate to find a one-bedroom, second-floor apartment less than a mile from campus. This location was important, because I could walk or ride my bike to the Chambers building to my cubby hole office and classes. My apartment also had a private doorway.

I started my summer classes and assistantship determined to do well. I began my masters program with eight credits and started my assistantship under Mr. Gerald Funk. My assignment with Mr. Funk was to assist him in the development and validation of the Pennsylvania Occupational Competency Assessment Test. This was a four hour written and performance- based test, measuring the key technical skills for mastery of a specific trade such as an electrician or a culinary arts chef. Our goal was to revise five new occupational trade examinations that year. (Many of the national occupational competency examination tests are copies of the original Pennsylvania examinations). Anyway, I found the test development process interesting and felt this assignment was a good match for my interest and abilities.

The job and classes were going fine: I still secretly cross dressed in my apartment, and I missed Martha. Determined to still save the marriage, I planned to attend Martha's graduation for her dental assistant program in late August at the Cottonbowl Vocational Center. I wasn't sure if she wanted me to come, but I did want someone to be there to recognize her accomplishments. I knew her parents were not planning to go, even though they lived only 200 miles away. I finished my summer classes and had just enough time and money to catch a bus for the 1,100 mile trip from State College. I slept half the way there, arriving in the northeastern Arkansas town Blytheville bus stop. Martha was nice enough to pick me up. Although it was a cool reception, I could tell she did appreciate my being there for her. I didn't know if this trip was going to be the end of our marriage or a third reconciliation; everything rested on a final talk.

That warm Saturday after graduation, Martha agreed to take a ride with me to make a decision. We drove to the country to find a quiet spot, and we walked down a path which led to a stream. We sat down on some large rocks and tall trees canopied our spot. Martha was understandably skeptical of my ability to put my feminine feelings behind me. On the other hand she admitted she still loved me and wanted to make the marriage work. While still having no real answers to my feminine feelings, I did not want to let her down and sincerely thought with willpower and the Lord's help, I could learn to be happy as a man, be a good husband and fulfill her needs. We had been through too much to quit now. So, I held her in my arms, looked her straight in the eye, and said with all my heart, "Martha, I want you to come back with me, and I'll try my very best to put the feminine conflicts behind me and be a good husband. If I can't keep this promise to you, then I'll let you go." She embraced me and said that she wanted to make our love and lives together work. We returned to Jonesboro to pack, and against the wishes of some of her friends, we headed back to State College with high hopes and faith that this third start would work.

Upon returning to State College, I began my fall classes and assistantship work, and Martha found a job as a dental assistant, practicing her new skill. We attended the Bethel Church of the Nazarene (as in our undergraduate days) and tried to enjoy rebuilding our life together. However, storm clouds were brewing and as winter blew into State College, the feminine feelings I was trying so desperately to suppress began to dominate my thoughts and feelings again. I had to do something, but what? The only knowledgeable counselor who knew anything about my turmoil was Ms. Fitch, my former Abnormal Psychology professor. I would not go back to the counselors at the student mental health clinic. While I did not know what kind of reception or help I could expect from Ms. Fitch, I had to try. I checked her office appointment hours and went to ask for her assistance. Upon arrival, I re-introduced myself to her and after a few minutes, she did remember my earlier request for help, a year and a half before. She was kind enough to hear my request, and after learning of the poor help I received from the student mental health clinic and my current struggles, she apologized for not helping me earlier. She agreed to assist me. With her teaching schedule and private counseling center in downtown State College, she was still a very busy professional, but she would see me at her private practice for a reduced fee, one I could afford. I was pleased to get counseling with someone who could help me reach some conclusions about my identity crisis, and I started my counseling on a weekly basis. I did not tell Martha about the counseling at first, because I did not want to raise her fears or have a final separation. I needed more answers about who I really was — male or female.

It became clear through counseling that my dominant identity was female. But the reality was I could not make the bold steps necessary to begin my female life. I had allowed society's pressures, friends, family, and religious values to suppress my real feelings, my true self. I could not bring myself to put my needs over those of others, but I still had to be honest with Martha. One night after dinner, with fear in my heart, I told her of my new struggles and the results of Ms. Fitch's counseling. We both cried that night. Once again, I had hurt the one I so desperately tried to love. Martha realized her worse fears; her husband could never be the man she wanted, nor would he overcome his true feminine identity. I asked her what she wanted to do, and she said she wanted to leave, to end the marriage, move out west, and rebuild her life near her brother, Dan, who was studying to be a minister at Mid-American Bible College in Olathe, Kansas. The next weekend, we packed the brown Buick Skylark and Martha left with a sad and heavy heart. I was also heartbroken that I could not live up to my promises. Deep down I knew this time the marriage was really over. She wrote to say she had moved into an apartment with her brother and found a new job as a trainee for assistant manager with Tandy Craft; a leather goods store. After that first letter, she did not correspond with me, and I had to pray she was doing okay in her new life.

My college classes and my assistantship kept me busy enough to make time pass, but I felt like a personal failure. A calico cat adopted me and became my new roommate. I continued counseling periodically with Ms. Fitch, but the threat of losing my new career, one I'd worked so hard for, and of disappointing my parents kept me from making the transition I knew was still best for me. Mentally and emotionally I was unable to pay the final price for true happiness. I had been well-conditioned by society. I was 31-years-old and trapped in my own body.

I finished my assistantship and received a $5,000 grant to produce 15 bound copies of my 150 page masters thesis, "The Development of a Centralized Occupational Competency Assessment Program." I had an overall 3.67 GPA in my masters degree, and I graduated in May 1978. My parents and other family members were present at graduation. At this educational level, it was a proud day for all of us.

I had two weeks off before beginning additional graduate classes (still using my GI bill benefits) and starting a job I had agreed to take in Asheville, North Carolina as a carpentry instructor. A stubborn Hoyman, I used that time to drive to Kansas, one last chance at reconciliation with Martha. Even though I knew I didn't deserve it, she agreed to see me. Upon arrival, I was allowed to stay in a spare room in her brother's apartment. I was stricken with remorse, and I cried for two days. I wanted her forgiveness. Desperate, I went to Sunday service in the large, beautiful chapel at Mid-American Bible College and responded to the alter call, asking for God's help and understanding. A few men came over to help pray with me and asked me what I prayed for. I told them I prayed for forgiveness and reconciliation in my marriage. They responded by saying that sometimes, if you love someone, you have to be willing to let them go and trust in God to determine in the other person's heart the best answer. I left, trusting in what they told me, and trusting in God.

On Monday I got Martha's car serviced and bought new tires. I left that afternoon and went to St. Louis, Missouri to visit a former minister I knew back in Irwin, Pennsylvania. The minister and his family greeted me warmly and gave me a place to pray and fast for a few days. I hoped God would hear my concerns. My friends thought my prayers would be answered, but Martha did not respond, and I decided to go back to Pennsylvania, knowing in my heart I had gone the extra mile to make things right; now it was out of my hands. I guess this was part of my grieving process. To make matters worse, I drank a pint of chocolate milk to feed my starving body (after the fasting). The last thing I needed on an empty stomach was milk. I was doubled over with stomach pains, reminding me of my ulcer attacks back in Okinawa.

I arrived back at Penn State in time to complete eight more graduate credits before leaving for Asheville. I was interested in this job because of the beautiful mountain area and the opportunity for two weeks extra pay in early August. I was to set up the vocational building construction lab at Asheville High School. However, when I arrived for the job, they informed me that the yearly pay would be almost $4,000 less than what they'd promised because of the state-wide pay scale. I said I would stay and set up the shop, but if they couldn't correct the difference to our earlier agreement, I would not accept the position — scary since I didn't have another job. The school system could not live up to their commitment, and I wasn't going to start with a low wage, so I thanked them for their consideration and drove home, not knowing what my prospects were to be.

Luck was with me. When I arrived home on Sunday afternoon, my parents said the Howard County School System in Maryland (with whom I'd also interviewed before graduation) had an unexpected vacancy in their carpentry program. They wanted me to come right down for an interview. I called first thing that Monday morning, set up a two o'clock appointment, and drove four hours to the interview at the Howard County Vocational Technical Center. I interviewed with the school principal and county vocational director. After an hour-long discussion and tour of the facility, they offered me the job, and I accepted. I signed the contract the next morning and drove home to pack and move to Ellicott City as quickly as possible. I worked the first two weeks before Labor Day writing my program's curriculum.

Totally new to Maryland and the Baltimore area, I didn't know a soul in the community until Sunday when I attended the area's largest Nazarene Church. The pastor was nice enough to announce that a new teacher in the area wanted to rent a room temporarily and asked if anyone could help. A very nice young military doctor and his wife had a spare room. I could stay with them until I found an apartment. They also had a weekly Bible study in their home for younger adults, which I naturally participated in as their guest. Unbeknownst to me, this was where I would meet my second wife, Alice. I was fortunate to find an apartment I could afford a few weeks later, and I moved into a nice one-bedroom apartment just above the courthouse in Ellicott City.

I really wanted my own place, because it gave me room to settle into the community, and I needed privacy in which to express my feminine side. The job started well, but it was challenging, as I worked extra hard every evening trying to finish and revise my daily lesson plans. I was only working a month when I received a surprise call on a Thursday evening from Martha. She said she would attend a no-fault divorce hearing in the judge's chambers of the Olathe courthouse the next afternoon. The divorce that I did not know about until that moment would be final the next day. I knew it probably wouldn't change anything, but I had to try and be there to say my part and goodbye to Martha. I immediately called the airlines to book a ticket for an early flight the next morning to St. Louis, Missouri. I flew to St. Louis because my next call was to my former pastor friend; he knew the territory and could drive me the 200 or so miles to the Olathe courthouse. I also wanted moral support from a friend who loved us both. We made the 4:00 p.m. hearing with a few moments to spare, and Martha and her brother looked shocked when we walked into the judge's chambers. The judge acknowledged everyone present and read the plea for a no-fault divorce. He asked if anyone wanted to speak, and I raised my hand and said that there were difficulties in the marriage, but I still wanted to work on them, and I objected to the divorce. He thanked me, but said if one person wants the divorce, it doesn't matter what the other spouse says or thinks. He struck his mallet and granted the divorce; case closed.

Dan stayed close by Martha. As we entered the hall, I turned to her and said goodbye and wished her happiness. She walked down the corridor and through the stairway door — I never saw her again. Years later, she called once or twice to arrange financial assistance to her. Eventually, she remarried, but I have not heard from her since 1984.

My heart was heavy as we drove back to St. Louis, and on Sunday, I flew back to Baltimore and my new job. I had given the marriage and Ron's existence everything I could. I had tried to live up to God's expectations as a man and a husband.

Over the next six months, I spent more time than ever getting in touch with and trying to understand my feminine feelings. I took a great risk and agreed to be part of a group of transsexuals who gave their personal stories in a Baltimore Sun news article on transsexualism. My picture and comments appeared with four others, and I used the name Debbie to cover my male identity. Ms. Fitch, the counselor from Penn State, even called, saying she had a friend with a cabin outside State College. I could use this place to start my life transition. I was as close as I could come to reaching for the brass ring and taking her up on her offer, but I held back, afraid of the unknown, once again.

I had little money, and there was the risk of my teaching career, my parents, friends, and the church. I allowed my conditioning and everyone else's views dominate my very existence. If I had known then what I know now, I would have thrown caution to the wind and started my female journey. Instead, I tried to continue suppressing my feminine side and find a way to lead a socially acceptable male life. I celebrated my 32nd birthday in May, 1979 — 16 more years of frustration and turmoil to go.

Chapter 10

The Second Time Around

I was unable to muster the nerve to quit what was just the beginning of my teaching career, disappoint my family and friends, and overcome religious expectations. I started 1979 just as torn apart on the inside as ever. I was being relatively successful for a first-year teacher, but the job took a lot of my evenings and personal time. My biggest work frustration was an administration unwilling to back teachers who tried to implement strong classroom discipline and moral values. Feeling alone, I suppressed my feminine feelings and began dating women once again. With church being my primary social, as well as my spiritual outlet, various friends would introduce me to single women.

One particular lady by the name of Alice impressed me. She was someone I could relate to and we shared some common interests. We got to know each other better during the weekly Bible study (at the doctor's home where I'd lived temporarily when I first moved into the area). A few of the men from Bible study and I helped Alice move into a new apartment. I especially remember the fellows' comments on how one person could have so many clothes, which is funny, considering that 19 years later I have a wardrobe much larger than Alice's.

Alice and I began to date, yet she wasn't sure she wanted a serious relationship. As the months went on, we realized there was an emptiness in our lives. Our growing personal friendship seemed to fill this void. By April, I had a strong sense of love for Alice and I asked her to marry me. Alice had always had difficulty making up her mind, but she only took a short time to consider my proposal. Her answer was yes. We had the blessing and support of her family who lived close by, and of our many mutual church friends. The excitement of the pending wedding swept both of us up into the routine turmoil of planning: invitations, flowers, cake, ceremony, wardrobe, and other details. It was to be a church wedding in late July.

During the same time, I was becoming increasingly dissatisfied with the lack of support from the "good ol' boy" administration at the vocational center where I was teaching. I began to look into other options for employment in the educational field. Fortunately for me, I learned about a new position at the Frederick County Vocational Technical Center (50 miles west of Ellicott City and closer to my hometown in Western Pennsylvania) for a vocational evaluation/support services instructor. This position related to a new initiative in Maryland to evaluate and help special needs and at-risk students gain the additional guidance and support necessary to select and be successful in a vocational training program. Given test development experience, an assessment development assistantship at Penn State, a special needs instruction minor and my feminine caring personality, I seemed to be a perfect match for this new job opportunity. I applied, completed the interview, and was offered the position. Even though the job was grant funded ("soft money"), I was confident in my ability to make this new program succeed, and I accepted the position — a choice I have never regretted.

Alice felt good about this opportunity, although it would mean moving and starting our new life together all at the same time. Alice's parents had lived in Frederick, she'd graduated from Frederick High School, and her grandmother still resided there. Everything seemed to be falling into place when Alice began to have second thoughts about marrying me. We brushed it off as pre-wedding jitters and went ahead as planned. Even her family reassured me that all her misgivings would pass. I had been honest and shared my feminine feelings with her months before the marriage; we both agreed this would not be a problem in the marriage.

The big day came, late July, 1979. The church was full of Alice's friends, from work mostly, and our mutual friends from church. Of course both immediate families were there. Fifteen minutes before the wedding, Alice said she had to see me. "Ron, I have to talk to you now," she said.

"Now?" I said.

"Yes," she said.

We slipped into one of the rooms in the church basement. "I can't go through with the wedding, Ron. I know I should have been more definite about this earlier, but I can't do it."

I looked back at her, and said, "I love you. I still want to marry you and give the relationship a chance. If after a while you still don't want to be married to me, then I'll give you a divorce and help you on your own way."

I thought it could work, and with wedding music playing and a church full of people, I didn't want to go up in front of everyone and cancel at the last minute. She said she couldn't do that either, so with an undecided heart, she agreed to marry. We composed ourselves, and the wedding ceremony went fine (at least on the surface).

Our first night together was in a hotel about 100 miles west of Baltimore. The next morning we would head out for a two to three week honeymoon to see the sights across American — our final stop the Grand Canyon. We visited many of Alice's close girlfriends in Ohio and Missouri along the way. Money was limited, so we drove in my Chevrolet Chevette, but it did not have air conditioning and the summer was unusually hot. The honeymoon started out slowly. Alice was still going through with the marriage, the heat was sweltering, and Alice wanted to spend more time with one of her friends than we'd originally planned. Finally, we agreed to cut the trip short and return to Maryland. I guess you could say it was an abbreviated honeymoon, due to the heat, Alice's avoidance of interacting with me, and her commitment to the marriage.

We returned to our new apartment in Frederick. I had to prepare for my new teaching assignment, as well as try to develop a marriage, which was getting off to a rocky start. To regroup, I suggested we take a daytime trip to one of the local state parks. We needed to see if we could find any answers to the frustrations we were both experiencing — already. As we walked along a path among the tall trees of Catoctin Mountain Park (a few miles from Camp David), Alice confided in me. Her troubles had little to do with us. She'd had some bad relationships with men, and her father had been a negative influence in her life. Basically, Alice said she would have difficulty adjusting to a relationship or trusting any man in a marriage. She appreciated my willingness to end the relationship, as I'd promised, but agreed with me that the marriage deserved more time — a chance to succeed — a good try to make it work. I felt the same way, but the turmoil of the last month made it more difficult for me to live up to her expectations, meet her needs sexually, and still bury my feminine feelings. The marriage was in reality more a close friendship than a marriage.

I agreed to see a counselor recommended by our pastor and attend marriage counseling. A year into the marriage, at age 33, I drove to Washington, D.C., to see a special Christian counselor (who was also an expert in sexual identity issues). I remember the first time I met this stately looking gentleman. He had grayish hair and a beard; he looked like the classic, textbook counselor. I thought he might really know his stuff. I saw him on a weekly basis for a few months, explaining my history and feminine feelings — a spiel by now. I even began to change from Ron to Debbie in the cab of my truck (always a nerve-wracking experience), so he could interact with both aspects of my life. We were just beginning to discuss how my feminine identity issues related to his own opinions and the Biblical/religious values I was trying to live up to. Then I saw a sad newscast, he was arrested for sexually molesting one of his patients. My faith in counseling was shattered once again, and I reverted back to suppressing my feelings, living for others, and feeling a deep sense of hopelessness.

My job was going well, and I enjoyed my new vocational evaluation/support services duties and teaching/coordinating responsibilities, I poured countless energy and hours into building a successful career. However, it was financially difficult to get ahead on a teacher's salary or purchase a house in the Frederick area. This was a high cost of living area in a booming suburb of Washington, D.C. Thinking a move might breathe new life into a struggling relationship, we moved west to the South Mountain area and more affordable town of Hagerstown, Maryland.

Alice agreed we needed a change of scenery, plus she wanted her own home. Our decision proved that you can't buy happiness. A new house couldn't fix our broken down relationship. Anyway, we looked around Hagerstown and purchased a 30-year-old California- style rancher. We'd stretched things a bit financially. But we liked the older, quiet neighborhood on Phylane Street; it seemed a reasonable compromise to improving our housing needs and the stability of our marriage. Alice liked the house, neighbors, and the local Nazarene church. We set up housekeeping in our first real home.

Difficulties arose as we began our third year of marriage. The lack of sexual closeness pulled us apart. Alice enjoyed being a housewife and she liked her new friends. I escaped myself by remodeling the house. This superficial life could not last forever. About a year after we'd moved into our home, also our fourth year of marriage, signs of personal frustration were evident, something had to give. I was trying, but unsuccessful at fulfilling my role as a man and husband. One night after supper, I got unusually sleepy and went to bed early. The next night Alice confessed she had put sleeping pills in the scrambled eggs I had eaten for supper the night before. A desperate way to send me a message — slow down. I was failing at being a husband and using work to find a purpose for living. Alice got little of whatever energy was left. I did not know how to make her happy. Life as a man was forced and contradicted who I was. On the other hand, Alice wasn't happy, and she admitted the real reason she stayed in the relationship was because she liked the house more than me. She withdrew and at times refused to talk to me for weeks.

We both had our faults, but the marriage was becoming increasingly unhealthy. Something had to be done. It was painful, but I told Alice that the only way for both of us to be happy was to separate for a period of time to see if any answers were still possible. I was feeling extremely guilty that I had failed her, but Alice needed space to to do what was best for her. As if things weren't bad enough, I was mowing grass Saturday, April 23, 1983, when I received a call from home. My father had passed away from a massive heart attack. I was sad for him, for Dad wanted so much to make up for lost time — enjoy his forced early disability retirement (due to heart surgery seven years earlier) and watch his grandchildren grow up. He basically wore his heart out working to support our family and trying to get

Mother & Ron at Home in Pennsylvania

ahead. He was a person who never said a lot about his true feelings. He could never have a heart to heart talk with any of us children. I had always been there for him from my early childhood to the last years when I helped maintain the home repairs he was physically unable to do. My father always knew he could count on me; he was proud of my accomplishments. I was sad, but there were no regrets, no times when I wished I could have done things differently, no guilt over disappointing him. He never really knew of my total frustrations and dominate feminine identity. I guess one of the lessons I learned from him was to take pride in everything you do and always do it to the best of your ability. The strong work ethic he instilled in me was counterproductive in some ways; it repressed the daughter he never knew, but it did provide me with a purpose for living. I guess one of the reasons I could not do what was right for me early in life was because I didn't want to disappoint him or Mom. A short time before his death, we were riding in his truck, and we talked about some of the good times we'd had together. He said he was proud of me. I sensed in those silent moments of closeness he was, in his own way, saying goodbye to me.

I was proud he was my father, and I did not have any bitterness that we never went fishing, or all the other father-son things, which many would say I missed out on. Our times together were made up of mixing mortar to brick the house or building the front porch. We did chores, but we were still together. I resented counselors who felt his lack of traditional fathering was part of the reason for my femininity. I would have liked more fun times, but these environmental conditions would not have changed the female feelings and personality I was born with and craved to express.

The summer of my 36th birthday, I moved into an apartment in Hagerstown, and Alice went back to live with her grandmother in Frederick (temporarily until she could move into her own apartment). We signed a separation agreement, which allowed us to sell the Hagerstown house, equally dividing the profits. With all the improvements I had made, we each had a little nest egg to rebuild our lives, although we were still legally married under the separation agreement. For many reasons, the second time around and the last four years of life had brought just as many disappointments as answers. I had failed once again to prove my manhood and to be a good husband. My personal life was like a puzzle with so many pieces missing. I didn't know how it could ever be put together or how I would find acceptance or happiness as a man. Work continued to be my only success and escape to find a meaning for living.

Chapter 11

The Three R's of Life

It was time to face *reality* and *regroup* again. I began searching for answers on how I was going to *rebuild* my shattered life. I moved into an apartment from the summer of 1983 to 1984 on the outskirts of Hagerstown. It was cramped but reasonably-priced, temporary housing (until I could figure out just where my life was heading). Some close friends also lived in this area, and most days, we were able to car pool together to the Frederick County Vocational Center, where I not only worked, but also had many supportive and caring friends. I would later find out this support system meant more to me than I realized and was, in many ways, my surrogate family.

Work was the only stable part of my life; I continued to build a strong educational student support system that gained local and state recognition. It was the only secondary education program in Maryland in 1984 to receive the *Outstanding Vocational Education Program* award from the Maryland State Department of Education. This success was followed by my submission of a detailed proposal and evaluation, leading to the selection of the Vocational Evaluation/Support Service Program (I had built from scratch over the last five years) as one of twelve model programs in the nation to be honored by the U.S. Department of Education Secretary's Award for Outstanding Vocational Education Program. I received a lot of personal fulfillment from the delivery of education services, which made a real difference in students' lives, especially special needs students. This career-oriented success justified and validated at least a professional reason for life's existence and helped me regain some of my self-confidence, as I continued to recover from life's recent set backs.

I was a work-a-holic, and I know that if I were ever going to be able to afford a home again (especially in Frederick County), I would have to use my evenings and weekends, to do side jobs. So I used my talents and personal time to work and earn extra money for a home and a nest egg. Over the next 15 months, I responded to about half of my coworkers' requests to help them rebuild or remodel their homes. This work included building family rooms or extra bedrooms or finishing out basements or attics. I preferred finish work, like paneling rooms. A master with the portable circular saw, I could also complement the job with plumbing and electrical work. I would do a job from start to finish. I can't begin to count the thousands of hours, including holidays, I spent working side jobs over the years. Many of my friends still affectionately call the room I built in their homes the Hoyman room. My efforts paid off, and while my personal life was nonexistent, I earned and saved over $15,000 to start my own new home.

In the summer of 1984, I began to look for a home or property in Frederick County. Realizing that I still did not have the income or financial assets to purchase a single family home, I decided to set my sights on building the home of my dreams — a custom log home. I researched and checked seven different log home dealerships. I wanted value and quality and also a rural setting with a wooded lot. My efforts paid off in late summer. On a quiet Sunday afternoon, I noticed a "For Sale by Owner" sign on a single lot, close to Frederick, and heavily wooded. I knew it wouldn't last long, so I called the number, hoping the price wasn't too high. The gentleman who owned the property quoted me a price that seemed fair, but it would take all of my savings and then some. There was also the risk of not finding water, and I couldn't afford this potential problem. The property was set on nearly two mountainside acres (more suitable for sled riding); it was too good to pass up. Within a week I signed the contract.

But there were bigger questions looming. How could I afford to build the house, and afford the house payment on the loan once I built it? Interest rates were 10-12% and changed quickly. Mr. Lanyard, the property owner, was nice enough to use the land I had just purchased as collateral, and he loaned me $60,000 to build my home. Of course, I paid interest and had a limited time in which to complete the home. Then I'd have to acquire a permanent mortgage. With fall coming, I had to use every waking moment to clear the site for the house, find water, put in a foundation, get the log home shell up, and under roof before winter set in. I went through the County permit process as the main contractor, sub-contracting the foundation, septic and well drilling, while selecting Timberline (now Asperline) Log Homes as the source of my log home kit. I chose them because of the smooth milled log style (half round on the outside and flat on the inside), and the fact that they had a complete material package from the subfloor to the finish windows and finish stain. If I bought their special Timerline B model, a saltbox, two-story look with an open loft and connecting bridge walkway on the second floor, I could get the package by early fall and receive a free unfinished set of kitchen cabinets as a bonus.

My dream home was starting to become a reality, but I had to use all of my talents and energy to work like a squirrel, storing up my shelter for the winter, as the winds of autumn began to blow. Four of my friends from work kindly donated a Saturday to help me cut down sixteen, 50' to 70' oak trees to clear the setting I had marked for the house, driveway, carport, and well. By that evening, the trees were on the ground, with five of the straightest chopped into 10' to 12' lengths for sawmill lumber; the others were made into 18" to 24" firewood chunks. The next day I wore blisters on my feet moving the firewood pieces, one by one, to the top of the hill above the bulldozer excavation line. Within a week, the stubby four foot tall tree stumps were pushed over, removed from the property, and the initial bulldozing/excavation was completed.

Knowing I could not afford to drill more than two deep wells (the neighbor down the road drilled 10 wells to find adequate water), I sought out a well driller who used the old fashion witching method (like the Indians used to perform) to find water. The fork-like pointer said the best location for water was at the end of the future carport area. We maneuvered the well drilling rig up the steep driveway and, to my neighbor's surprise, hit a two-gallon per minute stream three hundred feet down. He finished and capped the well in one shot. This was truly a blessing from God.

Next, I poured 10 yards of concrete to make a driveway base in the moist, clay-like hill, so we would be able to get the trucks in place, and I poured an eight inch, solid concrete foundation with a brick mold facing. The three-ton log home section units were delivered, and the wooden floor joists and subfloor were nailed down just as a major hurricane moved in to hit the East Coast (I think it was Agnes). I postponed putting up the log shell for a whole week. Instead, my brother, Bill, and I sloshed through the ankle deep mud and drenching rain to build the front porch deck for safety purposes and to make raising the log home easier.

As brightly colored leaves painted the landscape, the weather finally cleared, and I hired five strong guys to swing

Laying the Foundation for Ron's Dream Home

the sledge hammers. We drove in the 10" spikes and fastened each row of the log home kit together. The log rows were numbered, and the exterior log shell went up in five days. Within seven days the huge beam rafters (with tongue and groove-exposed, interior roofing, covered with black felt paper) were up. With a crew chief from the log home company, a group of hired concrete workers, temporary rough carpenters, and some key friends, I beat the odds and turned a heavily wooded lot into the rough exterior of an unfinished log home shell (with foundation) in just two months.

For the next 11 months, I worked six to eight hours every evening, long weekends, and long summer days doing nearly all of the electric, plumbing, carpentry, staining, and finishing of the home; I got my permanent mortgage and moved in during October, 1986. The only work I did not perform on

Ron's Dream Home Becomes Reality

the house was the furnace installation and laying the finished carpet. I finished the kitchen cabinets and laid the red brick-style ceramic floor (the New Year's day Penn State beat Miami for the National Championship at the Fiesta Bowl).

My two companions during these long, cold winters and the following summer months were a portable television and a kitten I named Nittany. I adopted Nittany right after I began building the house. We survived on hot dogs, baked beans and fast food each night. For housing during that time period, I was fortunate enough to have a friend at work who rented me her finished basement to keep expenses manageable; it was a place to sleep and shower. In 13 months of construction I only missed three nights of construction work on the home.

My personal life as Ron did not exist. But at least I had managed to rebuild and refocus my life, something I would not have dreamed possible. The three years of living in the home continued to be busy ones, as I put on my interior decorator hat, landscaper hat, deck builder hat, retaining wall builder hat and carport builder hat to finish turning the two-acre plot into a completely finished home. By the time my 41st birthday came around, I had finished the home of my dreams, a natural retreat, nestled in the woods, just five minutes from Frederick.

My accomplishments were rewarding, but my life was still empty. I learned more than ever that materialism could not bring happiness or peace to a troubled soul. This emptiness made me question the value of life more than ever. I wondered if I would ever find the joy that was constantly eluding me.

It had now been three years since Alice and I had separated, and we still had not finalized the divorce. I had a die-hard spirit which made me think maybe the time apart would mend the frustrations of before. I did not want to just walk away from my commitment and marriage vows to her. Since we were both now relocated to Frederick, I had seen her now and then while I was building the house. She liked the home but we both had learned by then that a house wouldn't make a happy marriage. Not living together did ease the tension and strained interpersonal disappointments, and in many ways; our separation confirmed that we did at least have a good friendship. She had managed to get a steady job and rebuild her life, but she still struggled financially. While not legally required to help her financially, I continued to provide her with substantial financial help over the years, so she could maintain a standard of living and not face some of the struggles many wives have to face during a divorce and separation.

Inside Ron's Cozy New Home

She appreciated the assistance and knew that I was not trying to buy her love or manipulate her with money. I even went with her to pick out and negotiate the purchase of her new car a short time before we finalized the divorce. We both wanted the other to be happy, and after eight years of marriage (more separated than together), we knew it wasn't right to stay together simply for the sake of a piece of paper. Alice remarried and I learned once again that it was difficult to find happiness as a husband or a man. How could I realize happiness and love someone else when I couldn't love or be my true self? The questions still remained unanswered, as I drove home each night to my beautiful, empty, log house.

Chapter 12

What Next?
How Much Can a Guy Take?

Summer of 1989: I was 42 and had been living on my own for over five years, working myself to exhaustion. I longed for more than a home that could be on the cover of Better Homes and Gardens or a job for which I had gained state and national recognition. I needed to feel and be loved for who I was, not what I had accomplished.

Once again, I chose the only avenue which society allowed me and considered dating — rusty and inexperienced as I was. I was the leader for a workshop group of counselors; they affectionately referred to me as their "mother hen watching her chicks." I organized and led a summer workshop in June, 1988, where I took a group of twenty counselors and teachers to about fifteen different businesses to gain a first-hand understanding of the world of work and job opportunities in our community. This being the fifth year in a row that I had run the popular workshop I had gotten to know and develop friendships with many of the participants.

That year I met one particularly attractive and intelligent single lady, Kathy. She had a great personality, and we began joking and teasing each other throughout the week. Enjoying her company, I mustered up enough courage to ask her out on a date, and she accepted. With more freedom in our summer schedules, we would do inexpensive but fun things: walks in the park, tennis (she was good, and I was a novice), theater, or hiking in Harpers Ferry, West Virginia. We shared confidences with each other and we were both recovering from failed marriages. I did not tell her of my feminine personality, because I still didn't feel this would ever have a chance of becoming a reality, given all my unsuccessful attempts to express the real me in the past. I was hoping to find that magic formula that would bring some happiness to Ron's life. One thing Kathy taught me was that no one can ever take away a person's memories and that we should try and capture or create time for happy memories as we walk through life — before it's too late. I will always thank her for teaching me that simple but priceless thought.

As our friendship developed, Kathy shared with me that her former mate had not treated her with the respect she deserved. Like many ladies, she was taking a step of faith by allowing herself to trust a man again. My lack of the traditional male aggressiveness was a plus in building a trustful and respectful relationship. Rebuilding her life as a single mom also left Kathy with financial hardships, a struggle I had finally overcome. When I found out she had spent the last winter wearing a coat to drive most of the time, because she could not afford to get the heater in her old car fixed, I wanted to help her out. No one should have to make those kind of sacrifices. She did not even have a garage door opener on her house, a luxury she couldn't afford. So, one day I surprised her and put one in for her, since I had those talents, not only as a friendly gift but as a security measure for when she came home late at night.

I was blessed financially, and I had talents that God had given me to build my new home. I decided to give her a gift which would be considered, in most cases, going overboard, and it probably was. But, since I had been used to and conditioned to do more for others than myself, I had set up a special surprise for her birthday in early fall. On a day we both could arrange to take a personal day off from work, I took her to the Inner Harbor in Baltimore for an afternoon lunch/dinner on one of those special harbor cruises. On the way back to Frederick, I took the scenic route past Ellicott City, where I used to live and asked her if she would mind stopping by the large Honda dealership just to look around. As we walked in the showroom, I created a memory both of us would never forget. As she saw a bright red, sporty model 1989 Honda Accord with California style custom wheels and a big bow on the roof, I yelled, "Happy birthday, Kathy!" She was shocked and said she appreciated the thought but couldn't accept that kind of gift. I looked at her and asked her if she liked it. "Of course, I love it!" was her response. I told her that God had been good to me, and I wanted to bring a blessing to her life — no strings attached. I told her I had already signed the contract and paid for it (through a car loan) with the title in her name, and they couldn't take it back. A gift is not a gift unless you give it freely with nothing expected in return, and I meant that. She said I shouldn't have and reluctantly but happily thanked me, knowing she had little other choice. Of course, that made her birthday, and I probably should not have given such an expensive gift to her from a common sense point of view, but I have never regretted doing it, and I know she has enjoyed many happy and safe moments driving it.

We continued dating, as she showed me how to cross country ski early that winter and helped Ron pick out a better professional wardrobe. It was with mixed emotions that I applied for and was preparing to start a new job, which was offered as the Maryland State Supervisor of all trades and industry teachers. The job was in downtown Baltimore at the Maryland State Department of Education (MSDE), and since Ron was not into clothes, I had to improve my wardrobe for this new, professional arena.

I appreciated Kathy's friendship, and by Christmas, I had hoped to start moving the strong friendship into a more personal relationship, since we had been dating for six months, and I had never even kissed her. I tried to respect her initial need for space and trust. At Christmas, we exchanged gifts, but for whatever personal reasons she had, she said she did not want to move forward and make our friendship into a relationship. She wanted to put all of her energy into raising her two lovely daughters. She appreciated all of the good times we had shared together and all I had done for her, but it was time to go our separate ways. She said, under the circumstances, she wanted to start repaying me for the car or give it back. I knew money was still tight for her and had given the car to her without any strings attached. I would eventually pay it off and said it would not be right to expect the car back, for I gave it as a gift. She said I was truly a man of my word, and I had shown her a true Christian spirit she would never forget. I had come to the point in my life where the happiness of others meant more to me than my own. If I could not be happy myself then at least I could bring happiness to others I was fond of, no matter what the cost. I also believe you should treat others with the kindness and respect you would like them to show you in return. What goes around comes around, and others have been so kind and supportive to me in their acceptance of my true self, Rhonda, that I feel that God is giving me back some of the blessings I had shown Kathy and so many others in Ron's life. Life is not always measured in dollars and cents.

I was heartbroken yet again by the recent turn of events, but life had to go on, and the challenges of my new job awaited me to start in 1990. What I didn't realize (and no one has ever known) was that the disappointment of pulling back from Kathy and leaving my close friends at the Frederick County Vocational Technical Center (where I had worked for the past ten years), left such a personal void in my life that I went into a very deep depression. Feeling totally alone in life, I spent many of my first few months driving the 50 miles from Frederick to Baltimore and back again, crying my heart out. I questioned the price I paid for this career move. By the time I got to Baltimore, I was so mentally and emotionally drained that it took all the will power and physical strength I had to even walk from the parking garage to my new cubicle office on the third floor of 200 West Baltimore Street. I had too much to lose to quit, but that's what I wanted to do. Life was just a matter of going through the motions and putting on a happy face and act at work. If I had not gone through my former battles in life to gain some toughness, I would have definitely had a nervous breakdown. It took me until late spring and my 43rd birthday to regain my self-confidence, physical strength, and hope.

One of the blessings of my job as Trades and Industry Supervisor at the State Department was the many new friendships I began to establish with my peers and especially with my immediate supervisor, Maggie Caples, the Section Chief of our department. We would spend many long hours working together on program issues for the "40 plus" trades and industry occupational careers I supervised. I supported 760 teachers throughout Maryland.

I began attending Faith Reformed Presbyterian Church, and I made some good friends and began supportive counseling with the pastor and his wife. By early fall, I was adjusting to my new work environment, but it occupied more time than I was accustomed to in Frederick, especially the extra three hour commute each day. A new couple had moved to the area at this time and learned about my interest in establishing a personal life and introduced me to one of their single friends, who still lived in Northern Virginia, 50 miles south of Frederick. I wondered if I should start dating again, but I was still lonely and had to start rebuilding my personal life sometime. Laura was almost my age and seemed very nice.

I asked Laura to go out, and we began dating throughout the fall, finding we had many similar interests. She liked my log home and appreciated my carpentry skills, which I used to build her and the couple she stayed with a nice dog box. She had a Shelty Collie, which was also my favorite dog. Laura had never been married. Like Kathy, we took the time to become friends before starting a more serious relationship. It was not easy working in Baltimore, living in Frederick, and dating a lady from Northern Virginia, so we only saw each other on weekends, and I spent some late sleepy-eyed nights on the road.

Because I was becoming fond of Laura, as much as Ron could, I told Laura of my feminine identity struggles so that the issue would not stand in the way of the honesty and trust I was trying to establish with her. I also wanted her to know that I would never hide anything from her and that I was trying to put this issue behind me, personally hoping I could still find peace and happiness as Ron, especially with God's help. After sharing this delicate and difficult issue with her, Laura confided in me she was seeing a counselor who was helping her understand and improve her personal life issues. I even went with her to her counselor one time to show my good faith and prove to both of them the kind of man and person I was. Being 44, I was basically void of feelings from all my recent struggles and felt like if life was going to mean anything to me personally, I had to put all the energy I had into living up to life's expectations as Ron.

Laura had her concerns, but she liked my maturity and the fact that I did not have a shallow personality like many of the men she dated.

Regaining my confidence from last Christmas' disappointments, I asked Laura to marry me. She said she needed time to think about it; she would consider my proposal. Laura wanted a home, a family, and someone who cared about and understood her needs. During Christmas vacation, we both had more time to spend with each other, and as the week went on, I began to wonder if she would say yes. To my surprise, on New Year's Day, before I went to pick her up for our trip to Baltimore and New Year's Day party with some of her family and friends, she said yes to my marriage proposal with a big hug and kiss.

Her mother, stepfather and real father all lived in the Baltimore area. It looked like 1991 was starting off just the opposite of 1990, as we talked about a summer wedding. However, as spring came into bloom, doubts began to surface in Laura's mind, as she told me her counselor had concerns about our marriage. She said because of my past feminine life struggles, she wanted me to have a psychological personality test by a Christian counselor her family knew and trusted in the Towson area; ironically, not far from where I live now. Having nothing to hide and wanting to reassure, I set up an appointment with the doctor and paid $600 to go through tests such as the ink blot (tell me what you see), a long multiple choice psychological personality test, and a long personal interview with one of the staff associates. Finally, the afternoon came when he was supposed to review the results with Laura and me. During the analysis of his report, he concluded, with limited real knowledge from me, that I was a person with deep-seated anger, emotionally and psychologically troubled in life, a person seeing things from a negative versus a positive side. He advised Laura to think twice about marrying me before counseling with him. I left shell-shocked. I knew I'd had my share of struggles in the past and that I had a suppressed feminine identity, which I still felt like nothing could come of, but I was doing a pretty good job of trying to find happiness as Ron, and I was up front with Laura. I did not then nor had I ever had an angry bone in my body. I did not feel emotionally unbalanced, and I was a person who looked at the positive versus the negative side of life. Laura was understandably upset and said she needed time to be alone that day as I drove her home.

I felt betrayed. While I was not perfect, I was once again being misjudged and mistreated by the Christian counseling profession. Personally, I felt I had just paid to voluntarily go in front of the firing squad, and they'd hit me with both barrels. Laura agreed to meet me the next weekend. She was depressed herself, feeling like her dreams were being taken away from her. We both cried and agreed the marriage was off. I saw her once again after that to help her move from the home she was staying in to a house with one of her girlfriends. I never saw her again after that. I respected her wishes, treated her respectfully and let the relationship go.

Maybe it was God's way of keeping me from hurting her later in life. But I felt I was not given a fair trial; certainly, I was not treated with the same trust and honesty I had shown. Heartbroken once again as I turned 44, I wondered what else I could do. How much disappointment could I take in life? I questioned all the countless efforts I was making to be a man. Still I ignored and suppressed the cries of help from the little girl and woman inside me. Indeed, what would come next? Was life worth it? Would I ever find happiness? These became bigger questions than I could ever imagine.

Chapter 13

Ron's Last Struggle to Find Happiness

With Ron's personal life taking another recent knockout punch, I began to bury myself in my busy schedule at the Maryland State Department of Education and with side carpentry jobs. I built a deck around my sister's new above ground swimming pool back in Pennsylvania, and I remodeled my dentist's office and did some home improvements at his house as well. Helping family was always a priority and earning some extra money was a productive way to pass the limited personal time I had.

I had become successful with my new job as the state's trade and industry supervisor, and I was gaining a reputation as a knowledgeable administrator. Unbeknownst to me, Mr. Camron, a terrific gentleman, top notch career and technology education director, and pillar of his community in St. Mary's County, Maryland, was watching my performance, considering me as his future successor at a job he'd had for 28 years. Mr. Camron had tragically been diagnosed with Lou Gehrig's Disease and began losing his ability to carry on his responsibilities and function independently in life. I wasn't happy with the hands-off, state-level administrative position in Maryland, and I wanted to have more impact at a local school system. I followed up on a request to interview for his high-profile and influential position on rather short notice.

Not thinking I would have as good of a chance as one of the local applicants, I drove down to St. Mary's county one early morning for my interview on one night's preparation. The interview went well, and I left the county two hours after arriving, as I had an appointment back in Baltimore that afternoon. To my surprise, I received a call the next afternoon and was offered the job, which I happily accepted. I felt honored to be selected. The job meant a $5000 pay raise, and it was my first local administrative position. My friends and boss at the state were sorry to see me go, but pleased for me, and I would still be working with them in a different capacity.

Not wanting to sell my beautiful log home, which was so much a part of me, I rented it out to an Army colonel and his family who worked at the Department of Energy. I phased out my state responsibilities and moved to St. Mary's County in the fall of 1991. I didn't have a place to live, nor did I know the area, so I was fortunate to be able to rent the upper floor of the former headmaster's quarters at the Sotterly Plantation, a 100-year-old, U.S. landmark. The county leased the plantation for historic and instructional purposes; the first floor of the house was used as part of an outdoor school for students to learn about early plantation farming. St. Mary's County still had many cotton, tobacco, and soybean farms, as well as a good representation of Amish people. You can still see horses and buggies, traveling up and down the country roads, a simple life style. In some ways, I thought I was going back in time or moving to the deep South. Ironically, the Patuxent Naval Air Corps Training Base and hub of defense contractors are right smack in the center of the county.

The old white frame house I moved into had low ceilings, limited electricity, and a crowded old bathroom; it was not the modern log home I was used to. But, the trade off of living at a beautiful old plantation mansion was worth it. I soon found out that it also fit my new lifestyle — a demanding new job which allowed little time for anything except eating and sleeping, even on weekends. No one could ever fill the shoes of Mr. Camron, but I was able to keep the wheels moving as the new supervisor of trades and industry, business education, family studies, technology education, and school-to-career cooperative education. I was also a part of a three-county consortium, a national tech prep model demonstration site, and one of only two school systems in Maryland to serve as a model for the integration of academics in vocational education. I earned every penny of my new raise, as I usually worked 14 to 16 hour days, six to seven days a week. I rose to the challenge, learning a lot along the way, finding it easy to lose myself in the job and continue my workaholic tradition.

Nine months passed as did my 45th birthday. I yearned for a personal life and companionship, which seemed impossible time wise and questions regarding my manhood still haunted me. There were so many failures in Ron's life as a man. I would have to throw away my career in order to give my feminine side a realistic chance. I had no real support system. The male side of life would get one more chance. Summer of 1992, I purchased a nice, one-acre, wooded lot in a new housing development, Chestnut Ridge, three miles from my office at the St. Mary's County Technical Center. I chose a nice, 2,000 square foot colonial style house with a wrap around front porch, vaulted ceilings, white vinyl siding and royal blue shingles — a modern version of *The Walton's* home. I oversaw the construction, but with my busy schedule, I only had time to build the exterior 6'x 6' retainer walls and lay the bathroom, foyer, and kitchen ceramic tile floor work; a general contractor actually built the house.

By late fall, the house was starting to take shape, and I wondered how I would begin dating again or meeting single women. I certainly was not into the social scene. My younger sister, Darlene, asked if I would be interested in dating one of her friends, who worked with her at one of the local supermarkets. Her friend, Susan, was a single mom with two young daughters (ages five and seven); Susan was 12 years younger than I. On my next trip home, a five to six hour drive, Darlene arranged a blind date. I met Susan at her mobile home and took her and her daughters to the nearby King's Family Restaurant where she liked to eat. We had a good time, and while we came from different backgrounds, we both had our Western Pennsylvania roots and had graduated from the same high school. Susan was an attractive lady with a nice personality and caring attitude, who was looking to settle down with someone who enjoyed the simple, more traditional things in life. We decided to see each other more, but that meant long-distance trips to Pennsylvania for a weekend date twice a month. It also meant late Sunday night return trips to St. Mary's County for me and many nights sleeping at the Breezewood, PA rest stop on the way home. I knew this long-distance romance could not last long before becoming serious (faster than it probably should have).

During Christmas vacation, I had enough time to bring Susan down to the new home I had just moved into in St. Mary's, and we both decided to plan for a late spring wedding; she would move when the girls finished school in May. Winter flew by, and we had a Saturday wedding in April, 1993, at the Frederick Nazarene church I had attended, halfway between Greensburg and St. Mary's. Our friends and family could easily attend. Many of my friends in Frederick wanted to participate and helped with the details of the nice, but simple wedding, which was performed by my pastor friend, Reverend Lathrum. While limited by distance, we did have premarital counseling with Reverend Lathrum and his wife on Saturdays before the wedding to make sure we were doing the right thing. We wanted a Christian foundation to the marriage. I had discussed with Reverend Lathrum whether or not I should share my feminine personality with Susan, but he said since it was not part of my life now, I should be able to be a good husband — with God's help. I still wondered if this was the best choice, but decided not to bring up the issue, a decision I would later regret.

We left the day after the wedding on a week-long honeymoon to the Bahamas. After all, I was trying to do things right for a change and start the marriage off on the right foot. We both enjoyed the trip; unfortunately, we had our rough moments from the start. Susan missed her girls more than she thought she would and worried, even though they were staying with her parents. I could not perform sexually in a way that would please a younger wife, and since this was the first extended personal time we'd had together, we ran out of common interests quickly. By the time the trip ended, the honeymoon was literally and philosophically over. I felt like such a failure, not meeting Susan's needs, and she missed her kids and Pennsylvania. We both began to wonder if we'd done the right thing by getting married.

The weeks passed and Susan sold her mobile home to her brother. As planned, Susan and the girls moved to St. Mary's County in late May. Unfortunately, the culture of southern Maryland was a lot different from western Pennsylvania. I still had to work longer hours than I wanted, and our value systems began to clash. I was too strict in my expectations of her children. With the summer free for the kids, and her requirement to take the girls and spend one weekend a month with their biological father, they made extended trips back to Pennsylvania; things were rocky. Not only was I under constant pressure at work, but the continued failure in trying to have a good personal relationship, and my less than positive attempts at being a man and good husband were quickly creating more stress and frustrations, as I began my third marriage.

It was totally unexpected at this time, but the position of technical program supervisor became available in Baltimore County Public Schools. I was interested in applying, and could once again work for Superintendent Berger, with whom I'd worked in Frederick County. This opportunity would allow me to specialize my services and expertise in trade and industry technical program leadership. It would mean another $5,000 raise, and allow me to move back to Frederick County. The drawback — another 55 mile (one way) commute. Even though Susan had just moved to St. Mary's County, she liked the idea of being two hours closer to Western Pennsylvania, and she liked the community of Frederick better than St. Mary's County. So, I applied for and went through the three-step interview process and was offered the job. My experiences and credentials in the trades and industry/technical program area were strong; so I knew I had a realistic chance and could do a good job if selected.

The renters in my log home were getting ready to retire from the military and move home to Florida, so we were able to move back into the Frederick log home right before the girls started school. With the St. Mary's house in a good location and like new, I was also able to sell it in late summer without taking a loss. If only the rocky marriage and our personal lives would get better. Perhaps I could find success all the way around.

As we settled into Frederick and our first year of marriage, Susan and the girls liked the home, the neighbors, their school, and their new friends at church, but they didn't seem to like the one other part of the equation — me. We were able to manage finances; Susan did not have to work, so she could spend more time with the girls, take some beginning classes at Frederick Community College to improve the educational and job skills she never had a chance to develop, and become more involved with the Presbyterian church. I was almost a source of irritation and felt out of place, because I could not spend as much time at home. I worked long hours, traveled a long commute, was too strict, and conflicted with Susan's more lenient child-rearing rules. I continued to fail at understanding Susan's personal values and meeting her womanly needs sexually.

The disappointment and frustrations were taking a toll on me also, as I not only felt like a failure at the marriage, but also began to question my manhood, found it difficult to suppress my feminine feelings (especially living in a house with three females), and wondered if I would ever be happy or could make Susan and her girls happy. By the start of 1994, I realized Susan and I both would need help or some form of counseling if the marriage was going to survive. We talked to Reverend Lathrum for a few sessions, and he suggested a male Christian counselor that Susan and I could see individually, as well as jointly. Susan began counseling with Mr. Clark for a few months to help her with her personal needs as well as the marriage issues. Then, I started seeing him a few times each month before we started joint sessions. The counseling helped both of us realize the differences we had, and he gave his recommendations. Susan benefited from her separate sessions. On the whole, we had such different values and family raising expectations, more than we realized, and it was not easy to make the progress we'd hoped. I told Mr. Clark about my personal frustrations and increased battles trying to suppress my feminine identity feelings; everything was on the table. He appreciated my honesty and tried to make suggestions, saying he was impressed at how I was trying to give the male life and marriage a chance, even when I knew he was telling me something I'd already tried. But truthfully, I was trying to live up to manly and religious expectations which didn't appeal to my dominant feminine side. By August, 1994, I decided that no matter how painful it was, I had to tell Susan of my increasing frustrations and unhappiness as a man.

We had a week without the girls when they were visiting their father for a late summer vacation, so when she returned from dropping them off in Pennsylvania, I said I needed to talk with her about some personal matters. We took a ride that Sunday afternoon after church, and gently as I could, I told her of my personal identity struggles, apologized for not telling her earlier, thinking they would never resurface, and for not being able to fulfill her needs sexually. Naturally, this surprised and upset her, but she said she was glad I had told her, and it helped her understand why I acted the way I did. I also apologized for spending what little free time we had building an addition onto the master bedroom instead of spending that time with our family. After a short while, she told me of some personal shortcomings she'd had that were not best for her or the marriage. Now that I had shared my personal shortcomings, she could share hers. I thanked her for being brave enough to share them with me and forgave her for keeping a secret. That was not an easy or happy afternoon, but a necessary one. It was clear that we were two troubled people suffering a troubled marriage.

I told her that I didn't want to hurt her anymore, and I couldn't go on in life without some resolution to my conflicts. It wasn't fair for her to be married to a man who could not meet her needs mentally, emotionally, physically, or financially. We both agreed we would continue counseling. If in nine months, the end of our second year of marriage, things didn't improve I would help her move back to Pennsylvania and rebuild her life. She liked Frederick a lot, but her family and childrens' visitation needs made Pennsylvania a better location.

We continued counseling, but I knew I wasn't benefiting or finding any answers to my individual issues, so I tapered off counseling with Mr. Clark. All the while I became less of a man. The desire to become a total woman filled my thoughts obsessively, more than I knew how to handle. I began looking for help.

I heard a speech therapist, Dr. Linda Spencer, on a Baltimore radio station talk about the differences between male and female voices. I was impressed by her knowledge, and since achieving a realistic or passable female voice had always been my goal, I made an appointment with Dr. Spencer. She was very nice, as I told her my real feminine identity issues and asked her what I could do or if she could even help me if I made the transition. She tested my voice, said she could and would help me if I needed her services, but at this time it was not appropriate. She said progress is not made when going back and forth. If I decided to make a female life transition, I could seek her expertise. She asked if I had a personal counselor who was experienced in serving transsexual life issues. I told her I didn't. She recommended I see Dr. Gregory Lehne, a licensed psychologist, an expert in this field of counseling. I thanked her for her honesty and recommendation.

I did make an appointment with Dr. Lehne, because if I were to ever be able to make it as a man or husband, I really had to understand the depth and true nature of my femininity.

I went to see Dr. Lehne in November, 1994, with an open mind, desperately needing to make sense of all that was going on. Dr. Lehne warmly greeted me and went through the standard "Why are you here?" life history questions, then ones with which I was so familiar. By the end of our second session, I asked him his opinion of me and my marriage issues. He said I had to make the decision, but in his opinion, I was a classic case of a male to female transsexual, and in my heart I knew what I needed to do. There was only one solution for real peace and happiness. I looked back at him and told him that I knew that meant becoming a total woman if I were ever going to be happy. He said I had to resolve my marriage and family issues, and when I was ready, he could help me. I left that afternoon, a 47-year-old man, knowing what I had to do, but that didn't make it any easier.

I told Susan of my two sessions with Dr. Lehne and said I wanted to arrange one more session with him, so she could ask questions. He could explain why I felt like I did and what his diagnosis was, without my personal biases. We made the appointment, talked with him jointly. Although Susan didn't agree with everything Dr. Lehne said, she did understand more of what I was going through. Susan continued to see Dr. Clark for her personal counseling needs and support, and we continued periodic joint counseling. By now we knew we had talked all we could, and as sad as it was to admit, the only way for Susan and I to have any real future happiness was to end the marriage and go our separate ways. We started 1995 knowing what had to be done when summer came. We tried to make the best of our current situation until the girls finished school in May. I felt like a royal heel, but I knew to continue the marriage would be worse for both of us.

Susan did have two work-free years to spend time with her daughters, and she appreciated my efforts and honesty, and in many ways, was a stronger person than when we had first met. Still, it was hard to accept that the end of our marriage was near.

To help her rebuild her life, I agreed to a separation agreement which gave her a vacant building lot next to a mobile home we'd bought and rented out a year earlier in South Greensburg, close to her parents. With an additional monthly alimony check for two years, and the money she was receiving from the sale of her previous mobile home, she could make ends meet and build a new small home on the lot. To make this possible, I put my personal time and needs on hold. I researched the best, affordable modular home options, subcontracted out the excavation and building of a full basement foundation with a built in garage, and by the end of September (in less than four months), we had a new 24' x 42' modular home set up, approved to building code and ready for Susan to move into and own. She had moved back to Pennsylvania over the summer to live temporarily with her parents, so the girls could start school back in Pennsylvania. It wasn't easy on her, I know, and I didn't get much sleep on weekends, but at least she and the girls had a new home they could call their own. I continued to travel back and forth every weekend until late November, doing landscaping, setting up the sidewalk and the driveway, building stairs and a small deck for the back porch, inside basement steps, a dividing wall between the garage/basement and laundry room, plumbing and electric work, and all the essential finish jobs needed to make the house fully functional and livable. My brother, Bill, was also a big help with these projects. Without his extra help, I couldn't have completed the work so quickly. Susan loved the home and appreciated all I did to help her reestablish her life, but we both knew it was time to move on, and I didn't see her very much after this. We had to work out the details of transferring the mortgage and

Another Hard Day at the Modular Home

construction loan I had taken out, and I was exhausted, using all of my construction talents and waking hours to pull off a small miracle. God was good to me, as he gave me the extra energy I needed to work beyond my limits and guide me safely back to Frederick each weekend with limited sleep. Once again, I spent most Sunday nights sleeping at the Breezewood Rest Stop.

Now, halfway into my 48th year of existence, I knew I had given my all to finding happiness as a man and husband — three times without success. It was now time for the biggest challenge in my life to begin. I would become the woman I had always wanted to be.

Chapter 14

Jump Starting Rhonda and Life's Transition

The first steps of preparation to my full time transition really started in August of 1994, when I finally began to break down some of my defenses and allow Rhonda her chance to exist. While attending a two day training conference in Southern Virginia (almost three hundred miles from Frederick) and in an area where no one really knew me, I could check out the local mall and other stores on the availability of women's clothing and accessories. I wanted to be discrete in making a first time purchase (even in an area that was safe and far away from home). I had been resisting this temptation for so many years, but this was the beginning of a final, make-it-or- break-it quest for the answers to my true identity. That Wednesday evening, pretending I was looking for a gift for my wife, I went window shopping. So conditioned to suppress my feminine identity, I didn't have enough nerve to make a purchase.

I returned the next evening after dinner to buy the initial items necessary to start dressing as a woman. Not wanting to spend a lot of money on items I didn't even know if I would use often (or if they would be the right size), I began to put a rough wardrobe together. First I went to a department store and purchased some make-up: foundation, powder, compact, lipstick, eyebrow pencil, eye shadow, mascara, and rouge. So as not to be so obvious (which I probably was), I purchased these items, took them to the car, and went back for size 10, white, flat shoes, an off-white purse, a size 32-B bra, and some pantyhose. This took care of the undergarments, but what about the dress and wig? They did have a wig shop with a pretty good variety, but how was I supposed to select the best color and style without trying on different selections? I must have spent half an hour walking up and down the mall, back and forth, past the wig store, building up my nerve, and hoping for a slow time when no one else was in the store. Finally, on the fourth pass, I walked in nervously and approached the young lady standing behind the display counter. I told her I didn't exactly know how to approach her with the subject, but I let her know that I had feminine interests and wanted to select a wig for myself. I asked if she would be willing to help me. She was polite, smiled nicely, and said she would help. She'd been asked that question before and sensed my obvious nervousness. She asked me to look around and pick out a few different styles and colors, and she would put them in the back room where I could try them on in private. I made about six selections and slipped into the small back room, as someone else came into the store. I found a simple and basic style, which seemed to suit me. Too many curls were unrealistic, short styles were too masculine, and blonde was too light for my pale complexion. The sales lady slipped in, made a few suggestions, and I purchased a light brown wig with bangs — an almost shoulder length cut. I felt lucky to find such a good choice for a synthetic wig (human hair was too expensive). Along with the wig I bought a pair of clip on earrings from their accessory department, thanked the clerk for her understanding and kindness, and slipped out of the door, still embarrassed, but relieved to have pulled it off.

With only 30 minutes before the stores closed, I strolled into the women's section of a small Sears store and started sorting through the dresses on a sale rack. I guessed at a

Rhonda Emerges

size 14, traditional A-line cut, red with a white lace collar, and reasonably priced. I hoped it would fit okay. Like Cinderella just as the clock struck twelve, I left the mall at 9:00, hoping I too could be a princess some day.

I returned to the privacy of my own hotel room, and unloaded my purchases, curious to see how my feminine appearance would come out from my best guess shopping spree. Compared to my current wardrobe and full transition appearance, you could say I was pretty rough looking, but still I liked it. It was a good first step in passing as a woman in public. The conference over, I wanted to start the long drive home to see how I felt as a woman even if only in the privacy of my car. With my nerve up and confidence growing, I slipped into a unisex restroom to change into my new clothes. I changed and got out to the car (undiscovered) and drove about an hour up the road; my courage and self-confidence as Debbie grew faster than it should. Since I was still far from home, I decided to try another brief shopping stop in public, just to see how things would go. I pulled into a strip shopping area along the roadside and went inside a dress store. As I entered, one of the girls in the store asked if she could help me. In as soft a voice as I could, I told her I was just looking. I tried to remain calm and picked out two summer dresses to try on — one aqua the other green and form-fitting. I went into the dressing room and squeezed myself into them. They both looked better than the red one I was wearing. I shouldn't have bought them, but my ego was growing, and I felt I could lose weight, so I made my purchase and left the store without anyone questioning my feminine identity. Looking back on things, I can't believe they didn't pick up on who I really was; perhaps they were just being nice.

I drove another hour and pulled off onto a side road just as dusk settled in. I changed back to Ron for the remainder of the trip home and stopped for a late burger. I did not plan on making these purchases on the trip, but was glad to know

I had at least a starter wardrobe to begin my test process as Debbie. Over the next year, I didn't allow myself to dress as Debbie much or purchase a lot of other items, but they did come in handy when I introduced Debbie to my new counselors and to Susan (one time only). It was not a full transition, but a girl has to start somewhere.

By the winter of 1994, it looked like I would make the transition to my real self. I had shared my identity conflict with Susan, talked with our joint counselor, and visited the transgender counselor, Dr. Lehne, in the early fall. Beard removal is one of the longest and most expensive processes for a male to female transition. Unfortunately, I had a normal beard, so I mustered up my nerve again and stopped one evening at a new salon, Blue Ridge Electrolysis. I nervously walked in and introduced myself to the electrologist and owner, Karen Crawford. I told her I would probably be making a male to female life transition and asked her if she would be willing to help me. She said she had worked on men before, but I would be her first real transsexual patient; she was willing to help in any way she could. She explained what electrolysis was, gave me a free sample treatment, and said if I was serious about this, it would be a long painful but eventually successful process. Even with laser hair removal becoming more popular, electrolysis is still the only (medically proven) way to remove hair permanently; waxing and shaving just really make matters worse. Karen suggested trying an hour appointment once a week until I made a permanent life transition decision. This would start things out and keep costs and the time commitment reasonable. I began and did this plan of service until the start of my full time feminine life, then I moved up to two hour sessions.

Electrolysis was a necessary process and an alternative to shaving and a five o'clock shadow at the end of the day

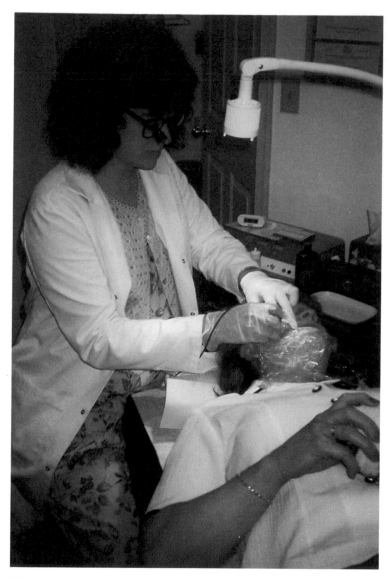

Electrolysis Process—Paying the Price of Hair Removal

(just what a new girl making this transition doesn't want).
Like everything else in this major life change, I got used to
the pain and the cost of hair removal, especially on the face.

Electrolysis is a process in which you insert an electrically charged needle into the hair follicle, down to the root, for a second or two, then the hair is plucked out with tweezers. You keep repeating the process as long as you can for the entire session. The reason it takes time and determination is that there are thousands of hairs in a normal beard, and it takes four to five zaps to finally weaken and kill off each little hair.

In addition to my initial electrolysis and brief counseling session in the fall with Dr. Lehne, I needed more understanding and information about the experiences ahead and possible support to help with my transsexual life adjustment. In late winter of 1995, I followed up on recommendations by Dr. Lehne to visit and participate in the local transgender/transsexual support groups. On Tuesday, February 7, 1995, I attended a meeting of the Baltimore MAGIC support group, which met the second Tuesday of each month on the second floor of the Gay and Lesbian Community Center of Baltimore. I'll have to admit that I felt a little uncomfortable going the first time for several reasons: I did not associate myself in any way with the gay and lesbian issues; I was not comfortable meeting in a location associated with that group; the meeting was from 8:00 to 10:00 pm in Baltimore, and I felt a little threatened being out that late (especially dressed as a woman); finally, I was not totally comfortable with my appearance, and I had to change in my car while parked in a dark lot. Regardless of these issues, I presented myself the best I could and arrived a few minutes before 8:00, parking close to the community center building. I felt scared and nervous as I crossed the street in the crisp, cold air and walked up the dimly lit stairwell of the old building to the second floor. As I walked into the room, I joined a small group of other transsexuals. They extended a nice, friendly welcome to a first time participant in their group. The leader did a nice job of explaining the purpose of the support group and sharing information in a newsletter about transsexual life issues, other groups, and related medical care providers. Everyone introduced themselves, said a little of why they were there, explained what was going on in their lives and discussed other life transition issues. I enjoyed learning about and meeting other transsexuals who had many of the same life transition issues and questions I had; I knew I wasn't alone any more.

I felt good and was glad I attended the meeting. However, I felt I wanted to learn more and meet transsexuals who had a broader base of experiences. The bigger Washington D.C./Northern Virginia area MAGIC group met the third Friday of each month in a Falls Church, Virginia Protestant Church. Thus, I made plans to attend the Washington group the next month even though it was about 70 miles from my Baltimore office and Frederick home. On Friday, March 17th, I nervously changed in the corner of a parking lot near work and made the almost two hour, traffic jammed trip down I-95 and the 495 Washington Beltway to Northern Virginia. The beautiful stone church was a definite upgrade to the meeting location in Baltimore, and I felt a lot safer and more comfortable attending this group. I didn't arrive until almost 8:00 and was surprised to find the parking lot and third floor meeting room full of about 45 transsexuals. The group was diverse — first time participants, persons in current phases of life transition, and a few experienced post-operative members.

The meeting started off in a similar fashion with everyone briefly introducing themselves (I felt like a really rough rookie). We discussed general topics like current transsexual legal issues: then they handed out a monthly newsletter, and everyone picked three focused topics and attended separate meetings to discuss their specific needs. I, of course, attended the new members group with about 8 other persons that night. A few veterans who had gone through most or all of their transsexual transition led the discussion and gave out a nice beginners information packet on transition issues like "Bathrooms and the Law," a topic a non-transsexual person would never have to consider. I felt I learned a lot, enjoyed meeting and talking with such a diverse group, and decided if I was to attend a support group, it would be this one in Virginia. After the general meeting, most of the group took over a large section of an Italian restaurant; we had a late supper and socialized on a more personal basis. I tagged along and enjoyed the unplanned dinner group, but we didn't finish until almost midnight.

I was still married and even though Susan knew what I was doing, I still could not go home as Rhonda. So, I had to change back to Ron in my car after the meeting and drive home, finally getting to bed around 1:30 a.m. I knew I could not do this each month; it would have to wait until after our separation in the summer. The most important contact I made that evening was with a tall, attractive, black lady who briefly shared her very successful plastic surgery experience with me. You couldn't help but be impressed with the results, as she gave me her surgeon's name, Dr. Converse of Severna Park, Maryland.

Since I was considering plastic surgery for my nose, I followed up on the tip and made an appointment for May 10, 1995, just four days shy of my 48th birthday. I originally wanted to use what I thought to be a really feminine name, Debbie, for my new identity. However, I realized it would be easier for me and the comfort level of others who knew me as Ron, to use the feminine derivative, Rhonda, for my new life. I scheduled a few hours off work that afternoon to allow time to find my way and to change into Rhonda. It was a tricky day. First, I got lost finding his office, then, I had to change clothes in my new raspberry pink 1995 extended cab S-10 Chevy pick-up in the corner of the remote parking lot in broad daylight. During my entire pre-transition experience, I had learned to quick change from Ron to Rhonda in 15-20 minutes time. For example; it was difficult to take off my pants and slip or my pantyhose while in a sitting position with the truck bucket seat adjusted all the way back. Still, it was always nerve racking, and I prayed no one would notice me. If they did I would just move to another parking area and finish; the lighted make-up mirror on my truck visor was a girl's best friend. You learn quickly that you have to take risks and go for it if you're going to make transition work, especially in less than ideal circumstances. At this point, I was meeting at least one of my medical care and other service providers as Rhonda on a weekly basis.

After changing, I was running late and knew I needed better directions to find Dr. Converse's office, so I spotted a consignment shop called Mary's in a small shopping area and decided to ask there; besides, I needed a better wardrobe and thought she might have some nice things I could use. At Mary's, "nice" is an understatement to the styles and selections she carries. I stopped in, asked for directions, and told her I would be back. After my visit with Dr. Converse, I stopped back at Mary's around 6:00 p.m., and we started talking and picking out clothes with the help of her assistant, Dawn. Mary was not only compassionate and understanding of my needs, but she had a friend who was going through a similar transition experience; she went way above the call of duty in helping me.

We tried on clothes that night for over three hours and I rounded out my initial wardrobe: professional clothes, a few casual things, and my favorites — an emerald green diamond sequin and silk short evening dress and a black and white sequin, open back evening dress. I love them and wear them to the theater and special events, because they really show off my figure. In getting lost, I found a friend who would turn out to be a very special person in my life. I can never repay her kindness. God was leading my path, as I drove home that day with a blessed heart, a great wardrobe, and an affirmation that things were going to work out fine.

My appointment with Dr. Converse was very important to me, because I was self-conscious about my feminine appearance and my large hooked-shaped nose. I finally found his office about a mile from Mary's and walked in. I was greeted by a warm and friendly staff — the office manager and the nurse. After filling out the initial medical history forms, I was directed to a small room, which had a camera and computer imaging system. Dr. Converse came in and asked how he could help me. Again, I explained my transition plans, and asked what difference plastic surgery could make in my appearance. I explained that if I scheduled any surgery, it would have to be in December, between my transition at work. I believed strongly a total, rather than a gradual, transition when I went back to work in January was my best game plan. I wanted everyone to see me for the first time as feminine as I could be. One of the real differences between Ron and Rhonda was that Rhonda had a little vanity.

Dr. Converse started off by saying he could help me more than I thought. He took a before picture and then enhanced his recommendations on the computer. He explained what the procedure, care, and healing process was like for a face lift. While I was interested in the nose, his first recommendation was to take away the more masculine double chin, then straighten the nose, take away the wrinkles and loose skin from under the eyes, puff up the cheeks, and generally tighten up the entire face from the eyes down. The possibilities were clear when the computer image was finished, and he suggested my best option was a full face lift to achieve my desired goals.

Pat, the office manager worked up the cost estimate, and we had a nice, long talk. She explained what would happen during the surgery, showed me some former patients and their results, and answered all of my questions to put any fear or concerns I had to rest. Since I had never been in a hospital or had surgery in my 48 years, this whole process was a big leap of faith for me. But my concerns about surgery and finding the right doctor were eased after this first visit. I left with a scheduled appointment for surgery on December 6, 1995.

Dr. Charles F. Converse recalls:

It was indeed a pleasure having Rhonda as a patient. She was very committed to her massive undertaking of a total life and sexual change. Her attitude was always up and we enjoyed seeing her progressive change from a not very handsome male to an attractive woman.

I was not only in good hands, but more optimistic than ever that I was making the right choice to start off my transition and female life looking the best I could be. A face lift is expensive but reasonable for the services. Besides, when I pro-rated the benefits of plastic surgery over a 10 year period, the face lift and other plastic surgery came out to be about $5 a day, a very good return for my finances and self-esteem.

While Ron could not, Rhonda would spare no reasonable expense to maximize her appearance and enhance her femininity. Although most of my major transition costs are behind me, I warn people that I am a HMW, or high-maintenance woman; you get what you pay for, and I'm worth every penny of it.

Chapter 15

Hormone Therapy and the Real Life Experience

The summer and early fall of 1995 kept me busy. I helped Susan get moved to Greensburg, Pennsylvania to the modular home I was setting up for her on the vacant building lot from an investment property we had bought with the assistance of Lil Bradish, a year earlier.

Lil Bradish, my real estate agent, says:

In my eyes, Rhonda has made the right decision for her. It has made her a vivacious person, more outgoing. She truly loves what she did. Most people reach times in their lives when they wish they would have done this or that. But Rhonda knew what she wanted and made her dream come true. Good for her!

I had few precious moments to prepare for my planned transition just six months away. My evenings and weekends in October and November were pressure-packed months, the beginning stages of life as a female, the pre-transition services, the preparation for my full time life as Rhonda.

One of the biggest steps in this phase of transition was to find a local Baltimore doctor who would be my primary care physician (preferably female), as well as the doctor who could prescribe my female hormone therapy. In July of 1995, I looked in my Baltimore County approved physicians directory and selected Dr. Judith Thompson to contact, internal medicine physician at Johns Hopkins Greenspring Station Medical Center, just a few miles from my office. I called to ask if she was taking new patients. Fortunately, she was and agreed to see me. I made an appointment for a routine physical, which I was overdue for. I decided to see Dr. Thompson as Rhonda, even though I was 5 months away from full transition. This meant changing from Ron to Rhonda during the midday hours in my little pick-up. This made me more nervous than usual, but I didn't have any other choice. Cautiously, I went into the main entrance and up the elevator to the third floor office and checked in at the front reception area. Concerned about how I would be accepted, the big moment came when Dr. Thompson came into the room and I explained my transition situation. I also explained that my dad died of a heart condition and said I needed a good internal medicine doctor. I also hoped she would be able to prescribe my hormone medication. Feeling more comfortable, I asked her if she would agree and be comfortable in having me as a patient, just like any other woman. She was impressed with my honesty and sincerity, complimented me on my initial appearance (still rough), and said she would be glad to be my primary care doctor. I thanked her and told her I was pleased to have such a competent and caring woman as my physician. She completed my physical, took blood tests, and did a preventive EKG. However, she told me she could not prescribe hormone therapy for me. I left with a good medical report and felt confident that I had found a doctor in whom I could entrust my life — monitoring my medical and surgical procedures was no small part of my transition plan.

Wasting no time, I contacted the endocrinology department of a local hospital the next day and asked for the name of the best person to see for preoperative transsexual hormone therapy. The nurse said the expert in this area was Dr. Elizabeth Cranston, and I set up the earliest appointment possible, on September 28, 1995. The early morning appointment allowed me to dress and leave home as Rhonda, since I was now living alone. All was going well until I got lost for almost two hours trying to find the hospital's Outpatient Center in Baltimore. Finally, I arrived late, apologizing for getting lost. They seemed almost used to this problem and kindly squeezed me in at 11:30 to see Dr. Cranston. She completed a thorough exam, along with a counseling session and had me wait for her results. When she returned, she said I was a candidate for transsexual hormone therapy, but she would not approve it until I went through a psychological assessment with Dr. Raymond Jones of a reputable transsexual patient clinic. I told her I was disappointed and already had an experienced counselor in Dr. Lehne, but that didn't matter. Even though Dr. Lehne was a credible transsexual therapist, I still had to go one step further. So, I made the soonest possible appointment with Dr. Jones' group, which wasn't until Friday, November 10. They only saw new transsexual patients for their four hour, $300 (prepaid) screening process on Fridays.

Once again, I worked in the morning and did my switch-in-the-car transition, getting to my appointment on time for a change. At that point, I was looking forward to the time when I didn't have to switch back and forth in life's daily routine, because living a double life was one of the hardest parts of a preoperative transition. I went to Dr. Jones' clinical area and started completing the standard patient forms. One of the nurses came out and called my name. I guess my transition appearance was starting to pay off; the nurse asked if I was there for Dr. Jones' screening test, and I told her yes. She complimented me, saying I looked so good that she couldn't tell if I was a transsexual candidate or not. We walked back to a clinical room. I sat down and completed the intake form. Then the nurse came back and handed me a 250 question multiple choice test. I was instructed to read and complete it. For the next hour, I completed the test, knowing I had done similar ones previously, even given similar tests in my profession. I wanted a fair analysis and honest results, so I didn't try to slant my answers.

Just as I finished the interest test, a team of three counselors who worked in Dr. Jones' group (two men and one woman) came in to question me with the standard history-of-my-life questions that I had been through so many times before. The counseling stage was really set when they asked me why I was there to do the transsexual screening. I told them I was referred by Dr. Cranston, a well-known endocrinologist, and I was just jumping through their hoops. They were surprised by my response and asked what I meant by that. I told them I knew what I was doing, as a 48-year-old adult, and that I was required to do the screening so that an endocrinologist could prescribe my future hormone therapy. We continued the interview, but I could tell they did not like such an outspoken, self-assured patient.

After they left, I was asked to take one more test full of personality questions and asked to wait when finished. Well, I must have impressed someone, because I was asked to stay and do a special interview/questioning session with a group of doctors and interns inexperienced in transsexual patients. I walked into a room full of white lab coats and sat down in front to answer questions about my life and transition experiences for about 45 minutes. I left, truly feeling like I had just jumped through one of the many hoops to come if I were ever going to get them to approve my hormone medication. This fear was confirmed the following week at the Washington transsexual group. I told them of my experience with Dr. Jones' clinic process. They said that unfortunately, some of them had experienced the same problems with many hospitals reluctant to prescribe hormone therapy to anyone without counseling with their group and a prolonged waiting period (one thing I did not have time for).

My January, 1996, status as a full time female was coming up fast. Sensing a need to find another source for hormone therapy, I was advised to call Dr. Beth Evans, an endocrinologist at the Medlantic Research Institute and Washington Hospital Center. Dr. Evans served a number of transsexual patients. Knowing it was less than a month before my plastic surgery and start of my new life, I called Dr. Evans' office on Monday, and she was kind enough to see me on Wednesday, November 29th — quite a contrast to my many months of seeing specialists in the Baltimore area with still no answer or approval for hormone therapy.

I took a half day off from work and took my first trip to Washington, D.C. — as Rhonda. I was nervous about my appearance, as I drove to the Shady Grove metro parking lot and took the crowded subway train for the first time on that cold, fall morning. My trip started on the red line, then the blue, and finally the orange. I exited up a long escalator to the bustling city streets of Washington. Out of my element, I found my bearings after going down one wrong street to 650 Pennsylvania Avenue and the Medlantic Institute. After completing the standard new patient forms yet again, I was given a blood pressure check, weigh in, and drawing of blood by a lab technician, whose caring and jovial spirit put me at ease and made me realize I was at a patient-friendly medical center.

Anxious to meet Dr. Evans, I was escorted to an examination room, asked to change into a medical gown, and sat on the examination bed until she came in. Nervously, I wondered what her impression of me would be. Would she prescribe hormones? What hoops would she make me jump through? My questions and fears were answered, as a smiling and attractive lady walked into the room. She introduced herself and I explained my life transition and year-long preparation for eventual surgery. I also described my frustrations of finding a doctor in Baltimore who could specifically serve my needs. She examined me for over a half hour, physically and mentally, before giving me her diagnosis. I was on pins and needles as she told me I was in good physical health. She was impressed with my candor, appearance, and transition plans. She thought I was an excellent candidate to achieve my transsexual goals. While she didn't always prescribe hormone therapy for patients the first time she saw them, in my case she was comfortable in doing so. She wrote me a prescription for a moderate dose of Premarin and Progesterone, which would be increased in three months at my next visit, provided my blood work and physical changes showed everything was going well.

I have never had any negative side effects from my hormone therapy. I experienced the customary changes, some loss of physical strength, slowing in body hair growth, moderate breast development (size 34A in my case), more emotional sensitivity, weight shift to my buttocks, and a bit of a female tummy, which Dr. Evans' called my baby bulge look. Unfortunately, hormones would not soften or change the voice pitch in a male to female as they do in a female to male transsexual. I was very relieved and happy to start my hormone therapy and also relieved to find such a caring and professional doctor. I thanked Dr. Evans for seeing me so quickly and left the medical center a happier and more confident woman. My transition was moving in the right direction.

Once I traveled back on the metro rail train, I made my (now customary) change back to Ron in my car — back to a man's role and my work objectives. The change was harder that day, because my feminine identity had had a good time earlier in the day; it'd been a good positive meeting with Dr.

Evans. To put things into perspective, my final diagnosis from Dr. Jones' transsexual clinic screening did not take place until Friday, December 15th, a week after my plastic surgery. Still in major recovery and just free from having my facial bandages removed on the 13th, I patched together a rough Rhonda and made my diagnostic session with Dr. Jones and his team to review their findings and recommendations. I felt bad physically and was barely able to walk on my own (a friend drove me to the appointment), but I was mentally prepared and self- confident, because I had already been on my beginning hormone therapy for two weeks. Still, I didn't let on that I had made this progress without their help.

I was nervous and curious as to their findings and recommendations, as I finally met Dr. Jones and his team of psychologists in my 1:00 p.m. meeting. I sat there, feeling cautiously optimistic and confident, believing I was on the right track for my transition. I was told my screening results and tests revealed I was a good candidate for a transsexual life transition, but the group was concerned, because I did not have a lot of questions about why or what help I would need in my transition. I responded that I was not a young, naive person. I was taking charge of my life and transition care needs, explaining that a proactive, confident approach to my change was a plus, not a negative. We talked a little more. Finally, Dr. Jones told me their final recommendation would allow me to start hormone therapy in six months — and if everything went fine, I could have my genital surgery in two years. Personally, I was amused. Obviously, their recommendations did not take into account individual cases. To me, it seemed these doctors wanted a standard plan for patients. I did not need to be led by the hand every step of the way. I didn't take no for an answer; I would go to Plan B.

They thanked me for coming in and said I could come back for more counseling and services if I wished to do so. I thanked them for their opinion, but explained that under their conditions I would not need to do so. Not only would I never go back, but I would never refer any transsexual person to such a narrowly-focused and controlling group. Their recommendations confirmed the information my friends in the Washington MAGIC group had warned me about and made me even more thankful that I had found an open-minded, progressive doctor in Dr. Evans.

I have found you can never do enough when taking charge of your own medical care and other transition services. One of the most important things that a transsexual person can do to maximize successful life adjustments is to be proactive. Don't be held back by trepidatious care providers. The only one who can take responsibility for your needs is you, no matter what they are. Many times I have had to re-evaluate and take charge of my transition when it would have been easier to feel sorry for myself or make excuses that something wasn't happening because of someone else. Life is not fair. You have to work hard to balance the odds in your favor.

Chapter 16

Putting the Package Together

Just like the bride getting ready for her wedding (hopefully I will experience this soon), I was making progress and had outlined the process needed to prepare for my January 1996 debut as Rhonda. But, there were still so many things to do and people to see before the big day, in my case the big year. My time to express myself and learn the experience of being a woman (practice makes perfect) was still limited to one or two evenings a week and an occasional weekend. Focusing on my appearance and presentation as a woman was more involved than I had realized, but I was looking forward to it. I knew I needed to continue to improve my clothing style, professional work wardrobe and make-up. But, where was the best place to go and would anyone understand or help with my personal needs?

With my initial success at Mary's, I started to identify local consignment shops in Frederick. I hoped to find a good selection, fair prices, and compassionate sales ladies to steer me in the right direction. Fortunately, lady luck was on my side again one Saturday, October 28, 1995, when I stopped at a quality consignment shop called The Fashion Exchange in a popular part of Frederick's renovated old rowhomes, Shab Row. I deliberately chose to stop by the shop at 5:30 (just 30 minutes before they closed), so I would not have to be in the store when they had a lot of other customers. Again, I was nervous, but looked forward to another new shopping experience. I walked up the steps and entered a room filled with racks of women's casual to dressy clothes. I walked up to the counter (in my rough but passable Rhonda garb) and told the clerk I was preparing for a full-time male to female transsexual life adjustment. I needed some help picking out clothes and styles flattering to me and asked if they would be willing to help. The sales ladies all responded with a warm welcome, told me their names (Janine, the owner and Sharon, her sales assistant), and said they would be glad to help. I couldn't have asked for more considerate and helpful ladies.

We buzzed around the racks, picking out skirts, work suits, blouses, two evening gowns, and a few slacks. They gave me some good pointers on dress and recommended I stick with a size 14. I did find a size 12 strapless, metallic purple dress with a black velvet top — my first evening dress. I'll never forget when I first walked down the steps from the second floor dressing room in a short skirt. Sharon said, "Damn, the bitch got legs; they're even better than mine!" We all had a good laugh. I appreciated the honesty and needed the compliment. I walked out of the shop two hours past their 6:00 p.m. closing time with two new friends and an armload of clothes (at very reasonable prices). I still go back once in a while to check out their new items. I even bought a black velvet dinner dress with a green sequin jacket, an outfit I couldn't originally fit into. Now it's one of my favorites and a size 10.

Since some of the clothes needed minor alterations and shortening, the ladies at the shop referred me to a seamstress, Barbara Allen at Creative Expressions. The next weekend I made an appointment for Barbara to come over and help customize my new wardrobe. Not only was she very knowledgeable about clothing styles, as we must have tried on and pinned up clothes for almost two hours (a real treat for me), but she was also very interested in me as a person.

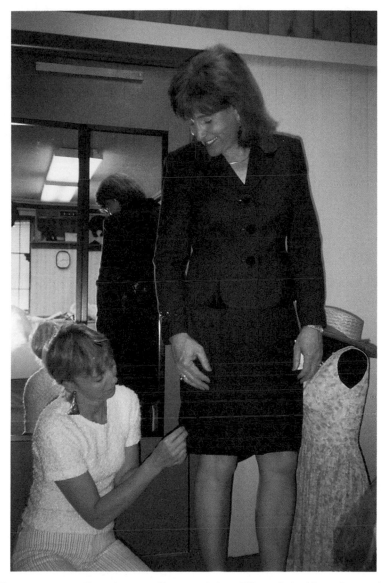

Steamstress Services—Customizing Rhonda's Hem Length

She was accepting of my transition experience, and we hit it off right from the start.

Barbara Allen says:
*It has been incredibly fascinating to watch and be a part
of Rhonda's transition from male to female. The face, the
hair, the plastic surgery, the clothes, have all been so neatly
chosen, to complete her package. I began as Rhonda's seamstress doing alterations for her female clothes since 1995. But
as the years have gone by, we've become friends. We talk about
our personal lives, men, fashion, money, etc. We've been to
the theater together as well as worked side by side, building
clothes racks in my shop. Rhonda's confidence and conviction
are fabulous attributes for all women to follow. Rhonda is
the only female who comes into my shop who does not attack
the flaws or shape of her body, totally accepting herself! This
is refreshing.*

We get along so well that whenever I buy any new dresses,
I don't even take them home, but leave them in my trunk
until I stop by her shop and have the usual 2"+ to 3"+ raising
of the hemline. Some women may like the length below the
knees, but that is not nor will it ever be my style. As Sharon
said, "The bitch got legs," a girl has to maximize her features.

I felt a real need for a breast enhancement, something
that would feel and look natural until my hormones took
over to help me form my own breasts. For the time being, I
had used my ingenuity and bought $5 worth of toy material
called "slime" and carefully sealed it into two plastic baggies
to act as a temporary breast substitute. It did work, but who
wanted lime green breasts, and I feared I would have quite
a mess on my hands if one of the baggies were to spring a
leak. With no prosthesis or breast form stores in Frederick,
I checked out the phone book and speciality breast form/bra
stores in the Baltimore area.

I finally located a store that I thought could help me which
specialized in bras, undergarments and breast forms for

women — usually, a service for women who have the unfortunate experience of having had a mastectomy. I was very nervous about how I would approach a sales lady in this type of store, explain my need, and purchase the right size breast form. With no easy way around it and my strong desire for a natural breast substitute, I once again completed one of my Ron to Rhonda changes in my car after work and drove to the suburban shopping area. I finally built up enough nerve to walk in this store on Thursday, November 8, 1995.

As I approached the sales counter, two mature ladies were standing near the cash register and asked if they could help me. Nervously, I explained my unusual request. I could see it sort of surprised them and made them feel uncomfortable, but I was not going to walk away easily. They said they thought I should talk to the head sales lady and store manager. I agreed and waited for her to return. Once again, I explained my need, and they said they weren't used to this kind of request. They suggested I would be just as satisfied with an inexpensive push up style cloth pad, and I told them I wouldn't be satisfied. The sales lady saw how serious I was and said she would be willing to help me, but felt I should come back early Saturday morning when there would be no other ladies in the store (for privacy reasons). I agreed and asked what time. We set up 9:00 a.m. appointment (an hour before the usual opening), and I drove back down from Frederick that Saturday morning to purchase my breast forms. I was greeted kindly, but there was still a feeling of unease in the air. I talked some more with the sales manager, and she began to realize how important this issue was to me. She showed me some of the different breast form styles and explained that they were expensive because of the material and silicone used to make a natural feel and look. Medical insurance usually covers most of the $500 to

$600 cost of a pair of breast forms. That was more costly than I expected, but I really wanted the natural effect and asked if they had any alternatives which would be cheaper. The lady was caring and said she had some one-of-a-kind mismatches in the back, similar in size, but not an exact cup or shape match. We looked in the closet and found two size 36 breast forms, but they did have slightly different style and cup sizes. She said she could sell me those for half price, so I said okay and tried them on. She directed me to the dressing room and also suggested some pocket bras which were also rather expensive, but especially made for a breast form to fit in to and stay in place. I tried on both breast forms and the bras and realized they provided the natural feel and look I desired physically and mentally. It was important for me to feel the natural weight of breasts, not just a stuffed for-effect-only bra. I purchased the mismatched beige breast forms and a black pocket bra (size 36) and left the store, more self-confident about my feminine feel and appearance. I also thanked the lady for her assistance. I thought we both learned from each other about the significance this type of service is to a transsexual person.

As I prepared for my "new life," I also knew I wanted and needed a better and more permanent hair piece. As I researched options, I was fortunate to get referred by one of the cosmetology teachers to Eldorado Hair Services and a top notch cosmetologist and hair restoration specialist, Penny, and her store owner/manager, Marty. Again, dealing with the unknown, I learned about a speciality hair replacement system which was customized for every person. I made my first appointment on Wednesday, August 9, 1995, to see how this option would compare to the Rogaine cream hair growth method, surgical hair replacement, or hair weaves. Penny explained the advantages and disadvantages of dif-

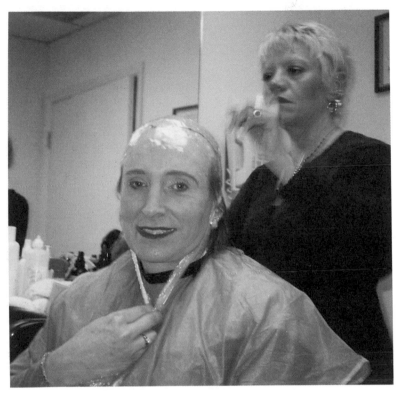

Performing Customized Hair Services

ferent methods and said, from her experiences and my hair condition, that a full hair piece system would fit my needs.

To start the process, she made a mold of my head with a plastic wrap to form a cap, which they used to order and make a full (human hair) system to compliment my own hair (what little was left). I spent hours learning about and selecting an initial style to suit me. The hair, if fastened to my head with a special adhesive would stay put for five to six weeks before needing to be refastened. Caring for it was no different than my own hair. I chose to go with #660 Clairol Audacious Red as the color, since I was born with red hair and that color best matched my complexion and freckles. A

Speech Therapy with Dr. Spencer

wig is nice for special occasions, but not what you want for a more natural, long-term solution to balding and thinning hair problems. For me, this service was especially important because I always had real thin hair. As I placed my order, I knew that I'd begun another new friendship with Penny.

Penny Fox notes:

Rhonda came to me as Ron who was going through the transitional phase of her change. I respected and admired her for the courage this woman had for such a serious undertaking, that would change her life forever. It takes a special person to be Rhonda. I don't think I would ever meet in a lifetime the special person I know as Rhonda Hoyman. It is my pleasure to know her, she has touched my life.

Over the fall, I continued seeing Dr. Lehne about twice a month to prepare for my transition. I also started preliminary speech therapy with Linda E. Spencer, Ph.D., 30 minutes every other week in October. Finally, I went full time. My voice was my biggest fear, as it is for many transsexuals.

Linda E. Spencer, Ph.D. recalls:

Rhonda understood very early on how important it would be to present an appropriate vocal image of her new, feminine self. Having had no previous speech or voice training, the process was slow and tedious, but Ronda persevered. Today, Rhonda's total image is feminine.

In my clothing purchases, I was treated and served with compassion in small, privately owned stores, but going into a busy regular store was still something I was not comfortable with. I wondered if I would pass as a woman among other customers. Would I offend them? Would I get fair treatment from the sales staff (not used to serving transsexual patients)? Things were starting off so well, but I was afraid of failure and rejection, so much so that the first time I went to a regular store called the Dress Barn one evening, I chickened out.

I liked what I saw in their window display, so about two weeks later I returned to the same Dress Barn and went in on Monday, November 6, 1995, as business slacked off one evening. The sales lady, Sharon, never knew how scared I was. I walked in, looked around some, and went to the counter to ask if they would feel comfortable with me and could they help me with the new look I was still polishing up on. My first appearance at work was just two months away. I don't know why I was surprised, but they said they appreciated my honesty, that I looked nice, and they would be glad to help me. This clothing chain has much nice, professional and casual women's clothes, especially suits, at reasonable prices. I instantly connected with their clothing line and bought a few suits and blouses that night. I had to resist the temptation to buy too much until my future dress size was determined.

A transsexual person has to consider the effects of hormone therapy, body weight shifts and weight gain or loss for at least one year after transition. For me, I saw my transition as a total life enhancement, not just a sex change, and dropped 20 pounds the first year to my current size 10, which I have been able to maintain. The sales ladies recommended I use the larger dressing stall at the rear of the dressing room for more space and privacy, which I still prefer, and helped make color and style suggestions. Once again, I found supportive, courteous service and the beginning of new friendships. Since then, about 90% of my new clothes have been from the Dress Barn, and I could be a walking advertisement for them. I am a loyal and devoted customer, and when I wear a new suit to work, the other ladies at the office just look at me and say "Dress Barn." I just nod my head, smile, and we all laugh.

Last, but not least, preparing for my natural, feminine appearance meant I would have to do a better job with my make-up. The drug/department store look was not going to cut it. Susan and some of my other girlfriends had been using a product called Mary Kay, which looked interesting. I did not have to be hit on the head with one of Ron's two by fours to figure out I should try it. I decided to see if Mary Kay would work for me. I called the independent senior sales director for the Frederick area, Jane Newman (the same person Susan saw a few times), and asked if she would help me. She said it was the first time she had worked with a client's spouse, but she was sympathetic to my situation, knew I needed good cosmetic services like any other woman, and was a fine Christian lady who demonstrated God's love in not prejudging me. I made an appointment for a make-over session and went over to her home office for my first real education in make-up on Friday, November 3, 1995. As I entered her lovely home, her husband and business partner greeted me warmly. He lead me to her customer-care center, where she had a table and make-over station all set up. It was such a pleasure to be treated like a real lady, equal to any other woman. Not only did I learn about the different colors and types of cosmetics which would be best for me, I also learned about Mary Kay's skin care cleansing system.

Jane says about meeting Rhonda:

I met Rhonda first as Ron when she was first implementing her transition and was referred to me for assistance with proper skin care and color cosmetics application. It has been exciting to see Rhonda blossom into a lovely woman whose courage, self-image and confidence are an inspiration to everyone she meets. She displays the very best attributes of femininity with her careful grooming, her can-do spirit and her generous heart. It is a privilege to know Rhonda.

The products Jane introduced me to seemed to be reasonably priced for the dramatic improvement just one session made in my appearance. Of course, a senior sales director's knowledge and make-up pointers helped, as I tried to soak up all the tips and techniques I could in one evening. We had a lot of fun, as I really enjoyed and appreciated using make-up, a personal need I was denied since childhood. I knew, once again, I had made a new friend and met a woman who would have a more meaningful impact on my life in the future. I purchased the basic skin care system and color cosmetics I would need to start off my new look. Besides, with my plastic surgery coming up, I knew I would need to take good care of my new face. Ladies, just like the car care commercial that says, "take good care of your engine with proper oil changes or you and your engine will pay the mechanic later," it pays to use a good skin care cleansing system to avoid the wrinkles and aging effects of the future.

One final step to my transition from a paper chase, legal perspective, was the need to not only change my appearance but also my legal name for personal, work, and financial records to match my new female life. In the past, I had worked with an attorney in the Frederick area named Mr. Thomas Slater (he'd processed my last divorce). I now wondered if he would help me as a transsexual with the process of a legal name change? With time closing in, I arrived back in Frederick on Monday afternoon, November 6, 1995, to start the legal name change request. I felt nervous as to what I would say, but I mustered up my courage and walked into his office to set up an appointment. I was first greeted by his office assistant, whom I'd met before. She had always been nice to me. I said hello and asked to set up an appointment with Mr. Slater. She asked what service I needed, and I hesitated a moment. I told her the request was new for me. I explained to her that one of the reasons for my divorce was that I had always struggled with a dominant feminine identify, and I needed to go through the process of a legal name change from the Ron she knew to Rhonda. As I prepared for a total male to female life transition in the next few months, I asked if Mr. Slater could help me with this legal process. She said she and Mr. Slater had never handled what I described as a transsexual life legal name change, but she was considerate of my request and surprised about the topic. She didn't really know how to handle such a case, but she said she would help in any way she could.

She asked me to wait a moment, and went in to talk to Mr. Slater about my request. Fortunately, he had time to see me and asked me to come into his office. As we sat down, he told me this was an unusual request; it was new to him. He had never legally processed a male- to-female name change or really knew anything about the legal aspects of transsexualism, but he said he would help if he could. He explained that a name change in Maryland would cost about $400. He explained that I would have to advertise the name change in two local papers for three weeks, so as not to deceive any creditors or try to escape legal obligations. Then, it would have to process, similar to my uncontested divorce. He also suggested I talk about this with Dr. Lehne, my transsexual counselor, for his recommendations, and find out what he knew about a transsexual name change process in Maryland. I also needed to get a letter from him saying I was under his counseling and that he supported my name change request. He had me fill out some standard name change request papers and get back to him as soon as I could, since the whole process would take about three months. Naively, I had thought it would only be a few weeks when I first went into his office. I thanked him for his willingness to help; he said he guessed we would both learn about this process together. I left his office, relieved that things went well and that the process was starting, but I knew I didn't have any time to waste. Fortunately, that next week, I had a counseling session with Dr. Lehne, and he said it didn't require a special process for a transsexual name change, but you had to do it legally, in the county where you lived. He would be glad to write me a supporting letter for the judge. He also advised me to use a completely feminine name like Rhonda, not my middle name Dale. While Dale is female in some cases, it was still gender neutral. I reported back to Mr. Slater the next week, and he filed the name change in the newspaper, processed the paperwork, and sent Dr. Lehne's letter and some pictures of me as a female to the judge. I didn't have to appear in person.

The judge accepted my name change plea without question and on January 19, 1996, my name and life as Ron was

EX PARTE   *   IN THE CIRCUIT COURT

IN THE MATTER OF   *   FOR FREDERICK COUNTY,

RONALD DALE HOYMAN   *   MARYLAND

                               *   CASE NO. ___95-2157-CV___

              *   *   *   *   *

JUDGEMENT FOR CHANGE OF NAME

Upon consideration of the aforegoing petition and affidavit:

It is thereupon, this _19th_ day of _January_ , 1995, by the

Circuit Court for Frederick County, Maryland, and by the authority

of this Court,

ADJUDGED, ORDERED and DECREED, that the name of RONALD DALE

HOYMAN be and the same is hereby changed from

RONALD DALE HOYMAN

TO

RHONDA DALE HOYMAN

as is prayed in said petition; and that the said petitioner pay the

cost of these proceedings to be taxed by the Clerk.

/s/ JOHN H. TISDALE
_____
JUDGE, CIRCUIT COURT FOR
FREDERICK COUNTY, MARYLAND

TRUE COPY TEST:

CLERK

Jan 22

Name Change Approval

legally changed to Rhonda. Not a moment to soon for my
needs. Since I was already living and working as a female,
I could now officially request and change all my legal paper-

work and business dealings such as bank accounts and credit cards from Ron to Rhonda. You can request and complete a transsexual name change without an attorney, but I found it helpful to have Mr. Slater's assistance. It probably would have taken me longer to have the name change approved on my own. Every change was one more permanent step to erasing my male identity; my female identify was taking place.

It takes time to research, meet, and select the services needed to make a successful male to female life transition. But, it has all been worth it and proven to pay off then, now, and in the future. The second year of my five-year life transition plan would be to finely tune my looks, a job made easier because of the homework and quality services I found to start off my first year of major transition needs.

Chapter 17

Setting the Stage at Work

At the same time I was helping my third wife regroup and reestablish her life by building a modular home in Greensburg, I was also researching the medical support system I would use to make my initial entry into the world as Rhonda. I was also dealing with the many issues and questions as to how I could make my transition at work. It was not easy, but an essential process to gain the approval and support of my co-workers, teachers, and school administrators. Could the Ron they knew and respected be accepted as Rhonda? My initial plan was to keep a low profile with everyone except my boss, the school system's top-level administrators, and my teachers until mid-November. This plan would minimize the controversial period when everyone would know I was going to make the big change to Rhonda, but still had to interact with Ron.

On July 23, 1995, I started to test the waters and break the news as professionally and discreetly as possible. I wrote a seven page letter to my immediate supervisor, Mrs. Roberta Brown, the Coordinator of the Career and Technology Education Office, and to Elaine Gorman, the Director of Applied and Technical Sciences for Baltimore County Schools. The next week, I set up an appointment with the coordinator, and we sat at the meeting table in the privacy of her office, as I shared why I wanted to talk with her. As she started to read the letter, we had open, honest, and caring dialogue.

Rhonda's First Glamour Photo

Dear Mrs. Brown,

To prepare for the positive start to another school year, my service to you and the Career & Technology Office staff, and my own personal wellness, I have written this letter so that I may use my energy effectively for my work, and personal life. I appreciate and respect your opinion and enjoy working with you professionally and as a friend. While I am taking a risk sharing my thoughts and concerns with you, I hope you will see that I do this out of respect and ask that you keep it confidential unless we agree to share it with others.

As you know, I have been trying to do my best in a very demanding position, and I am pleased with these efforts and feel success in many of my contributions to Baltimore County. However, the long hours, travel time on the road, and limited personal time and satisfaction in my life do not always allow me to be my best or even just to relax and find enjoyment in life. I am trying to make changes which impact my personal wellness as well as be a more productive worker.

I want to continue to work with Baltimore County, but I must make some major changes in my life and how I operate if I am going to take any real steps in changing the stress and conflict I deal with. At work I don't mind extra hours, but one of my problems is that I lose myself in the work to fill time productively as I personally run from the inner conflict I face. At home, the conflicts and difficulties of living in Frederick (57 miles from the office) and working in Baltimore do not help the marriage, and a counselor who Susan and I are seeing wants me to consider quitting my job, but I do not see that as a solution to family or work improvement issues.

Most importantly and most difficult to put into words is that as a person I have never had a lot of happiness and feelings of fulfillment because I have been struggling with a transsexual life personality conflict. I am dealing with the reality that, while I am accepted as Ron on the outward appearance, my inner feelings and dominant identity are those of Rhonda or feminine. To help determine if I have the personal rights, guts, feelings or support to gain some resolution to this inner conflict and personal wellness, I have recently tried to gain some limited experiences, professional counseling and special/consultant help in living and preparing to transition to a female life. Dr. Lehne and Patty Cummings, the counselors I have been working with, feel that I have a classic case of transsexual identity conflict and see me as a female who needs to make a total life adjustment.

I have said all of this not to seek sympathy, offend you, or to do anything that would negatively impact on carrying out my responsibilities. Just the opposite, I want to do everything in life better. To say the least, dealing with all of this has not been easy and I have come to the point that I do not have enough energy to manage the job demands, relationship issues, and personal conflict much longer without some decisions being made.

The reason I write this letter is because it was too much to say easily in a brief discussion, and I wanted you to understand all that I was dealing with before discussing the issue further. If for my own well being and if I can learn to begin living life for myself as well as the benefit of others, could you accept Rhonda instead of Ron as someone you could work with?

Thanks for your understanding, supervision, and friendship,

Ron / Rhonda

Mrs. Brown was understandably surprised and said that with my construction background and personal male actions, she had no reason to believe this was an issue in my life. But, she would do what she could to help me, and we continued to have personal dialogue after reading the letter.

From her perspective, she would try to understand, support and accept Rhonda, but she did not know how the school system as a whole would handle or be able to accept this major change in my life. It felt good to have her initial acceptance and understanding; she was a very professional and classy supervisor. I asked her where I should go from there, and she said I needed to talk to Ms. Gorman, the Director of Applied and Technical Sciences, next in the chain of command, as soon as possible.

So, I set up an appointment a few days later and started off my meeting with her by sharing my same letter. I was surprised when she sat there without even so much as a change in her facial expression. She read the entire letter before saying a word, but she was gracious and caring. She said it was really a surprise to her and quite a contrast to the male image my life portrayed. She also wanted me to be happy as a person, as well as a productive worker. She said she would support my transition needs however she could. I asked her what she would recommend I do at that point. She said I should talk with the Assistant Superintendent of Curriculum and Instruction. She would even go with me to lend her approval and support during the meeting. Since she already had a meeting scheduled with him the next Monday, we agreed I would join her at this time to share my request for transition on the job from Ron to Rhonda.

Around this time I also approached a teacher, Barbara Francis, whom I worked closely with to ask her opinion about my proposed life change. While I almost chickened out, we did discuss the sensitive topic in an open, caring, and professional manner. It was good to get feedback from a teacher as well as my administrators, as I tested the water of how people might feel about Ron becoming Rhonda.

Barbara Francis says:

Rhonda has worked harder to be a total woman — more than any other woman I know. When I first met Rhonda, she was Ron. Ron was a workaholic who tried to help everyone. I remember visiting him in his office at Greenwood and the amount of materials and resources he had collected to advance curriculum was overwhelming! I offered an area at our school to help him get organized. Little did I know, reorganization of his persona was of paramount importance to him at this time. As I left his office, he gathered enough courage to ask me a personal question. He was wrestling with a sex change and wanted to find out if he would be more comfortable as a woman. I listend and later referred him to my dear friend and incredibly kind and knowledgeable counselor, Patti Cummings. As time went on, Ron became Rhonda. In retrospect, she is much more relaxed and open as Rhonda. Of course, her work ethic and the kind ways Ron had, transferred to Rhonda.

Nervously awaiting how things would go and what acceptance I would have as I moved up the chain of command, the rest of the week seemed to move slowly before our 11:15 a.m. Monday meeting. As things often go with meetings, the director was tied up in another meeting and running late. The secretary asked if I wanted to wait for her or go in to see the Assistant Superintendent on my own. Feeling like this was really my responsibility, I told her I would go in as scheduled. I walked in nervously, and we exchanged morning greetings. He asked how he could help me, in his usual pleasant manner. Knowing time was limited, I did not use the letter, but instead, briefly explained my desire to continue to do a good job for him and the County, but to bring a balance and personal satisfaction to my own life, I felt I needed to make the personal life transition from Ron to Rhonda. How could I do that without any negative repercussions with his staff and my job responsibilities?

He was very open-minded and received my request graciously, but said he really didn't know what could or could not happen. He said he would try and support what was best for me but would have to check with the Superintendent's office and get back to me. We talked a little more, as I asked if I should share this with the Superintendent's office. He said no that he would handle it. I left, feeling I was making progress; I had now passed three hurdles with caring support and acceptance of my request to transition on the job. Now the ball was out of my hands.

The following week I was in my office on Thursday afternoon when I received a call that the Associate Superintendent of our school system (the 25th largest in the country), wanted to see me in his office at 3:30 p.m. the next day. I was surprised about the call and on pins and needles that warm Friday afternoon, as I walked up the hill of our administrative complex to the renovated mansion building, which houses the superintendent and staff. I walked up the long, stately, spiral staircase to the second floor and into his office, hoping for the best. This was the big moment of decision. After waiting a few minutes, I was told I could go in as I knocked on his door and entered. I struggled to display a calm exterior, but my emotions were performing cartwheels on the inside.

As I entered the room, he said that I guess I knew why I was there, and I said I think I did, as he invited me to sit on one of the small couches in the formal conversation area of his office. As I sat down, he put me somewhat at ease and started off by saying he wanted me to know up front that he and the Superintendent of Schools wanted to support my request and help make my transition as smooth as possible for all concerned. I told him I really appreciated this. Then he dropped the bombshell on me. They were going to tell the school board of my request during the following Tuesday's meeting. This news really surprised me and put my transition on the fast track, a full two-and-a-half months before I'd planned on telling the schools and teachers with whom I worked. However, it was a very considerate move in that it cut out the rumor mill to the board members and explained why the system supported me and wanted to minimize any controversy and dissent on their approval of my transition.

Even though it shocked me, I really appreciated this decision. Secondly, I was surprised when they said they also wanted to offer me a new job in the school system. They thought it would be easier on me to start off working as a female with new coworkers who did not have a history or predetermined ideas of Ron, just as I was starting my new life as Rhonda. This was also very considerate, but I did not think this was best for me or the school system, and I responded by saying that I appreciated the opportunity, but there would be enough changes going on in my life during my transition. I was good at what I did as the Technical Programs Supervisor, and I wanted to stay in my present position. I felt that I could handle the adjustments in the same job. He saw my commitment to my present position, said okay and recommended I start sharing my transition plans with my schools and teachers and report back to him on what they said. We talked further on why I felt I needed to make this change in life so he could understand the reasons a little better. He wished me luck in my new and challenging plans and hoped life as Rhonda would bring me satisfaction and happiness. I thanked him and the Superintendent of Schools for the professional and compassionate way in which they responded.

I left with an assignment to talk with my instructional staff, other co-workers, and one of the school system's wellness coordinators. She would be the person who could assist me in my transition plans. The walk down the hill to my office was much more relaxed and pleasant on that early September evening. Knowing the chain of command was giving its blessing and approval to continue my employment with them as Rhonda was all I or anyone could ask for. Now the responsibility to prove I could make a successful transition was on the shoulders of the only person who could really assure this was the right thing to do — me.

I had just two working days to stay one step ahead of the rumor mill. I knew I had no choice but to talk to the administration and teachers in five technical high schools and eight other high schools in which I supervised instructional programs as soon as possible. With no time like the present, I was scheduled to perform teacher observations at the Carver Center for Arts and Technology the following

Monday. So, I intentionally made a point of arriving early to meet the principal and share what others would perceive to be the "big news" and ask how I should share my story with the carpentry, electrical, culinary arts, welding, cosmetology, multi-media communications and technology education staff whom I supervised. The principal, Mrs. Cary, granted me my request for a short meeting in her office before the day's events started and sat spellbound and a little taken aback with the news of my plans to start my male to female life adjustment in January.

While naturally surprised, Mrs. Cary was very understanding, said she appreciated me telling her first and wanted to continue working with me as Ron or Rhonda. She recommended I tell each of my staff members during my closing comments to them after my class observations. I quickly learned that there was no other way but to be to-the-point with such an issue. I took five minutes or so to tell each teacher what I was preparing to do and asked for their questions before moving on to my next class.

My simple and direct message was:

I'd like to take a few minutes of your time to share a very personal matter with you about my life, and ask for your understanding and honest feedback. I will be glad to answer questions now and / or later that you would have about this issue." I would continue, "For my entire life I was personally unhappy and dealt with many personal conflicts, broken relationships, and overcompensated by working too much, always helping others as a crutch to cover up my inner conflict and frustration. I was forced to live as a man when I always felt like and suppressed my dominate feminine identity or desire to live as the woman I really was. I have come to a point in my life that I cannot continue to live a lie if I'm ever going to find true happiness, and in January, after Christmas break, I will be transitioning from Ron to Rhonda

165

and my full female life personally and professionally. How do you feel this would affect our relationship and would it make you feel uncomfortable to have me as Rhonda be your supervisor? Do you have any comments or questions I can answer at this time? Thanks for your time and understanding.

After doing this explanation at least six times that day, I was pleased to find that, while it naturally took my teachers aback (they sat glued to my every word as I so openly and candidly shared my news), they all said what I was doing was a brave thing to do. While they didn't fully understand it, they wished me luck and wanted me to continue being their supervisor.

This experience drained me emotionally, but it felt good to receive an initial supportive response. You could sum things up in the comment one teacher said, "I really don't know why you would want to do this, but you have done more for me in two years than anyone else has done in ten years. I want you to continue to be my supervisor, and I'll get used to the new personality." This response became common over the next week, as I made a blitz around the County sharing the news personally with my principals and teachers — as much as I could before they heard it from someone else. The open-minded responses gave me reassurance and hope that things would work out and affirmed I could make the transition professionally and personally.

I guess the toughest moment in sharing my news was at my Sollers Point/Southeastern Technical High School, where I work with 11 different technical programs and overall school staff of about 25 to 30 teachers and support staff. The Principal, Mr. Parker, was also very accepting of my transition plans and asked me how I wanted to share my news with such a large faculty, just one week after sharing it with my smaller Carver Center staff. He said he was willing to tell them in his staff meeting that afternoon if I wanted him to. I told him I appreciated the thought, but it was my responsibility, and I thought I should do it. He said, "Okay, come back this afternoon, and I'll put you on the agenda." Again, the next few hours, as I performed other duties, seemed like days as I returned for my first large group sharing. About half way through the staff meeting, the principal said he wanted to give some time to Mr. Hoyman to briefly share some very personal information, which takes a lot of courage to do, and asked for their undivided attention. I appreciated this lead in and really wanted the staff to hear the news from me directly, no matter how many butterflies I had in my stomach. I shared my upcoming life change. The room got deathly quiet, as I quickly got everyone's full attention with such a surprising message. After I shared my brief story, I asked if anyone had any questions or responses. I could tell most teachers were in shock except for one of my female cosmetology teachers who was sort of chuckling to herself (this man is going to do what?). She broke the seconds of silence and tension in the air by asking, "Does this mean you can come and get your hair done in our beauty salon now?" I told her it did! Everyone had a good laugh, and I appreciated her candor as others responded with comments like "good luck," we support your personal decision," "that's the bravest thing I ever saw a person do in a group," and other positive/supportive comments. From male-oriented, traditional automotive or construction trades, to female-oriented cosmetology or allied health teachers, I couldn't be more appreciative of the acceptance, support and respect I received from the instructors, school administrators, and support staff I work with at my schools. While I'm sure there was still additional chuckling, jokes and negative comments from persons who did not (or still don't) fully understand why I have made this black and white change from a male life to my natural female life, I still value everyone's opinion and appreciated the chance they gave me to prove myself.

To complete the initial sharing of my pending life change, I spoke with our Career and Technology office staff and to fellow supervisors, individually after meetings or at the end of our usually long days. While they may have had a little tougher time accepting or getting used to the idea that the person they knew so well would soon become Rhonda, they also treated me with the caring, respect, and acceptance I needed in order to maintain my technical program position. In staff meetings, there used to be three men and three women among the supervisors (counting our coordinator), before I made the sex change. As we sometimes voted on decisions along traditional male or female viewpoints, after my transition the odds that year changed to four women and two men. The joke was, "Okay, Hoyman, which way are you voting now?" The men felt the odds had unfairly changed, and I guess you could say they did.

I shared my life adjustment news with as many staff members as possible the next few weeks. I then made an appointment with Ms. Wendy Mopsik, the wellness coordinator and the deputy superintendent to provide feedback from the news that now probably everyone in Baltimore County had heard in one fashion or another. The wellness coordinator was impressed with the way I was handling the issue, and said she would help when or if needed, but things seemed to be going so well, there didn't seem too much else she could do to help me at this time. The deputy superintendent was also pleasantly surprised with the response I reported. I'm sure he checked with other persons directly on their willingness to accept my transition plans. Based on this feedback, I was allowed to plan on staying in my present position as Technical Programs Supervisor in preparation for my January transition, still over three months away. Those three months were a little uncomfortable working with co-workers and teachers who wondered what the change and type of person Ron would look like and be as a woman or Rhonda. But, it was good to get everything open and out on the table to discuss before I walked through the door as a female for the first time.

The one key issue I personally raised so I could be considerate of and respect my fellow women's concerns or privacy was the famous bathroom question. Many schools and buildings had a single, privacy bathroom, but not our ESS Building in which I worked. What bathroom would the new transsexual woman use? Many of the women in the building said I respect your femininity, you are now living as a woman and should be able to use the ladies restroom. However, erring on the side of making all the women accept me and getting comfortable with Rhonda without controversy, I talked with the building administrator about the use of bathrooms in his building to reach a reasonable transition plan. During the first year of my transition (before I had my sex change genital surgery), I agreed to not use the ESS building restrooms during the day when most people worked. Instead, I would walk up to the Central Area office building at the top of the hill and use their single private restrooms, no matter how hot, cold, rainy, or inconvenient that was for the first year. This was not always easy, but I was glad to do my part to gain overall respect and acceptance from my co-workers.

The other part of our agreement was that in January of 1997, when I came back from my gender surgery and was physically a completely functioning female, I could use any of the ladies restrooms in our ESS building. If that concerned any of the other ladies, that was their issue, not mine.

Other small adjustments were handled as they arose, but I have to say that I feel my experience shows that an open, up-front policy of honesty and mutual respect for your peers and fellow co-workers is the best policy; it can work if given a chance. I'm grateful for the chance that Baltimore County Schools has given me. I think we are both winners for that.

Chapter 18

The Facelift:
The Agony and the Ecstasy

Determined to put my best foot forward and maximize everyone's first impression of Rhonda, I decided to schedule and complete my facelift before starting life and work as a female in January of 1996. While this was without a doubt the best decision I could have made, it would also turn out to be the most traumatic experience of my life.

The controversy escalated when I scheduled an appointment to color my, now shoulder length, baby-fine hair back to its original red color. In order for my sutures to heal, I could not have any chemicals or coloring performed on my head for at least a month after my December 6th plastic surgery. No matter how funny Ron looked with long, bright red hair, I was determined that nothing would deter me from the steps needed to start my new feminine life, an especially daring move, since I was going away to my annual American Vocational Association (AVA) conference in Denver, Colorado, that weekend before my facelift surgery.

I had to catch up on some last minute memos and paperwork before I would return as Rhonda in January, so I worked until 4 am Thursday morning, November 30, then drove to the Western School of Technology and Environmental Science and slept in the parking lot for a few hours in the cab of my pickup. It was cold that late fall morning. I slept in the truck because home was too far away and I needed the wake-up call of an early morning chill if I was going to be on time for my participation in a school-to-work transition conference that morning.

Susanne Gibson's comments in her cover story article on my transition in the October 22, 1997 City Paper of Baltimore sums up other's impressions of me that morning, saying, "Ron showed up at the Western School of Technology and Environmental Science in Catonsville in November, 1995, for a staff development day. The topic was 'School-to-Career Transition for Students: How do educational professionals effectively prepare students to make the transition from high school kid to college or professional?' It seemed appropriate that Ron was at Western to discuss transition. That cold morning we stood bleary-eyed near the coffee and doughnuts. I ate and watched other teachers eyeing Ron's new hair. He'd grown it shoulder length since the summer and dyed it purplish red (I wonder who sold him on that color). His clothing was androgynous; his gender seemed almost neutral. Dressing this way was a psychological technique to help co-workers prepare for the bigger change. After the Christmas break, Ron would come back to work in mid-January wearing a new face and a skirt."

I did feel uncomfortable and knew everyone was looking at me during the day's workshop events, as I sat in the cafeteria with large groups of teachers, fellow administrators, and business professionals — one of the prices of transition, like it or not. Late that afternoon, I boarded a plane with one of my automotive technology and computer drafting teachers whom I was taking to the AVA conference. *My last day as Ron in Baltimore County was now just a memory.* During the next four days we spent in Denver, I received more than my fair share of stares and unusual looks from business vendors and fellow administrators from Maryland who attended the conference (and knew nothing of my transition), as well as local restaurant, hotel, and store workers. I still had a job to do, and I did it.

I returned to Frederick Tuesday evening, December 5th; unfortunately, found the pump on my well wasn't working, and I had no running water. My surgery was the next morning. I called a plumber whom I had just met (who was also interested in possibly purchasing my log home) to do the repairs while I was away. He kindly put me on his schedule but could not have it repaired until the weekend. Knowing I was scheduled for plastic surgery, his parents kindly offered for me to stay with them for a few days during my recovery period until the well was fixed. Not having many options, I appreciated the offer and kindly accepted.

With spirits high, I made the 75 mile trip from Frederick to Dr. Converse's office early that cold Wednesday morning, December 6, 1995, ready to have the first surgical procedure of my life, ready to be Rhonda full time. The transition days of carrying around a portable wardrobe and make-up case, changing from Ron to Rhonda in the corner of a parking lot, and living up to everyone's false perceptions of Ron, were over. Rhonda would emerge from the operation table that afternoon to start the baby steps of her life, her rebirth. Eight-thirty, I was escorted into the surgery preparation room to undress, receive my surgery orientation, and review the steps I was to follow in my initial recovery period. I was a little nervous, but at this point, everything was out of my control now and in God's hands. I had to trust in Him and the skill of Dr. Converse that everything would go fine. Dr. Converse came into the room with a smile on his face, said good morning, and asked if I was ready to go. I was. He escorted me into the surgery room, and I laid down on the operating table. The room was intentionally cold, as they covered me with a light blanket and tried to reassure me that everything would be fine. I'd never had anesthesia; it took but a few seconds before I was fast asleep.

The operation lasted around five hours; they performed a standard facelift, and rhinoplasty (to straighten out my hook-shaped nose), removed the wrinkles around the side and under my eyes, puffed up my cheek area, fattened my lips, and took away my double chin. Fortunately, I did not know or feel a thing until around 3:30 that afternoon when I started waking up in the recovery room. I remember Dr. Converse came in around 4:00 pm and said that everything went fine and that I would be able to leave with my friend, Mary, in a few minutes. Mary was the lovely lady whom I'd met a few months earlier at her consignment shop. Since she lived close, she graciously agreed to let me stay at her home to recover that first night after surgery, at times when complications can occur. The nurses helped me dress. I looked like a Teenage Mutant Ninja Turtle. I was barely able to walk or see clearly. The bright sunshine and cold winter air hit my face like a snowball, smashing against my skin.

Mary drove me the short distance to her house and kindly helped me in the door and down the steps to her guest room. I was very appreciative of the help and felt out of my element since I was so used to being independent — the strong helper, instead of the weak patient. After slipping into my nightgown and bed, I tried to get comfortable and acclimated to my recovery routine. I had to lie flat on my back with my head and upper body elevated at a 45 degree angle, ice packs on my eyes and packing in my nose. I struggled to get comfortable, to get some sleep. Other than light broth, I could not eat that evening and needed help with every move I made. The lingering effects of the anesthesia and pain pills kept me comfortable, though, and I was able to get a little sleep that night.

Front View—Before Facelift

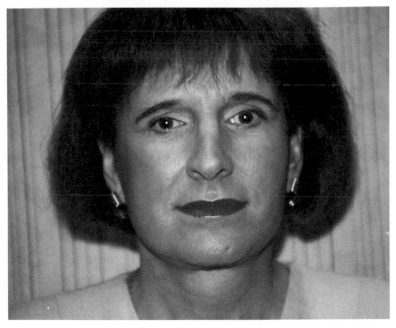

Front View—After Facelift

Side View—Before Facelift

Side View—After Facelift

The next afternoon, I was able to see and walk a little better. I went back for a quick check-up by Dr. Converse, who released me to go back to Frederick to start my recovery. One of Mary's salesgirls was nice enough to drive me back to Frederick that evening to my new friends, the Fosters, who had offered me a place to stay for the first few fragile days of recovery. While I was in some minor pain and discomfort, all was going well, and I settled into their home. We sat down to dinner around 8:00 p.m. that Thursday evening. Being a novice at taking pain medication and knowing I could not chew or open my mouth easily to eat, I took along a can of tomato soup and apple sauce for my first real food in two days.

What I didn't know was that tomato soup and apple sauce are high in acid, not good for an empty stomach. This combination, along with the pain medication upset my stomach in a way I never anticipated. Around 10:00 pm I started vomiting violently. As I stood in the bathroom vomiting, I could not control the heaving which continued. This strain on my face and neck caused the sutures on the left side of my face to rupture, and I could feel the blood beginning to seep out, between my skin and my chin area, under my bandages.

Pain now turned to panic. I stopped heaving, tried to calm down. I made my way to the kitchen. The Fosters helped me call Dr. Converse's pager number, and he called back about 15 minutes later. He asked what was wrong, and I explained my vomiting and bleeding. His exact words were, "Does it look bad?" I told him, "Yes, I think it does." He told me to come down as quickly as I could, and he would meet me with his nurses at the office. I thanked him and hung up.

Feeling blood continuing to ooze under my chin and neck, we didn't have a minute to waste. As we ran out of the house, I didn't even grab my purse or suitcase. I climbed into the back seat of the Fosters' Cherokee Wagon and my teeth started to chatter in the frigid air. By now, it was almost 11:00 pm We left Frederick for the Severna Park-Annapolis area, 75 miles southeast; I was the only one who knew the way. As we drove down Interstate 70 toward Baltimore, I asked Mr. Foster to go faster. He wasn't comfortable with that, so I gave up asking. If I could have driven, I would have gone 90 MPH, the way I felt. The older jeep was bumpy on the road, and I felt like I was in a war zone going to a MASH hospital. The blood continued to spread under my entire chin by now, my face started to swell, and I felt like I was in a life or death situation. I was barely able to see and give directions. We finally made it to Dr. Converse's office around 12:30 am. By now, my blood pressure needed monitoring, and I was very nervous, but also relieved to be back in Dr. Converse's hands. I was not only concerned about my emergency care, but also very worried this situation would damage my facelift results and care. The nurses quickly guided me back to the emergency room, took off my clothes and prepared me for emergency surgery. They placed me on the operating table I had just left the previous morning, put the IV in my arm and had me sign and emergency operation release form on the table. I couldn't even see the line on the page by this time. Dr. Converse came in and cut the bandages off my head. I heard him quietly say to the nurse, "This doesn't look good." While this certainly didn't reassure me, I knew I was in the best hands possible and receiving quality care—all I could ask for. I didn't want any regular intern at a hospital emergency room touching me. It had been three hours since my sutures ruptured; the bleeding was profuse. My blood pressure elevated; it was safer not to have anesthesia. The doctor operated with a few local injections to help ease the pain. I clutched my fists and tried to think good thoughts. Dr.

Converse had to cut open all three sutured areas, suction out the blood, recatheterize the blood vessels, and sew me back up; it took two hours to get things under control. By the time he was done, we were all exhausted. My upper chest turned black and blue from some of the related bleeding and tension. By 3:00 am the operation was successfully complete, and I was asked to try and calm down, and get some sleep. Under the circumstances things had gone well.

The two nurses were wonderful; they stayed up with me the rest of the night, monitoring my condition until 8:00 am. For safety's sake, they left me on the operating table. The nurse said it took me two hours to calm down enough to finally get to sleep. At 8:00 am, they took me into the recovery room to clean me up and get a few hours more rest before my friend, Mary, whom they'd called, kindly agreed to come over and take me back to her home for recovery. Dr. Converse wanted me to stay close by until I was out of the woods in my recovery and I agreed.

Because of the trauma of the emergency surgery, they rebandaged my entire head and face again, only now my face and eyes were completely swollen shut, and I could not see at all. Mary arrived at noon, and I was led like a blind person to her car and guest room. I now was faced with a longer recovery, on my back or propped up for five days. It was Wednesday, December 13th, before I could return to Dr. Converse's office to have my bandages taken off. The swelling went down enough so that I could see again. During that extended recovery time, my back was so sore from lying still (longer than I had in my entire life). I had to try to hold ice and moist pads on my eyes and wait to be led by the hand every time I needed to go to the bathroom.

Mary had to work in her store, so I had to call her by cell phone, for assistance when I just could not wait any longer. When she was home, I would beat a string of jingle bells she gave me against the wall, so she would know I needed her help. While not intentional, I could hardly eat and lost about six pounds that week during recovery. To prevent further complications, my pain medication was cut in half. I chose pain over another surgery.

To spare Mary that Sunday, two of my co-workers were nice enough to come down and stay with me while Mary worked. The first person, Mike, came in and jokingly said, "Boy, you look terrible. If you ever do anything like this again, I'll kill you!" We both started to laugh, and I told him not to make anymore jokes; it hurt even to smile. Dr. Gettle also came. He commented on how bad I looked, saying I had just been run over by a Mack truck, but I told him that I would do it again if I had to (and I would). He knew then that life transition was right for me, or I couldn't have gone through what I did and still have a positive attitude. I appreciated his comments and help he provided that day.

Dr. Karl Gettle says:

Perhaps one of the most interesting life experiences I have had is my relationship with "RhONda." My association with this person goes back 15 or more years. However, I really only got to be on a close personal relationship when Ron was appointed Supervisor of Technical Programs for Baltimore County Public Schools.

I remember one of my earliest conversations with Ron when he was about to marry Susan. He was so enthralled about the idea of getting married. He even carried a picture of her in his pocket over his heart. His conversations indicated he tried to do all he could to make married life happy. He even bought a van to transport his "new family" as Susan had two daughters.

Over the years he and I had many conversations, but his inner conflict was never mentioned to me. When I heard that he was getting divorced, I assumed that it was because of his work schedule and his untiring desire to help other people that caused his marriage to fail.

Then one day I heard that Ron was living with personal inner conflict. I did not pay much attention to the rumor. When Ron finally called me aside one day to describe what was going on in his life I was awed but not surprised. We had several long talks after that regarding what was happening in his life and how he was handling them personally and with his peers and colleagues. He and I did not always agree on what was happening but I feel we always had open discussions, we told each other what we really felt and not what the other wanted to hear.

When Rhonda had the first operation, she came to stay with Linda and me while she recuperated. I could see the agony and pain that she was going through and wondered why she would endure so much. Only after talking to her during that stay and reading and consulting with professionals, did I understand what a 'turmoil' she must have been going through her whole life.

Over the next year and several more operations Rhonda and I had many discussions over the change in her life. The change was amazing. A whole new spirit and person evolved. Rhonda became a person who dressed, as she likes to state, in 'killer outfits.' I never saw anything like this in Ron. Her personality also changed and she presented herself as a person who enjoyed life. This was something new and what I feel Rhonda had been seeking her whole life. She had really tried to be a happy person and thought that marriage (three times) or the military would do it. However, all of these events never gave Rhonda the satisfaction she was after, even though she tried her hardest to do what she thought a male should do. I believe that through these efforts her feelings of being trapped in a male body grew stronger and stronger until she took the steps that gave long sought after happiness. Today

The Facelift:

Rhonda is a happy person who presents herself in a professional manner. She will face hurdles, but with her determination and outlook, I know she will succeed.

Time moved slowly for me that week after surgery, but I finally received Dr. Converse's blessing to go home Wednesday for further rest and recovery. Dr. Gettle and one of the office secretaries came down over lunch break to get me that day and Dr. Gettle insisted I go home with him for a few days to be sure I would be okay. I appreciated his offer and was in no condition to disagree. I knew help would be best even though I was not used to receiving any.

The next evening, Dr. and Mrs. Gettle and one of their lovely daughters all sat in their living room and celebrated the Christmas spirit with the tree all trimmed and plenty of goodies for all. I rejoiced in my heart with God's blessings, as this evening was such a major celebration and contrast to the Thursday evening just one week earlier. When I was being rushed to Dr. Converse for emergency surgery, I'd wondered if I would ever have another day to celebrate life and my newfound womanhood.

It was sometime later, in June of 1998, that Linda Gettle, Dr. Karl Gettle's wife, wrote me the following letter about that time of my life.

Rhonda,

As you well know, as Ron, I had only met you briefly once or twice at the office. You were just "one of the guys" who Karl worked with. He spoke about you occasionally when relaying news about the office, but other than that, I really didn't know you at all. Then one day Karl came home with the news that you had told him you were about to make a big change in your life — and fulfill a long held desire to go ahead with the sex change process that you had already started. He explained some of the steps of the process and how you planned to carry through, including the physical operations.

Of course, I found this interesting, but beyond that I didn't give it much thought, because I really didn't know you. It wasn't until you stayed with us in December, 1995, that I began to think of all of the manifestations of what you were doing. Hearing what an ordeal you had just come through, and seeing first hand your optimism and determination made me realize the importance of this process to your personal happiness. I wanted to ask a million questions, (I hope I wasn't too invasive); but you were so open and willing to share that I just wanted to learn more about why a person would be willing to bear all of this expense and suffering. I came to realize that it wasn't simply a willingness, it was a deeply felt need that must be met if you were ever to find inner peace and contentment. Each time that we have been with you, Karl and I have marveled at how comfortable you are as Rhonda. Whether it be discussing clothes, make-up, hairstyle, or any other aspect of your new life you just seem to radiate happiness. Knowing what we know about all the challenges you have overcome to reach this place in your life we both feel a deep appreciation for your perseverance and determination. Both personally and professionally you hold yourself to the highest standards and we have complete love and admiration for you. We thank you for the confidence you have had in our friendship that has allowed us to be a small part of your miraculous life. We know that life holds much promise for you as you continue to enrich and evolve as a beautiful human being. It will be our pleasure to have our friendship grow with the years.

Linda Gettle

The next day, Friday, December 15th, was also a big day for me, as Dr. Gettle dropped me off for my final assessment report from Dr. Jones' transsexual clinic group. I was determined to look my best and make this crucial appointment I

Recovery from Plastic Surgery

had scheduled over a month ago. Getting ready for this meeting was so important to me that I put on my wig, my new Dress Barn outfit of a red jacket, black skirt, white lacy blouse, black pantyhose, pumps and make-up. Dr. Gettle and everyone I saw that day were surprised at how good and naturally feminine I looked, even with my face swollen from the surgery. Rhonda unveiled her new self for the first time that day and it felt great. Dr. Gettle liked my outfit so much that I still call it my "Dr. Gettle Look" and will never forget that day or the help and loving friendship he and his family gave me.

Not wanting to overstay my welcome, I wanted to get started back home for the rest of my recovery, which still had a long way to go, I decided to drive home that evening. It felt good to drive for the first time in almost two weeks, but my eyes were still so sensitive to light and tearing from the operation that I had to wear sun glasses driving home at 10:00 pm. That evening in the darkness, tears rolled down my cheeks. The last two weeks had been more traumatic than I could have ever anticipated. It wasn't Dr. Converse's or anyone's fault. I was a better person for what I had been through and now confirmed in my own heart, as well as others, that Rhonda was not only my true nature but a stronger person than I had even realized.

I enjoyed being home the next few days and tried to rest until Tuesday, December 19th, when I would go to the nail salon for the first time to get acrylic nails put on to feminize my hands. I prefer a medium tip length, a bright pearl plum color and a rounded, rather than square nail shape. While it took a while to get used to having longer nails, I loved the look and feel. Besides, it made it easier to eat popcorn.

Trying to maximize my time, I traveled to the Baltimore-White Marsh area later that afternoon to the Eldorado salon to have my hair system attached and my ears pierced for the first time. To attach my hair piece, Penny had to shave the few hairs I had on the top of my head and attach it to my scalp with a strong double tape and special glue made for the head and scalp. It looked and felt great to have a head full of hair that looked and felt natural. The color of my new hair matched the red hair coloring I had used in preparation for this day almost three weeks earlier. It was all worth it now. It would be four to six weeks before I could wear other earrings. Penny put in a pair of gold ear studs to finish off my new and more natural look.

Having other appointments in Baltimore the next day, I went back to the Gettle's home to stay overnight, and they were very impressed with the look of my new hair. However, it didn't take novice Rhonda long to mess things up. I was so naive in how to take care of my new hair that I dampened my hair before trying to curl it with my new curling iron the next morning. I was so embarrassed that I didn't know you use a curling iron on dry hair and curlers on wet hair. By the time I learned my first basic lesson in hair care, I had things so messed up I had to schedule and go back to Penny the next day for her to restyle my hair and learn how to use a curling iron. I can laugh about it now, but it points out how much I needed to learn about my new feminine life.

The next day, I also started seeing Dr. Spencer for my speech therapy on a regular basis and bought my first bracelet and piece of jewelry at S & N Katz jewelry store. That bracelet is still one of my basic pieces with a ½" wide gold band and diamond cut to compliment my one karat, solitaire diamond ring. It was now two weeks since my emergency surgery and things were definitely looking better and falling into place.

On Saturday, December 23rd, I returned home to catch up on some of life's necessities and to experience interacting as a woman. My car needed to have an oil change. Because I did not want to continue the grease monkey job of changing oil, which Ron always used to do, I went to Rice's Tire Center to use a coupon I had for an oil change. The counter man treated me warmly as he scheduled my oil change. He asked me to have a seat in the waiting room, which happened to have three other ladies in it. I felt at home with my counterparts and was learning the lady-like method of receiving and waiting for auto repair work when things got interesting. After about a half hour, the service manager came out and asked for Ms. Hoyman. He informed me that my air filter was dirty; he said they would change it for $15.95. I told him thank you, but I didn't want to have it done at this time. The advantage I have over most ladies is that I knew it only meant popping four clips to take the filter cover off and the purchase of a new filter for $6.95 at Pep Boy's auto supply. An easy job that Rhonda would do to save $9.00. I appreciated the repair shop offer, but it was interesting to see how I was approached and treated as a lady in a man's world.

That afternoon, I received an offer to attend a neighbor's Christmas party. I knew most of the other neighbors would be there. Since they invited Rhonda, I was nervous and a little hesitant, but said to myself that there was no time like the present to break the ice. So, I put on a nice lacy white blouse, red and black plaid vest, knee length red, pleated skirt, and black hose to round off a Christmas look. I walked through the snow with my boots on before changing to my black, low-heeled pumps and entered the neighbor's house. I was greeted with hellos as those close neighbors (who'd known Ron) had to do a double take to realize it was Rhonda now. As I expected, both of my closest neighbors were friendly, but it was harder for one of the families to accept and adjust to me as a female. One of the ladies said that other than the moderate voice tone, she never would have known I had ever been Ron. That was a nice compliment to receive just a few weeks into my transition. After about an hour at the party, I walked back home feeling good at the way things went. I had broken the ice and introduced

Rhonda. I have learned with these and other folks that it's better to not shy away from greeting people you know, but then it's better to back away and give them time to adjust to the idea that I am now, and always will be, Rhonda.

As dusk settled, I concluded a very interesting day by venturing out to Hechinger's, an environment with which I am extremely familiar. I went over to order a sheet of Formica or counter top laminate which I needed to resurface the desktop of my speech therapist's office. As I asked the salesman about the sizes and styles of Formica available, he kindly, but directly, asked me if I knew how to cut and apply Formica (he assumed I didn't know). So, I explained the type of saw blade used to cut the formica and methods used to apply it with contact cement. He was surprised that I could so easily explain the process and quickly took my order. While I appreciated his desire to make sure I knew what I was getting into before ordering this costly material, he would not have thought twice about taking the same order from Ron (or any man) without asking these questions. I was in a new world now, and, while it felt great to be accepted as Rhonda and female, I also was reaffirmed, that as a female, there are some areas in which I'm not perceived as being a man's equal.

On the bright side, it is not considered feminine to lift heavy objects; fortunately, I have found most men fall all over themselves to load or lift heavy items for me at the home improvement stores. It is to my advantage not to try and left heavy items, and if I do, I pretend they're heavy. For example, if I go to lift a 5 gallon bucket of drywall spackling compound onto a cart, I have to bend over using two hands and slowly lift it up, when in reality I can easily lift it with one hand without bending over. Besides, why should I wear myself out at the start of a home improvement job if the men are willing to do it for me? All I have to do is wear my shorts, a tight-fitting top, look cute, and act help-less.

The next week, I continued to make new purchases: a watch, hair dryer, fingernail polish remover, clothes, Kotex lightday pads, and other items I would need to live in society as a female. It was fun shopping but also quite a reorienta-tion to a world and culture that I was just learning. It felt good but unusual to be referred to as she, ma'am, or her as I shopped for items such as my Easy Spirit pumps. Ron could never have related to this experience. Every new day I interacted in society as Rhonda, I continued to gain a little more confidence in my femininity. Aside from shopping and my other brief outings, I continued to practice styling my hair, trying different make-up looks, and learning to read the washing labels of clothes.

In general, my recovery from plastic surgery was not only a physical healing, but a time for mental readjustment and getting used to living as a woman, putting all of Ron's old clothes, lifestyle and habits behind me. As Rhonda it was easy to leave behind my old male image and forced lifestyle. I would get some second looks at times or a feeling of discomfort about being accepted as a woman. But, whether real or perceived, you have to show confidence, no fear, no hesitation in improving your interactions as a woman. That was one of the hardest things to do in the beginning, on a day-to-day-basis.

I also continued with my electrolysis, a trip to Baltimore to see my speech therapist, counselor and other transition services. I had to build my medical services into life's routine on a weekly or bi-weekly basis. You have to be determined and disciplined to be successful and keep from sliding back-wards. I was so busy I even did a dumb thing like locking my keys in my car one day and running out of gas the next.

While it may sound demeaning, I learned that dumb mistakes like that are more acceptable for women.

The last week before going back to work, I had my more positive interactions, as I introduced Rhonda or my feminine self to Casey, my real estate agent. I also decided to become a Mary Kay beauty consultant to learn more and invest in my skin care and color cosmetics, and I traveled to have one last check-up with Dr. Converse, who was pleased at my recovery. Even though it would take longer, there would be no negative complications from my second, emergency surgery. I even attended my first Mary Kay consultant training session on Tuesday, January 2, and was received with great acceptance, like any other woman in the group. I didn't reveal my past identity. It felt good and different interacting with and being accepted in a large, women's group. For the first time as Rhonda, I really felt like a lady among ladies.

I realized I still had a long way to go, but the rough edges of Ron's old life seemed to be smoothing out nicely. I knew life as a woman would be more demanding, that it would take more time to present a positive appearance each day. I was not only learning how to do it, but also enjoying life as a female. Two-and-a-half years later, that feeling hasn't changed; life as Rhonda is so much more rewarding and fulfilling.

That year, I didn't need any material Christmas presents, or even to be with anyone to celebrate Christmas Day or the start of the new year. I had the gift of life, the love and friendship of close friends, and the beginning of my new life, which could not have been put into any package.

Chapter 19

Getting to Know Rhonda

My family back in Greensburg needed to meet their new daughter, sister, and aunt for the first time; I had planned on spending the weekend back home before starting my first full week at work. I could not go home for Christmas because of the extended recovery from my plastic surgery complications; besides, I did not want to make such a major re-entry into their lives when they were celebrating the holiday season.

I concluded my long first day back at the office by packing that Friday evening, January 5, 1996, for my first trip home as Rhonda. Of course, it took longer than Ron's standard "throw in some slacks and a few shirts, shaving gear, underwear, and off you go." Now, Rhonda wanted to make sure she not only had the right skirt, blouse, or dress, but she also needed the extra pair or two of shoes, make-up, curling iron, hair spray, and earrings for each day's planned outfit. Life was certainly more fulfilling, but also more time-consuming and demanding. But, as they say, it comes with the territory.

Saturday, January 6, 1996, I arose early to get my outfit ready. Before taking off, I had my usual two-hour Saturday morning electrolysis. That day, we started working on the hairs around my chest and breast area, avoiding my face so that my make-up would be smooth. During that first full year of transition (and also the second year), I found that my personal time and life were not really my own. In order

Rhonda Goes to Work

to maximize the transition, I had to allow time for medical services, recovery time, and learn all the techniques to become a woman. I had to be focused, dedicated, and determined to keep my priorities straight.

After lunch, I started the three hour, 160-miles drive home to Greensburg. My first planned stop was at my middle sister, Cheryl's home. I arrived around 4:15 in the afternoon. As I entered through the kitchen door, Cheryl, my brother Bill, my teenage nephew, and my niece all kindly said hello and unanimously "Boy, you look different!" We sat down at the kitchen table and got to know each other all over again. We talked about my surgery experience, Christmas, other family news, and how things were going for me as Rhonda. My sister Mary, who lives in Pittsburgh, could not come but called to say we would meet on my next trip; she warned me of a snow storm that was coming.

With my mother reluctant to tell my stepfather of my transition (fearing a negative reaction), I was not sure if I would get to see her this trip. Her presents and others were there for me to open. Since this was Rhonda's first time for presents, I wasn't sure what to expect, but things turned out well. I received a toaster oven from my mother, and a nice flowered picture frame with a music box song ("You Light Up My Life"), some chocolates, a big Hershey bar (I'm a choco-holic), a snake flashlight and a pair of earrings from my sisters and brother. I also gave gifts. It was nice and informal. A time for my family to get to know and relate to the new me.

After a sandwich, I left to go see Susan, my former wife, to catch up on personal business with the separation, check out the new home she was living in, and just have a brief, cordial introduction. I appreciated her understanding and guarded acceptance. Susan greeted me with a warm hello, and we unpacked some items I brought from the Frederick home. Her daughters were at their father's for visitation, and I honored Susan's wishes that, at least during the present time, I wouldn't meet them as Rhonda. It's hard to put into words, but it seemed like we were now both getting used to a new level of interacting with each other, maybe like a girlfriend or helping sister, rather than formal, strained husband-wife relationship.

When we'd first separated Susan was, of course, very hurt and felt like she could not trust anyone again in a relationship. I told her if she trusted in me, then I would help her rebuild her life and faith in another person, so she could start over in all aspects of her life, just as I was. By helping her get a new home, being understanding during the separation, and committing to assisting her financially, I hoped to show her trust and caring, something she was also giving me. Susan and Rhonda interacted on a limited but essential way during that first year of my transition before the final divorce. She really didn't want Rhonda to take over Ron's life, but we both knew Rhonda was the real person, Ron was not my true nature. We shared recent Christmas and personal events in each other's lives with one another that evening. She took a picture of me, and we exchanged some presents I brought for her and the girls.

With final move-in work still needed, I changed from the lacy white blouse, red jacket, black skirt, hose and heels to some jeans and a casual blouse to help finish some house carpentry work and hang some pictures. Many of Susan's friends and relatives didn't want her to associate with me, but Susan knew that at least staying friends would benefit each of us, and she had a more compassionate and Christian spirit than other's narrow-minded viewpoints.

A large snow storm was coming (three inches had already fallen since my arrival). I decided to call my trip short and brave a blizzard on the way home, even though it had already been a long day. Otherwise, I would have been stuck in Pennsylvania for an extended time, and I was not really prepared for that as Rhonda. As midnight came, I packed up and started home, hoping I could beat the storm and road conditions. I drove the three hour trip in five hours in three to six-inch unplowed snow. I parked my little S-10 pickup at the bottom of my driveway at 5:00 the next morning. I only made one roadside gas and snack stop half-way home, because I was concerned about going out in public or getting stuck at the end of the day when my beard stubble and make up was not as convincing. I made the right decision, by Sunday evening, we had 24" of snow on the ground, and the interstates I had just traveled were closed for the next three days.

I knew we would not have school for a while. I changed into my consignment shop, powder-blue (snowbunny), winter pants and jacket to shovel off my driveway in stages. Again, it felt different just shoveling snow as Rhonda. You should have seen the looks I got from some of the snow removal road crew and other neighbors. "This woman is doing all that shoveling!" Not my first choice either, but there was no one else to do it, and my driveway was very steep. Besides, shoveling snow those next few days was a blessing from God. It allowed me to have some peace and quiet, rest, and more preparation for my new life at work.

Having to change more than my physical appearance in this new total life adjustment, I had to think differently about money and borrowing. I would be okay when I sold the house, but to keep up with major transition costs and not slow down on any of my plans, I took the time to set up a $50,000 home equity loan to consolidate my mounting debts. My former hard work and home equity qualified me for the loan; but I can tell you, borrowing money for personal needs in the amount Rhonda was spending was something conservative Ron would never had done.

I enjoyed my few days at home and thought that if I was lucky enough to find the right man, I could get used to being a housewife and homemaker. I knew I was what many would call a three-time loser at marriage, but that was because I could never be my true self in building a good marriage. I was not there yet, but I'm old-fashioned and optimistic enough to feel that as I love myself for the first time in my life, in the future I could really love someone else and consider a relationship that would be fulfilling and lasting. Call me a dreamer, but I never felt I could be the Rhonda I am today and that dream has come true.

With the positive start to my re-entry back to the world of work on the previous Friday with my getting-to-know-you luncheon at Dr. Gettle's, and subsequent afternoon back at my office, I was ready to start off what remained of the month with a bang. The blizzard of '96 was over. Or was it?

That cold winter morning on Wednesday, January 10th, I got up extra early to put on my make-up, style my hair, and accessorize. Quite a different routine than Ron's old shave, quick brush of the hair, jump into a suit, put on the dreaded tie and out the door with little thought to his fashion and appearance. While schools were still closed, I was required to report to the office or lose a vacation day. Still wanting to meet fellow administrators and office staff for the first time on a positive note, I wore my suit with the red blazer with a blue collar and skirt, complimented by a red and blue small print blouse with a V-neckline. I did get some nice compliments on my outfit that day, which was especially nice since my mother would never let me wear red as a boy because of my red hair. "Rhonda, I could hardly recognize you!" "You better watch out that you don't look better than the other women!" "I can't believe you are the same person!"

After a morning at my desk, the big event for the day came in the afternoon when I went to the Baltimore County Timonium complex purchasing department. The women and men there were really nice, complimentary and supportive of the new me; again, I had to introduce myself to many who did not know I used to be Ron. Even one of my former automotive instructors, who was now a transportation specialist and a person for whom I'd sat on an interview committee said, "Can I help you ma'am?" He really didn't know it was Ron, his former supervisor.

The special event came when I was asked to show my Baltimore County Public Schools identification badge. I had signed in as a visitor since the only ID I had was with Ron's picture on it. Since this was also the area where they took the picture, I had a new picture taken on the spot and would receive my new Rhonda ID back in a few days. I was anxious to see the picture and looking forward to another affirmation of my official female status. I even had a chance to wear my new Naturalizer snow boots. It felt great to do things like regular grocery and personal shopping as Rhonda.

That evening I made the many requests for a name change on all my bills and correspondence. For example, my new home equity loan said on the closing statement "Rhonda, formerly known as Ronald" to assure proper legal identity. I thought this was a clever and very appropriate way to handle my change. There are many details and paperwork changes as part of a transsexual life transition. It was a necessity and I was happy to change all correspondence as fast as possible.

Thursday, January 11, I arose again at 5:30 a.m. to allow the time needed for my special look, as I was now introducing myself to new people on a daily basis. I decided to wear my new purple suit with a nice white blouse. It was a real treat to have such diversity in my look, style, and overall appearance. The old saying, *presentation is everything,* was true. "If it looks like a duck and walks like a duck, then it's a duck." I wanted to be perceived and accepted as a duck (female, of course, not a rooster trying to look like a duck).

My first stop of the day was Dundalk High School where I introduced myself to the principal and his secretary. They didn't recognize the new me. Mr. Janson offered to help me take off my winter coat, and I appreciated the gentlemanly help. It felt nice to be treated like a lady and different in a good way. Back at the office, I met some co-workers for the first time, and as we talked they would occasionally slip up and call me Ron, then catch themselves, and apologize. I told them not to worry about that — it would take time to adjust to the new me. I knew I couldn't wear my feelings on my sleeve or be offended by the unintentional slips.

Later that day, I needed to stop at the purchasing office in Timonium. Again, I received some nice compliments on my appearance. One lady told me how brave I was at taking this bold step and that I was really considered and accepted as female by their office group. That kind of affirmation and positive feedback was repeated many times those first months, as I re-introduced myself to everyone. It really helped me maintain and gain the self-confidence I needed to start my transition so successfully. Perception was becoming reality. The ladies all liked my multicolored, purple angora coat and commented that they didn't have to teach me anything about shopping.

As my working day ended, I stopped by the payroll department to have my direct deposit and paycheck records changed to reflect my new name. The payroll secretary was also nice enough to ask if I wanted the sex category changed from "M" to "F" and I told her yes, and I appreciated her asking. I thanked her for that extra consideration and this

assistance showed the professional courtesy and consideration I was being shown in my official acceptance as a female.

To help reduce the pain of my two-to-three-hour electrolysis appointments, I stopped by to ask Dr. Thompson, my
personal physician, for a prescription of a topical skin cream
called EMLA. When the white cream is applied to the skin
and covered for an hour with plastic wrap, it helps numb
the surface feeling of the skin. While it does not take away
the pain, it helps in real sensitive areas like the upper lip
during electrolysis. I usually apply it during my Route 70
interstate trip to my electrolysis in Frederick. I say, "I look
like a sandwich with the white cream and plastic wrap
covering my face." The affects or numbing of the skin surface
last about two hours after being wiped off.

I was still self conscious about my appearance in public.
On the way home that evening, I went to the pharmacy
department of a Giant grocery store to have my EMLA
cream prescription filled, I made the request as Rhonda.
Well, 15 minutes later the pharmacist paged Ronald Hoyman to come and pick up the prescription. When I went to
the pick up counter, he asked me if the prescription was for
my husband. This was a nice compliment but I said (having
to sign the co-pay form) that I was the same person but going
through a transsexual life transition. He said he understood
and would have my files changed to Rhonda, until I could
receive a new medical authorization card from work.

As I arrived home and quickly got ready for bed, I felt
good about my long but productive day of acceptance, realizing you have to take the discomfort or fear with the good
on a day-to-day basis. As I took off my dangling, purple
earrings and put on my gold pierced studs, I was still a little
clumsy in trying to easily change earrings; there is a learning curve to all aspects of my feminization and new life
routine.

Friday, January 12, brought another snowstorm and 12 inches of snow as my work week and introductions to my teachers and schools was cut short again. Friday and Saturday required shoveling snow to get to my electrolysis and the remainder of the day juggling bill payments and figuring out how I was going to continue floating money and charge accounts to keep up with my expensive transition costs. One important tip I learned from Lelia, my new electrologist, was that you can remove surface body hair without disturbing the roots and making it grow back stronger and thicker by trimming off the surface hair with a pair of fine scissors or even better, a small rechargeable electric hair trimmer. Saturday, I also went to Blockbuster Video to update my membership card, and, again, had to reveal my former male life with my request for a name change. The girl at the customer service counter made the name change without any questions and even asked me if I wanted her to destroy the old cards.

On Sunday, January 14, I caught up on my diary, which took time in itself to keep up with, as I wanted to keep track of the key steps and experiences in my transition. That day, my one significant step was that, due to my weight loss, I was able to drop a dress size and panty hose size from X-tall size scale to the smaller, large-size panty hose. I had started ordering, and still do, most of my hose from a mail order hosiery and nightwear/undergarments source called "Silkies." It felt great to order the smaller size, so my hose would not sag around my ankles or stretch too much after use. I was still learning the information that I did not have previously; as I continued to maximize my appearance and presentation to be a sharp looking chick.

With the blizzards of '96 finally under control, I knew the next few weeks would be the most significant of my interaction with teachers and schools. I prepared mentally and style-wise. My primary objective for the week was to complete my work duties, and simultaneously introduce myself to fellow administrators, instructors, and office staff as Rhonda. Knowing it would take time for everyone to get used to the initial shock of seeing me as Rhonda, I intentionally did not want to spend a lot of time with any one person that first day. Even though it was just a few weeks since I began living full-time as a female, it felt so natural to me, although I knew it would take other people more time (especially the ones who knew Ron) to get used to interacting with me as a woman. I wanted to create space for them to develop their own comfort zone, no matter how long that would take. Maybe for some it's still happening. To cut down on the rumor mill and gossip, I also wanted to at least say hello to everyone of my teachers when I visited their building for the first time. This I also felt would maximize everyone's initial acceptance of me — allowing them to judge me for what they personally saw and felt, not by what someone else's perceptions might be.

I started off Monday morning, January 15, working at my desk. I focused on my duties and anticipated participating in my first division meeting with the assistant superintendent for curriculum and instruction and 50 or so fellow administrative directors, coordinators, and supervisors. Wanting to look professional, I wore my plum-colored suit (which I love). Again, I was meeting more than half the people in the room for the first time as Rhonda. There was no special statement or welcome to Rhonda. The assistant superintendent intentionally wanted me to blend in and be accepted as a woman in the meeting, without drawing any attention to the fact that Rhonda had joined the group that morning. They did not realize it was me until I spoke up and addressed issues that related to my technical programs.

Again, a nice affirmation of my acceptance. I was blending in.

That evening, back in Frederick, I ended a very eventful day by attending another Mary Kay consultant training meeting, which my director, Mrs. Newman conducted every week. I was still self-conscious about my interactions with them, especially my voice. Just think, it was only a month earlier that I had been out in public for the first time from my plastic surgery recovery.

Tuesday, January 16, I was working back in the office when one of the secretaries from another section came over and complimented me on my appearance. That was the first time someone also said how they thought I seemed like a different person. I was more relaxed and self-confident as a woman. Another ice breaker happened in the afternoon when two of the principals with whom I worked closely came to our office for a meeting. As I had a chance to say hello for the first time as Rhonda, they were very kind, complimentary of my appearance and invited me to stop by their schools as soon as I could. While still a long way to go, these two examples demonstrated just how positively I was perceived in my personality, as well as my appearance.

To keep from fighting the weather and long distance miles I was facing in my drive back to Frederick each day, I was fortunate to have a friend offer to let me use the upper spare room of her Cape Cod home as a room away from home anytime I wanted. While it was not my log home, it was a place where I could set up personal items, make-up, clothing, and a make-up mirror (my first). I could now stay in town a few days a week, usually Tuesday and Thursday, to catch up on some much-needed rest. That night was one of the first times I used my new home base, and I enjoyed the pleasant company of Ms. Fisher and her two cocker spaniels.

Over those two weeks, God's hand helped with the harmony in Rhonda's first trip home. He provided safe travel in the blizzard of 1996, acceptance and support from co-workers at the office and building complex level, extra time for rest, recovery, and regrouping with life's issues and a safe and secure home away from home. I was trying to do my part, but I do not believe I could have coordinated the events that took place with my own humanly persuasions.

I was now as ready as I could be to face the students, staff, and school environment which would bring the real flames to test the fire brick exteriors of courage and will I would need to survive my biggest test.

Chapter 20

Rhonda's Return to the Front Lines

On Wednesday, January 17, 1996, the schools finally settled back to a normal schedule, the blizzards of '96 began to melt away. After office work began my day, I squeezed in a rare lunch-time counseling appointment with Ms. Cummings before I began my first real school visit to Eastern Technical High. At Eastern, I was greeted warmly by Mr. Kemmery, the principal, and I made an effort to see most of my technical program teachers before they left for the day. Most of the office staff and teachers did not even know it was me until I told them. Time went by fast as I nervously made quick stops to let my teachers meet me. I tried not to stay long for those first face-to-face encounters. As planned, the short meetings seemed to be best for them as well as for me. The day ended with a long, one-and-a half hour, (eighty-mile) drive to Hagerstown for a two hour electrolysis appointment. I drove home after electrolysis for the first time in three days.

Thursday, January 18, was a foggy morning. The snow melted, and I drove to Milford Mill Academy to meet with the school staff. As I pulled into the parking lot, one of my cosmetology teachers was getting out of her car. I said "Good morning, Brenda. It's me, Rhonda." She looked for a while, "Oh my gosh!. It's you! Rhonda? Don't you look nice!" We walked in together, having a nice chat before I introduced myself to over 15 teachers, administrators and office staff with whom I worked closely. Only a few recognized me without a direct introduction. Even the two teachers who went with me to the AVA conference in Denver (just six weeks earlier) didn't recognize me. It was a series of positive meetings, as we briefly discussed a number of work issues.

Brenda Stark says:

I met Rhonda when she was Ron. As Ron, he was intelligent, loyal, articulate, and worked very hard to secure the future of vocational- technical education. However, Ron was not very personable and didn't exude personality. Now she has all of the positive qualities I witnessed as Ron, and an abundance of happiness which is evidenced in the personality change, attitude, the carriage of herself, the positive way in which she is able to handle unflattering responses and remarks with a great deal of understanding and acceptance of how others feel about the issue of gender transformation. She has had the character and determination to see her way through all of the turmoil and pain, and has arrived on the other side, I believe a better person, not only because of what she has had to endure to get there, but because she is now where she has always felt she belonged. If you allow yourself the experience of getting to know her, you might be pleasantly surprised with the emotional and intellectual growth you experience in yourself. You realize that while each of us should have happiness in our lives, only some of us are truly fortunate enough to find our way to it.

After stopping at another comprehensive high school, my afternoon business took me to the male-dominated building maintenance department. Nervously, I walked into what could have been a much tougher crowd. As I walked by the various departments to my meeting with one of the maintenance supervisors, I tried not to show any signs of anxiety, which would erode my self-confidence and their acceptance of the new Rhonda. To my pleasant surprise, in my meeting with the maintenance supervisor, he said my transition was not only a non-issue, but that he was looking forward to a better working relationship with Rhonda than he had with Ron. Finishing up the workday back at the office, I was waiting to meet with Ms. Carter, the course scheduling specialist, when one of the secretaries who knew Ron very well came up to me and asked if I was Carol. I politely said no and introduced myself to her for the first time. After work, I ended with a session with my speech therapist, Dr. Spencer, who was helping me with my pitch changes. One of my problems was that I would get caught up in one of the many technical content subjects I was dealing with and not pay as much attention to the softer and slower delivery of my speech, which takes a focused, conscious effort. I still had a long way to go before I was comfortable with my speech delivery; practice makes perfect (or at least helps a lot). Some of my girlfriends would say, "Men like a woman with a raspier tone in her voice." With longer vocal chords, it is characteristic for taller women to have a deeper, less soft voice pitch. I was beginning to overcome the fear that came each time I opened my mouth.

Friday, January 19, brought an exciting conclusion to the end of my introduction week as I arrived early that morning at Sollers Point/Southeastern Technical High School in the industrial community of our southeastern area of the county. I intentionally wore my red suit that day because it was part of the school colors and a favorite of the principal's. I arrived early that morning. As I entered the building, I wondered how my new appearance and first meetings would go. I took a deep breath, trying to relieve my anxiety, and opened the door. As I entered the front office, I introduced myself to the two office secretaries. Ms. Derda, the head secretary said, "My gosh, Rhonda, I didn't even recognize you! You look so nice." Mr. Parker, the principal, greeted me warmly as he said, "Come on in and have a seat, Rhonda." He paid me some nice compliments on my appearance as he remarked on how different I looked. We caught up on school-related issues and he said, "Come on, I'll introduce you to the faculty, but I have to leave for another meeting in thirty minutes." We started and met about half of the faculty in brief stops as each person was very receptive and friendly, but you could also tell they were very surprised by my new appearance.

When the time came for Mr. Parker to go, he told me I was welcome to stay or come back another time to meet the rest of the staff. We walked back to his office. He and Ms. Derda said, "Rhonda, we know you have been through a lot, and we would like you to have this little gift as a token of our support and something we thought you could use." I was completely taken aback when I opened the long jewelry box to find a beautiful pair of pearl and gold earrings and necklace. You could have knocked me over! I did not have words to show how much this symbol of caring and support meant to me. "Rhonda" was being affirmed and cared for more than she could ever dream possible. I still cherish my jewelry set and wear it proudly in visits when I return to this school, along with a red suit or dress. After all, I have to show my appreciation for a kindness and day I will never forget. Mr. Parker and Ms. Derda are a class act.

Mr. Parker left for his meeting, and I continued meeting the remaining faculty members. I had to introduce myself twice to many of them before they realized it was me — three times to Mr. Bobian, one of my printing program teachers, who was very accepting but also very surprised at how different I looked.

The teacher I will remember most that day is Ms. Smith, the cosmetology teacher, who, four months earlier, was so surprised about my initial announcement in the faculty meeting. She was the person who broke the silence by saying, "Does this mean you can come and get your hair done in my cosmetology lab?" I wondered what her reaction would be as I walked up the steps to the second floor. She was the last person I would see on my first visit. She happened to be standing in the doorway, and I walked up to her and said hello. Ms. Smith was taken back by my new appearance and told me I really looked good. I could tell by her reaction that she was a little embarrassed. I said that was to be expected and told her I would see her at a later time. Her reaction in reality was a nice compliment on how feminine I did look. I wanted her and everyone to have time to digest the new Rhonda before interacting more. I went down to the office to thank Ms. Derda once more for the nice gift, and let her know that I was able to see everyone before leaving. As I drove away, I was a little emotionally drained from my own fears about meeting everyone, but also feeling good that things had gone so well, or at least I thought so for a first time meeting.

Friday evening I made the long drive to Fairfax, Virginia, 75 miles from my office, to the monthly transsexual group meeting — the first one since living as a full-time female and my plastic surgery. Approximately 40 to 50 people met that evening at the Protestant church. It was a good way to get tips. Everyone shares and supports each other. With my confidence growing, recent weight loss, mannerisms, and attention to dress and make-up, I was fast becoming one of the more successful members of the group. Some of the other girls did not have the resources, job stability, education, or proactive assertiveness I had in my fast track transition plan.

I was inspired that evening by one lovely post-operative lady who had just been married and brought her very supportive husband. That gave hope to many in the group that with the right circumstances, you can achieve mainstream acceptance in society, as well as a positive heterosexual relationship. They made a cute couple.

Over the weekend I had a chance to rest up, review my week, reflect on adjustments to my appearance and presentation, and even a stop at my favorite shopping spot, the Dress Barn. Some dress-coat style dresses had just come in, and I quickly learned that this form-fitting cut and shorter length style was a winner for the look I was trying to achieve. I wore my new black dress to work that Monday, and received lots of compliments. I was going a little shorter and sexier as my self-confidence continued to build. This day I took a trip to my Carver Center for Arts and Technology and introduced myself to the staff (the school where I first announced my transition).

As I approached Ms. Bridges, my cosmetology teacher, she did not recognize me until I said hello and introduced myself. Her reaction was, "Oh my God! You look great!" She continued to give me a constructive critique for self-improvement, which I appreciated. I never wanted sugar-coated responses; I couldn't have improved without honest feedback.

Ms. Bridges now reflects:

After several years of teaching, I was introduced to another Technical Education Supervisor! This one was a little different. He said, "I'd like to get together with you to see if you feel there needs to be any changes in your program." He called, and the changes began to happen. We (the teachers in my program) could not believe this person cared to hear our thoughts. After meeting with us individually, he put together our suggestions and needs, what he wanted, and what was possible. Each year things began to get better. Our confidence began to grow. After a couple years, Ron told me in confidence of his plight and that he wanted to become a woman. I was taken back, amazed, and confused. However, after 18 years as a professional Cosmetologist and 11 years as a high school cosmetology teacher, I knew Ron was serious. I am not sure if I was a help or a hinderence. Now Ron is Rhonda. She has a long way to go to be the woman she wants to be. But then, so do I! She still asks me how things look! I am brutally honest, but I am like that with my students. There are changes in Rhonda Hoyman's life, she has earned the respect of this Baltimore County Teacher."

That afternoon was my first meeting since my transition with the Associate Superintendent, who had earlier agreed to and supported my request to stay in my same position as Technical Programs Supervisor. He complimented me on my appearance and asked how I thought my transition and acceptance was going. I'm sure he had already received feedback from some of my schools and co-workers. He asked if I was coming back to work in Baltimore County next year, and I said yes. He was supportive and pleased about how I was handling things, and recommended I stop by and see the superintendent for the first time on my way out. He reassured me that after a few months the excitement of the new Rhonda in the school system would settle down to business as usual. I agreed.

As I went down the hall and entered the Superintendent's office, I was greeted by the Superintendent's Administrative Aide, whom I knew rather well, but she didn't recognize me, "Do you have an appointment?" she asked. I introduced myself, and she was surprised but complimentary, as we had a brief discussion on my transition and the old Ron. I then introduced myself to the Superintendent. He asked how things were going and said he was pleased to meet me, and promised he would be able to recognize me in the future. I left feeling good about myself and the professional and personal support I was receiving from the top officials in the school system.

As I walked out of the building, I noticed Mr. Burch, the principal of Western School of Technology and Environmental Science, and the last principal, of my five main technical centers in which I supervised programs, to meet. Not being bashful, I walked over, knocked on his window and said hello, as he asked if he could help me. When I told him who I was, he was so surprised he told me I looked great and would never have recognized me if I hadn't told him who I was. We talked a little and he invited me to stop by his school as soon as I could. As I walked back to the office, it began to sink in how much change was really taking place, how completely different I was being perceived and supported as a person and a woman. Just six weeks earlier everyone only knew Ron.

The final affirmation of my acceptance and newfound femininity came when I got back to my office and returned a call to Mr. Parker, whom I'd visited that past Friday. After greetings, he asked me if I wanted feedback on the staff's impression from my visit. I told him I did, as I waited with anxiety to the honest feedback I knew he would give me. His response had two main points: First, the staff thought I looked better as a woman than as a man (is that a compliment?). I said, "Yes it was." Second, as a group, they found it easier to accept and get used to me as Rhonda, because even though they knew it was me, I looked so different and like just another woman (versus the female looking Ron they had expected). It was easier for them to relate to me than they thought. I thanked him for the feedback and support. I hung up the phone feeling like my surgery ordeal, my emphasis on my appearance and the straight forward, but caring, approach to others' feelings, was paying off more than I could have even hoped for.

On the flip side, when I visited Mr. Burch's Western School of Technology later that week, I was, at least on the surface, received well by the faculty and staff members I supervised. However, I later learned in an article by Suzanne Gibson, a high school English teacher and free-lance writer whom I gave information and authorization to write an article about my life, (published as a cover story in the October 22, 1997 edition of the Baltimore weekly City Paper), that not everyone in the County was so enthusiastic about the change.

City Paper article excerpts:

But God could not protect Rhonda from the biting scrutiny of her colleagues. There were coworkers and subordinates indignant that Rhonda touted her newly found womanhood, that her suits were bright purple and her hair a flashy red; at least she could have had the decency to be dowdy. Rhonda remained determined to focus on the positive aspects of her change, but that did not prevent people from cracking jokes behind her back. There seemed no end to the wry smiles and eye-rolling, the comments and rib pokes. A number of well-educated professionals could be seen racing down school corridors, hoping to get a look at Ron Hoyman in drag. Rhonda had nerve, they seemed to be saying—not for deciding to become a woman, but for refusing to apologize for it. The rest of us are stuck with who we are and are prepared to suffer through it. Why couldn't she?

But Rhonda had her defenses. She had struggled to make do with God's intention for nearly 45 years. She'd suffered quietly with mousey, miserable Ron and what Rhonda called his "meaningless penis." She'd tried countless tactics, from intensive therapy, to marriage, to hone and preserve Ron's masculinity, and she'd failed. The lonely torment of living as someone she was not, had toughened Rhonda against the criticism of others. She often chanted her mantra, "I don't care what people think."

And that was true. She seemed to possess a divine shield against cruel words and hypocrisy. Her faith and her brick-wall will guided her, and when all else failed, she was, after all, still the boss. Higher-ups offered Rhonda a less visible but equally lucrative administrative position, but she resisted. "I had enough on my mind with becoming a woman and trying to be successful with that," she says. "I don't think I could've tolerated yet another major change. When I do a job I put everything, 100 percent, into it. I had to put all my extra efforts into becoming a true female, not learning a new job."

At work, the initial shock and outlandishness of the whole sex-change thing began to die down after a while. If forced, most people will adjust to almost anything. Some did remain critical, even angry at having to work directly with Rhonda. "I don't want to hear about her surgery. I don't want to know those kinds of details about someone." one female teacher said to me in a school copy room. "She tells me things about this situation and the surgery that I don't want to know!"

That much was true. For all of Rhonda's success during this transitional year, she hadn't yet learned that not everyone shared her excitement over her brand new life. While the teachers and students at the various high schools where Rhonda worked would just have to adjust, so would Rhonda. She was even verbally reprimanded for bringing too many of her life changes into the workplace. The touchy-feely humanitarianism had ended, and it was time for Rhonda to get over the novelty of being female. Her job performance had never wavered — "She's the best person who has ever been in that job," one coworker commented — but Rhonda had to learn not to bring her personal life to work.

As Rhonda struggled to be a normal professional woman who leaves her private life (and private parts) at home, one group didn't seem quite as ready to let her forget who and what she was. Teenage students have trouble adjusting to new seating assignments, much less dealing maturely with a woman who used to be a man coming to school in a dress to talk about carpentry apprenticeships and automotive technology opportunities. Ron was a master carpenter and had even built a luxurious log home in Frederick County, from scratch, but none of that mattered when Rhonda entered this traditionally masculine sphere.

The kids had known Ron Hoyman—his face, his voice, his persona. There was no way to hide the fact that after Christmas Mr. Hoyman had become Ms. Hoyman. "Hey, that woman's a guy" and, "Ooh, sick," were some of the loud-enough-so-all-could-hear comments among students. No one was sufficiently brave to address Rhonda's transition to her face. Teachers were left to handle kids' questions and remarks, or ignore the situation all together.

Again, Rhonda fell back on her mantra, "I don't care what people think."Like black-eyed Susans in an August blaze, she flourished in the heat, and a few resisters began to take notice. One supervisor kept commenting, "The lady is unflappable." A few others, even those so-called Bubbas, began to offer grudging respect: "You gotta give her credit." "Took some nerve to go through all that." Some still called it lunacy; others began to call it courage.

I have learned that you have to be positive and as Suzanne states, fearless, to survive in such a dramatic, life-altering transition, but you also have to be reserved in what you share with others. I believe one of the reasons the transition has worked overall for me is because there is no question I won't answer, that is, in a respectful manner. But,

I also learned people sometimes don't want a full or detailed answer, so I now ask people if they want the full answer or description to their questions, or do they just want a brief response.

As one of my teachers, Mr. Stetson puts it in his opinion:

It's a good thing that most people don't possess the same self- awareness as Rhonda Hoyman. Few have the courage and confidence to live as they wish they could.

Other experiences included a presentation to more than 50 head counselors for the middle and high schools in late January. This was a neat experience because half the group did not even know Ron or recognize that the Ron they knew was indeed Rhonda. I also appreciated the men at the Baltimore County Fire and Rescue Training Academy, where I had set up a special high school student training program. They treated me with acceptance and the courtesy they would give any other woman. It is interesting to note that when the *City Paper* article came out a-year- and-half after my initial transition, one Captain said to me, "While I accepted you as Rhonda, I never really knew why you would want to make your life change until then; it really helped me understand why."

On Wednesday afternoon, January 24, I took another step. I scheduled an appointment with a new optometrist. I not only had my eyes checked, but ordered a new pair of feminine style glasses; Ron's old frames were not going to go with my new look. I enjoyed selecting gold and purple marble, stone colored frames. Another step in the perma-nent life style transition: details, details, details.

Thursday, January 25, was interesting because I wore a dressed-down, yet still feminine, blouse and slacks to help two modular furniture sales representatives set up a new technical program laboratory I was coordinating. The gen-tlemen were nice but admitted it would take a while getting used to working with Rhonda versus Ron. As we worked, I had to get used to doing minor assembly tasks as the men did not want a woman doing the dirty or heavy work. I appreciated their courtesy, but it also took time to hold back on work Ron was used to doing. After all, I was a lady now. When we went out to lunch, I was the only woman at the table and it seemed a little funny now operating in a man's world as Rhonda.

A year later, at the Cincinnati National AVA convention, I saw one of the same salesman at his vendor booth. He asked if I minded a question. I didn't mind at all. I'd heard just about everything by that time. He said, "One thing I don't understand about your personal life change is how in the world can you want to have your penis changed and removed." I told him I understood how a man could feel that way, but the reason was because my penis was meaningless to me. The thing men don't realize is that I have always felt female from my earliest thoughts. My penis was never a part of me that I wanted or had any strong feelings for. In fact, it was a nuisance, and I was looking forward to the time I wouldn't have it anymore. I knew that was hard for him to accept, as it should for a normal man, but I never was a normal man. We are still good friends, and I appreciated the gentlemanly respect and caring attitude he demonstrated.

On Friday, January 26, I was attending a staff development activity at Woodlawn High School, just a stone's throw from the nation's Social Security complex. I was walking down the hall, carrying a large red book bag with presentation materials in it. One of the male vice principals came up to me and said, "Ma'am let me carry that for you." He kindly took it from my hand.

This set the tone of my transition again, as Mike, one of the male supervisors in our office, looked at me and smiled, "Are you going to let him do that?"

I smiled back and said, "Sure, that's one of the perks of being female."

"I always thought it was better on the other side," he said with a laugh.

Take it from me, the guys do deserve a break, because life is better as a female in many ways. I love it when a gentleman treats me like a lady and opens the door or carries something for me.

As I went to other schools, the respect and reactions were similar to those of my other schools — very positive on the whole. I guess the return of Rhonda can be summed up in the reactions of six of my technical program teachers (5 male and 1 female) at the Carver Center. I met with them on Monday, January 29, for a presentation of a new student-managed portfolio assessment model. This was the first time I had met with this diverse group of carpentry, culinary arts, electrical, multimedia, technology education and cosmetology instructors in a group setting since my initial visit to see them. I came to the meeting with a-business-as-usual attitude, handing out sample of the portfolio materials and moving right into an information sharing, interactive format from the start of my presentation. The interaction and discussion picked up as the presentation went on, and overall I thought things went well for the group's first extensive exposure and working relationship with Rhonda. What I did not know at the time was that while I was conducting the workshop, Ms. Bridges, my cosmetology teacher, the only other woman in the room, was watching the men's facial expressions and interactions with me as much as she was my presentation.

When the presentation was over, she came over to me and said, "I not only like the portfolio materials, but I found the meeting very interesting." I asked her what she was referring to. She said that as she observed the men, she felt they were still a little uncomfortable or curious about this new person, Rhonda, running the workshop. But as I stuck with the subject matter and focused on the topic without hesitation, they began to get more comfortable, relaxed, and more interactive about 15 minutes into the workshop. By the end of the meeting, everyone seemed to be comfortable and business-as-usual with Rhonda, just as they would have been with Ron. I told her that was helpful feedback and thanked her for her comments.

What she and everyone else didn't know was that I was just as nervous as everyone else but tried not to show it. I consciously did not want to show any hesitation or different delivery than Ron would have. This feedback confirmed Dr. Lehne's recommendation: people do need adjustment time to get used to the new Rhonda. It also affirmed my beliefs that while not easy, Rhonda could fit in and be just as effective in the traditional male-oriented job of Technical Program Supervisor as Ron was.

I could now move forward with a new month and year with the acceptance, confidence and can-do spirit that was needed to prove to myself and others that Rhonda could not only survive and succeed personally but also professionally in her new world.

Rhonda's Return to the Front Lines

Chapter 21

Rhonda's New Game Plan

With life as Rhonda getting off to a good start at work, I was gaining the strength and confidence needed to perform my work duties just as well (or maybe even better) and also find the time, stamina, and money to handle the medical aspects of transition services. The first year of transition from male to female life required weekly or biweekly appointments for counseling, speech therapy, and electrolysis (especially essential for someone who has a regular beard growth like I did).

I planned for my major sex change surgery in mid-December, 1996, which meant I would need to show steady progress in my work and full-time female life. I had a monthly monitoring session with Dr. Lehne, a weekly mindfulness counseling session with Patti Cummings, a biweekly speech therapy session with Dr. Spencer, two, two-hour electrolysis sessions in Frederick (usually Wednesday and Saturday morning) per week, and quarterly check-ups with my endocrinologist to monitory my hormone therapy. Throw in the new hair care (once every five to six weeks), two foot surgeries, a head lift, wardrobe shopping, the sale of my home in Frederick, my subsequent move to Baltimore, and some side carpentry jobs to make extra money. As my grandfather used to say, "I was busier than a one-armed paper hanger." There were many days when I went on four to five hours sleep, my personal goal of having two sit-down meals at a table per week was a rarity. I scheduled my life by the hour, not by the day or week. My former experiences with hard work, time management, denial of personal pleasures, and the attitude that nothing was impossible was paying off big time. I was operating at 100% all the time, and I learned that this was not the way to live. Looking back on the first year of my life transition, not just the sex change transition plan for 1996, I would not have believed I could have accomplished all I did. I was accomplishing the goals I set in my five-year personal improvement plan: Year one — Full-time transition services and life as a female; Year two — Fine-tuning life skills and feminine presentation; Year three — Public relations (my Book) and personal dating; Year four — Learning to relax, interpersonal relationships, and possible marriage; Year five — Settling down to the simple pleasures of life, having fun, and being a good wife. I may have to make some adjustments, but so far, I'm batting a thousand and looking forward to a fabulous second 50 years of life.

At work, we often set one, three, or five-year program improvement plans and goals of productivity and success, but far too often I have learned most of us let life's circumstances or other people's ideas dominate our personal lives, without any real plan to make our personal lives more meaningful or fulfilling. Don't let your personal life have second class status like Ron did. Strive to make a five-year proactive personal improvement plan and set meaningful goals for improving your life. My hope is that when you have finished this book, you will realize it's never too late to be happy or do what you have to do for the most important person in your life — you!

To make sure the classy and quality look I was striving to achieve was also properly perceived, I wore my diamond and sapphire ring on my right hand. I don't want to wear this ring on my left hand, which would indicate I'm engaged or married. A girl doesn't want to send the wrong message when she wants love to fill the air. There are so many more ways for personal expression as a female. After work, I could even talk about clothes, make-up, and shopping with the other ladies. Clothing or personal appearance was a topic Ron was never concerned about.

Things were going so well at work that one afternoon I received an invitation from one of the other secretaries. She wanted to take me to lunch to get to know me better. Of course, I kept that appointment and really appreciated her kindness. People wanted to know what Rhonda was really like, but they were also sincere in their respect and support of my new feminine life. Ron knew a lot of people, but Rhonda knows even more, and on a more personal, as well as professional basis.

One evening, after having my hair changed, I stopped by the Maryland Department of Motor Vehicles Administration (MVA) with my legal name change court order to have my driver's license changed. I was nervous, as I explained to the clerk my new identity, name change, and request for a new license. She was nice and approved the new license with my female picture and name, but the MVA would not let me change the sex category, which still had an "M" instead of an "F" until a year later, after my official sex change letter from Dr. Schrang, my surgeon, and another Maryland court order, which stated not only my name but also my sex was female. While I hoped people would not look at the sex box closely when I used my license for ID purposes, I was pleased to now have a license with my new legal name and female picture on it.

This month I started more interactions with business/industry members and professionals from outside the Baltimore County School system, and I had no choice but to prepare and reorient them to Rhonda. While it also took time for them to get used to interacting with me as a female, they were all understanding and accepting, without any change in our joint education/business partnerships. Continuing to be open, honest and up front was proving to be the best policy. Most of the business community, then and now, still find it hard to believe I used to be Ron and are amazed at the transition difference.

Early winter was rolling along as well as I could expect, and aside from curious looks and remarks from some students, I was feeling good about my acceptance in the work environment. This acceptance was reaffirmed when I received a phone call from Mr. Burch, the principal of Western, that one of his English teachers, Suzanne Gibson (who barely knew Ron) wanted to meet Rhonda. She wanted to see if I would be open to her interviewing me and allowing her to write a possible news article on my life's transition. Mr. Burch made the initial overtures to me about Suzanne's interest and request for an interview, because she did not feel she knew me well enough to make such a request. In mid-March, we had our first interview and eventually our work together resulted in the previously mentioned, October 22, 1997, cover story for the City Paper.

I appreciated Ms. Gibson's respect for my privacy, and I was honored she was impressed enough on how I was handling the transition (regardless of other's reactions) to meet me. But, I think the key point here is that she and others did not fully understand that I was feeling so good about myself and was so open about providing honest feedback to others in helping them understand Rhonda — even as a relative stranger, she could have approached me directly. Ron was such a plain, matter-of-fact, work-oriented person that people did not realize what a difference or change was occurring in my personality, as well as my more obvious physical appearance.

By mid-March, I had my second visit with Dr. Evans, my endocrinologist, in Washington, D.C. She physically evaluated me and checked my blood work, approved my hormone therapy of 1.25 mg of Premarin and 5 mg of Progesterone to my normal and still constant daily dosage of 2.5 mg and 10 mg respectively. I had to follow a regulated and progressive plan of medical transition services for my own health and well-being, as well as the obvious physical changes and benefits a transsexual patient must complete before authorization for her genital surgery.

On Sunday, March 17, I went to my first work-related conference as Rhonda. Ms. Walker, the Business Education supervisor, and I represented our office at the National AVA Policy Seminar on federal funding issues for vocational education at the Washington, D.C. Convention Center. What was unique about this event was that it was the first time as Rhonda that I interacted with such a large and influential audience as a woman. It felt good to mingle, interact with and be accepted as a woman without any question; we even went to the Hill to lobby our six Congress representatives and their aides in their congressional offices on our Monday session. This was also the time I learned that you don't wear high heels when you have a lot of walking around to do in Washington, and the reality is that the women's restrooms are never big enough for a major event. I waited in long lines with the other women to use the Convention Center facilities. Ron was used to the traditional male restroom accommodations and physical conditions which usually did not require such inconveniences. While a nuisance, I am glad to pay the price of waiting in a restroom line, to be my true self, but if the engineers who designed women's restrooms from fast food to concert hall to convention center buildings, had to experience nature's call, as I did then, the size of ladies rooms would be a lot different.

While my voice tone and the stress on my vocal chords (getting used to speaking at a pitch almost three times higher than Ron's low voice) was getting better, it was still my biggest source of discomfort while interacting with others in person or on the phone. I had to learn to breath deeper and talk slower, which was difficult for me in my diverse, fast-paced work environment. I ended March by attending my first regional conference as a Mary Kay consultant with my director, Ms. Newman, and our team from Frederick with about two thousand other woman. This was also a unique feeling, being a part of such a large women's group for the first time. I wore my nice mauve suit to blend right in.

With Easter/Spring break the first week of April, I started my so-called vacation doing home repairs and improvements for Dr. and Mrs. Stuart Berger (former superintendent for Baltimore and Frederick Counties). Ron had always been the Berger family handyman and now Rhonda was their new handywoman. While it took some time for the Berger's to get used to Rhonda, they were very accepting and still respected my construction skills whether a man or woman. While I didn't especially want to work so much in my spare time, I wasn't ashamed of using my skills as a woman. I needed the money to keep up with my personal transition costs, and they appreciated the honest and trustworthy, do-it-all service I could provide.

Mrs. Debbie Berger recalls:

I first met Ron Hoyman in the early to mid 1980s when he showed up at our house to handle some repair jobs. I don't recall what they were exactly — I know that he replaced the mailbox several times, built new steps in the garage, handled innumerable small household repair tasks that neither my husband (who couldn't change a lightbulb on his own) nor I had the ability, time or inclination to tackle. He was a close

friend of the husband of Stuart's secretary and I don't sup-
pose in those early years that we paid him much attention
at all. We were always grateful for his help but he was not a
particularly talkative or outgoing personality so I don't sup-
pose we had many conversations beyond the task at hand.
Because he was so skilled at what he did—and despite the
fact that he had a full-time "day" job—we eventually com-
missioned him to renovate the basement to provide bedrooms
for our eldest daughter, Jennifer, who was about 15 at the
time, and our son Chuck, who was 14. It was a project that
seemed to take most of the summer and at that time our
youngest daughter, Tracey, became Ron's (or Mr. Hoyman, as
we all called him) shadow. She talked to him and provided
him with scraps and spare nails and things. She watched
him work and went to sleep nightly with a stuffed dog he
had given her.

It was about this time that the Ron Hoyman "mythology"
got started. It was with great affection and a certain amount
of dependence that we started referring to Ron as "our"
handyman, and we were very possessive about his doing jobs
for others (since it meant he wouldn't be available to work
for us). When we moved from Maryland to Kansas the
summer after the remodeling job, we seriously gave some
thought to flying him there for a couple weeks to handle the
numerous chores that our newly purchased Kansas home
entailed. Ron could handle carpentry, plumbing, electrical
work, telephone connections — you name it, he could do it.

During our five years in Wichita, we kept in contact with
Ron through Christmas cards and word-of-mouth. I believe
he was divorced for the second or third time and we used to
say he let women just walk all over him. We knew he had
moved and when we were ready to return to the Baltimore
area, and the house to which we were moving needed sub-
stantial renovation, it was Mr. Hoyman to whom we turned.

He literally moved in right after closing and seemingly handled everything. We were delighted to renew our friendship and this time it seemed a stronger friendship — Ron and I, in particular, seemed to talk more; he joined us for dinner occasionally and when he met a young woman he wished to marry, we were among the first to know.

Still mild mannered and slight of build, Ron Hoyman was one of the last individuals of my acquaintance that I would have suspected of having gender difficulties. Not that he seemed macho, but he certainly didn't seem the slightest bit effeminate either, and it was more than just a shock when a mutual friend shared the news of Ron's impending sex change. We were incredulous, probably a little embarrassed and shocked. We simply had no experience with this and tended to equate sex changes with the kind of people who appeared on the most lascivious of the talk shows or the tabloid newspapers. On the other hand, Ron was a friend and, as Stuart quipped, "I don't care what sex he is as long as he still comes to fix things." Well, that sounds almost crass in retrospect, but I don't think we were alone in not knowing how to react." As time went on, we became quite concerned about what Ron / Rhonda might be going through at work and sometimes we were uncomfortable that she was so open about all the dteails of the procedure, the counseling, etc. On the other hand, we consider ourselves fairly accepting of all and any lifestyle, and there was never a moment that we considered not continuing as Rhonda's friends. Stuart probably had a harder time of it than I did, especially when it came to the details, but all in all we were more likely to be protective of Rhonda than shocked or titilated. And perhaps that is because Rhonda was so open about all that she was going through—we just sort of went through it with her. As she evolved more and more into a woman, we simply became acclimated. For a long time after the actual surgery, I con-

tinued to refer to Rhonda as "he" or as "Ron" when I was talking about her to other people though I don't think I ever mistakenly called her Ron to her face. Now that it is close to three years since we first learned of the impending change, I would say that both Stuart and I and all of our children think of Rhonda as female.

What we have found to be most interesting is the almost total change in Rhonda's personality. She has become gregarious, talkative, outgoing—the complete opposite of her personality as a man. This happened somewhat gradually and, for a time, we weren't sure we liked the change. But one observation remains undeniable. Rhonda appears to be a much happier individual than Ron was. I wondered if Rhonda and I might become close personal friends as women since we're close to the same age. We haven't, really, but that might be because I'm going through a phase of my life when I seem not to need close women friends the way I did in the past. It might also be because Rhonda is a far more "feminine" individual than I am and, to me, seems much younger than I am.

For certain we wish her well in her quest for personal fulfillment and applaud her ability to share this very personal journey with others. We trust she'll remain our family's friend for always.

The difference now was that my work had a bigger purpose, helping Rhonda meet her personal needs and expenses, not just a way to productively fill time as Ron did. That summer I really learned how to interact in home improvement stores like the Home Depot, as men went out of their way to lift things and provide advice for a woman in a man's world. My biggest concern doing construction work in the summer was sweating. I had to be careful not to wipe my face and smear my makeup. Even in shorts and a shirt, I wanted to keep my feminine appearance.

At the end of spring break week, I scheduled the first of two (unplanned) foot surgeries with Dr. Falston, a podiatrist in Frederick. I had corns on the sides of my feet. I was experiencing discomfort and soreness from women's shoes, a sharp contrast to the roomier, more square-toed man's shoe. To correct this problem I now decided to stop and see what could be done at Dr. Falston's foot care center. I explained my problem. He was very accepting of my plight and responded by telling me the only way to really correct the situation was to make each toe shorter by cutting about 1/4" of bone out, thus creating a shorter toe that would not rub against the shoe or cause a sore spot. While I was taken aback by this answer, I also wanted a permanent solution, so I asked him when we could begin and set up an appointment a week later. On Friday, April 5, 1996, at 4:00 pm, I sat in the foot care laboratory to begin the hour- and-a-half, out-patient surgery. I sat in the large, electrical patient chair. He raised it up and placed bandages, scissors, gauze, and other operating tools on a chair beside me. I was not only the patient, but also the assisting nurse. As we were ready to begin, Dr. Falston looked at me and asked if I wanted to watch him operate, and I said I didn't; I wasn't that brave. So, he placed a small divider that attached to my chair. He sprayed the small toe and longest toe (four parts over) with a cold, numbing spray. Then he proceeded with injections of Novocain in each of the toes and waited about 10 minutes for it to numb.

I could feel some tugging and movement, as he cut open each toe and cut about a 1/4" of bone from the center for each toe with the buzzing sound of his little hand-held, hobby shop-type, saw. Next, he pushed the toe back together and neatly stitched each one up as I handed him tools, gauze, and bandages. He wrapped my toes and foot up. I had a big hump at the end (where my toes used to be) then he placed

Unplanned Foot Surgery

an ace bandage all the way past my ankle. Finally, he placed a gray sandal shoe on my newly constructed left foot with two big Velcro straps on the top.

Since I didn't realize I would need crutches, I literally hopped out of his office on one leg to my car and drove myself to the drug store and also hopped in for pain medication before my short drive home. My foot was now throbbing, as I made it to the kitchen for a light supper and bed, where I tried to sleep with my foot propped up, mildly throbbing all night. The pain medication helped as I sat around that weekend paying bills and starting my income taxes. But on Monday, April 8, I hobbled back to Dr. Falston, this time with some crutches a friend loaned me, to have my foot checked and some of the bandages removed.

I drove to work on Tuesday, wearing a real shoe on my right foot and the gray medical sandal on my left for the next month. Even though it was still sore, it felt good and looked a lot better wearing two shoes again by mid-May. Just as my left foot was beginning to feel better, I went back to Dr. Falston on June 7 to repeat the whole routine again with my right foot. This time, I bought the pain medication ahead of time and took crutches with me. By mid-July, I was now a new woman. The operation was a success and I can wear all styles of shoes better, but it really took a year for the toes and stitches to heal back to a normal state.

I maintained my other weekly medical services during this time period and to show how well my transition was going on the job, I was the hostess to nine construction trade teachers, administrators, and industry representatives from Kansas and Missouri on April 23rd and 24th. We described our national model Associated Builders and Contractors (ABC) Apprenticeship Program, and we toured schools and industry training sites. The relationship I established with Mr. Ramsey, an ABC program director, led to my hosting two other groups over the course of the next year.

This year, there were many "firsts" for me. May 1st, now one of the ladies, I wore a corsage for the first time, as we honored our outstanding career and technology students at a large annual recognition banquet.

In May, I also experimented for about two months with a hair weave instead of my glued-on hair piece. I learned I was originally on the right track with my first hair piece. You have to experiment a little, but I learned the hard way; when you find something that works and looks good, you don't mess with it.

Mother's Day was on May 12th this year and only two days from my 49th birthday, and I went home to Pennsylvania for only the second time since my transition — this time with no threat of snow. I still could not go to my mother's house, because she would not let me tell my stepfather of my transition. So, as I was working on some outside yard repairs and planting grass around the house I had built for Susan, I arranged to meet my mother and my sister for the first time on, of all days, Mother's day, 1996. Knowing they would stop by for about an hour after church, I quickly changed into a nice skirt and blouse and freshened up my make up and hair as I nervously awaited their arrival. My mother arrived first, and as she came up to the door, I greeted her with a warm smile. "My, I hardly even recognize you," she said in a mother's loving way. She was also a little nervous as we sat down to talk about the last few months, my transition, and other family affairs. We also exchanged cards, mine a Mother's Day card for her, and her's a birthday card for her new daughter. I also gave her flowers and a choice of Mary Kay lipsticks I brought. She gave me a nice pair of earrings and other birthday presents. Emotions of newness, love, and caring filled the air. We hugged and kissed each other on the cheek before she left; a new chapter had started in our lives. I feel she missed and will always have a soft spot in her heart for Ron, but she also graciously accepted the new Rhonda she has known about since my early years. She accepted my life change, because she knew it had finally brought happiness to my life, and because she was and is the best mother a son or daughter could ever have. I am the person I am today because of her sacrifices, love and guidance. Thank you, Mom. I love you!

My youngest sister, Darlene, came in as Mom was leaving, and she also had a "Gee-you-look-different-how-are-you-doing-this-is-amazing!" kind of greeting and visit for the next hour. Knowing that I'm a chocolate lover, she brought me a supply of my favorite candies for my birthday. Having had her share of hard knocks in life, Darlene showed the loving, caring acceptance of her new sister — the same kind she has always shown her daughter, Melanie. She also needed time to adjust after an hour visit, but was also happy to see me finally doing what was right for me, no matter what other people thought.

Darlene, my youngest sister's impressions:

She is still the same person inside, loving, caring, kind, thoughtful, giving, just as Ron was; even though she is now my sister, instead of my brother. She has also been there for my daughter, Melanie and me, always going out of her way; especially in crucial times. Helping me through hard times providing me with inspiration, necessary to maintain a positive outlook on life.

My adjustment and feelings about having Rhonda as my new sister was not as hard for me because I still feel she is the same person I grew up with. I'm glad she is finally happy for the first time in her life.

I worked until 9:30 that night on Susan's house before making the long drive back to Frederick. Even though I was physically tired, I had a smile on my face and in my heart, knowing I had the love and support of my family, and was especially glad to finally meet my mother for the first time as my feminine self.

Chapter 22

Filling up the
Other Half of the Glass

I was now spending well over $1000 a month more than my budget allowed. I continued to work on Dr. Berger's house and do other small carpentry jobs throughout the late spring, summer, and fall of 1996. I tried to keep expenses as manageable as possible.

Maggie Caples says:

Ron—Rhonda. Ron...Rhonda. When I first heard about Ron becoming Rhonda, I thought it was a joke. We had listened when his engagement broke up. He was half-bald approaching middle age, a registered carpenter. He had been the Trade and Technical Supervisor at the state level and for two counties. Then I started hearing that it was true. He had approached the School Board to keep his position. A special bathroom had been designated for him — no, her. "Which was it?" I wondered. "What is the proper pronoun to use? How will I react when I first see him as "her?"

One of my colleagues who also knew Ron, returned from a meeting where Rhonda had introduced herself in her new life, complete with a short-skirted suit, earrings, bracelet, and heels. My colleague was fascinated, and said, "You'll have to see for yourself. I don't know if anything or anyone could have prepared me for it or made it less of a shock for me. Why don't you call her?" I still couldn't bring myself to make the first move, even though I was very curious.

Then one day I was at a meeting, and a new woman joined the group. I didn't really look at her because I thought she was from the agency that we had concerns with, and we had touchy issues to discuss. At the end of the meeting she came up to me and said in a raspy falsetto voice, "Hi, I'm Rhonda." It still didn't sink in as to who she was. And then she told me! I worried for days afterwards that I may have initially reacted in a way that hurt her feelings. Whatever I did, she seemed okay. We stood in the parking lot and talked for a long, long time. She showed me pictures of before, after, and along the way. She filled me in on her divorce and other people's reactions. She told me she sold Mary Kay cosmetics! I kept slipping, sometimes calling her "Ron" while we talked. (I still do sometimes, but she always says, "That's okay.") She tries hard to make everyone else comfortable with her change. For the next few days, I had such a hard time adjusting to it all. It isn't easy to know someone as one sex, and suddenly have to relate to them as another sex.

Rhonda and I see one another and talk more often now. It's hard not to accept her as a female when you see her with her red hair, classic clothes, manicured nails, and her snazzy red car. She's a much better dresser than she ever was as a man. And she does seem much happier. It's still a little hard to reconcile the voice with the physical appearance sometimes, because at times she still sounds like "Ron." But she is still one of the most giving people that I know, always sharing a new soft drink, curriculum tips, her expertise as a "handy person." You can never do more for Rhonda than she does for you. I don't even know how to try, because she is so high energy and knows how to do so many things. In her words, she can do almost anything. And she pays more attention to her phyiscal appearance than many of us who were born female. When she's all dressed up, she looks good!

Rhonda's transformation has given me an experience I never expected and would never have sought. But I'm proud to have her as a friend. It took me a few more times seeing her as a female to adjust to it all. But she would always say, "Are you okay with me now? Ask me anything you want to ask." Her openness made it easier for me to accept her as she is.

Rhonda and I have a fun relationship now. She's helped to do some more things around my house, but feels free to draw the line for what would have been her old, masculine self instead of her new, feminine self. I envy her knowledge for doing so many things around a house and equipment. I respect her opinions on how to arrange and do things. At first my husband was a little hesitant about having "Rhonda" do some of the repairs. But he quickly saw that she hasn't lost any of her skills that she had as "Ron." And one day when we were debating one of the changes, he said, "Why don't you just let Rhonda make those decisions. She really has good ideas on how to make it look really nice. Just listen to Rhonda." What he doesn't know is that Rhonda listens to what I say, helps me figure out what I really want, and then sets out to see if it can be done (with her improvements, of course!). Funny; she did the same thing for me when she was "Ron." She sometimes already knows what my decision is before I know myself. But she lets me go the gamut to reach my conclusions. And sometimes she pushes, "Well, we can stay in the store all night, but I already know that this is the one that will work."

"We can go to as many more car lots as you want to, but the one with the snazzy wheels is the one you should buy." "You might as well spend the extra money for the doors (lights, dress, etc.), because you only live once, you deserve it, and you're worth it." Our friendly bantering probably looks like arguing to some, but we understand one another very well, and don't really get angry with one another. One night,

a store clerk said we sounded like sisters as we debated about which ceiling fan to buy. We both snickered about that!

Ron — Rhonda. Ron — Rhonda. It really doesn't matter to me. She, once "he," is still a very intelligent, caring person who just wants to be accepted for her true female self that she always knew she was, no matter how hard she tried to live successfully as a man, Ron. She is truly Rhonda to me now, and the more I see her, the more that's who she always was to me.

To keep my energies up on my usual 16 to 20 hour days, I started taking an herbal-based vitamin and using a vegetable and fruit-based nutrition system called Juice Plus. I did, and still do, give great attention to my physical appearance, but I wanted to take care of my entire body and figure a lot more than Ron did. It was important in my overall life improvement plan to have the proper nutrients to compliment my long-term life improvement goals. Quality vitamins and a vegetable/fruit-based natural supplement system are essential for most people to maximize their physical health and wellness. Now, if I could get more exercise and sleep, I would really be doing all the right things. Like I tell people jokingly, "You don't want to confront me in a dark alley when I'm rested!".

My other unanticipated major project late that summer and in the fall of 1996 was when I agreed to balance out some of my co-pay counseling expenses with Patti Cummings, my regular counselor. This is significant not only from a money issue, or how I found time to do the work, but also because it allowed Ms. Cummings to see another side of my life outside of the counseling room. As I skillfully completed a variety of plumbing, electrical, painting, floor tile, carpentry and other major home improvement services, she asked me if there was anything I couldn't do and don't do less than my best. I had a simple answer. No, there isn't.

She said that she could now understand why my transition was going so well, because if I do something in life, no matter what, I will try and do it to the best of my ability, 110% effort. I am pleased to say, as I moved beyond my counseling services, I have maintained a close personal friendship with Ms. Cummings. She is now one of my girlfriends with whom we have a mutual respect for each other's talents and caring attitude. I strive to have friendships with people who have a positive outlook and respect for life, are into health and wellness, and live in the present, striving to live life to its fullest. People with a negative outlook on life don't want to stay around me, and I don't want to spend a lot of time around them. The glass is not half empty, but half full.

As if I wasn't doing enough to my body, on July 1, 1996, I went in for four hours of dental work. I had a six-tooth bridge (complete with root canals) taken off (after 10 years of service) and replaced it with a new nine tooth bridge. This unscheduled work was necessary to save my smile and the poor teeth I have had my entire life. So, for the next six weeks, I went back and forth to the dentist and wore temporary dentures until my new bridge was made and installed. Dr. Damson did a great job, and I'm glad I followed through on his recommendation, but I began to wonder if there wasn't anything on my body that wasn't going under major construction that year. If I were a building, I would have been condemned by the health department.

As I met different people interested in buying my log home, I struck up a friendship in July with Jana, the lady who would eventually buy my house. She was an artistic person and craft lover like me; so on Saturday, July 13, we decided to make the three-and-a-half hour drive up to Penn State's annual arts festival. It was quite an event, as we checked out the different exhibitors that lined the university, and State College streets. This was my first real fun

Rhonda's Return to Penn State

day and time back in Happy Valley as Rhonda. I especially liked the jewelry booths and bought a beautiful, purple stone necklace and my first lady's straw hat, which looked pretty good and kept the bright sun from my eyes. After a long but enjoyable day and dinner, we decided to make the trip home that night, sharing driving responsibilities in my little pick-up. We finally pulled into my driveway about 1:00 am Sunday morning with Jana in the driver's seat.

She said, "Rhonda, my stuff is on your side."

I looked at her and said, "I know how you feel. I've been on the wrong side my whole life."

She burst out laughing . Being able to joke and be light-hearted while making the transition has been good for me and my acceptance easier for others.

Jana Leigh says about the transition:

In the spring of 1996, I had the honor of meeting Rhonda Hoyman. Rhonda was almost one year into her new role as a woman, after 48 years of unhappiness. I was there to listen, watch, and help Rhonda through her transition into an incredibly beautiful woman. I immensely enjoyed each moment.

Initially, my husband and I crossed paths with Rhonda to purchase her Asperline log home she had built herself 10 years prior to our purchase. We had our grandmother move into our log home with us for nearly a year. Rhonda immediately befriended our grandmother as well; as have many others that crossed Rhonda's path. It's been nearly two years since I met my new friend Rhonda. I have faith that the good Lord will provide many blessings to her new life.

Things were continuing to go well at work, as I ran curriculum workshops for a variety of my 30 different occupational programs with many of my teachers still getting used to the new Rhonda. The short summer between school years was quickly coming to an end and I took my two-week vacation to have phase two of my facelift, or what Dr. Converse calls a head lift operation, on Tuesday, as scheduled. This procedure would require me to have my hair piece system removed, because they would cut the skin on my forehead just above the hair line from ear to ear. By pulling up and removing this excess skin, the top of my face would be smoother and my sagging eyelids would be lifted, allowing for a more open-eye effect, aided with proper eye shadow accents.

Not wanting complications as before, I learned my lesson and only took Tylenol III for a mild pain reliever and watched what I ate after the operation. I was grateful to have a close friend, Ed Roebuck, and his lovely wife, Linda, with whom I'd worked at the Maryland State Department of Education, offer to help me through this procedure. They only lived a few miles from Dr. Converse's office. I stayed at their house the night before for a good night's rest and was back in their spare bedroom again by 1:30 the next afternoon. The successful operation took place Tuesday, as scheduled. Since the surgery was not as severe as the main facelift, I had local anesthesia and awoke about half-way through the surgery, talking with the doctor and nurses as they stitched me back up. I left the doctor's office with my head completely bandaged and mild headache, none the worse for wear. By evening I had a light supper at the Roebuck's, and we chatted as the healing process began to show—my bruised raccoon eyes.

Since I was supposed to close on the sale of my house in the next few days, Casey, my real estate agent's husband, came down to pick me up and take me back to Frederick. I wanted to get a special key ring for the new owners, Jana and Walt, so I simply put on a green and purple head scarf and summer outfit (my black and blue look) and went to the local mall to purchase the gifts and have them engraved. I looked like I had just been in a fight, with my face all bruised and head bandaged. But, I wasn't going to let an operation slow me down, and besides, I looked so bad, people looked like they felt sorry for me and were afraid to ask what happened to me.

By August 6, a week after the operation, I looked bad, but was feeling better ,and I drove down to Dr. Converse's office to have the head bandage removed and the stitches taken out. The rest of the week and my vacation was filled with electrolysis, counseling, and speech therapy appointments, having my new dental bridge put on, and my hair piece replaced for work on Monday, August 12th. It took extra make-up to cover some of the remaining bruise marks and

Photo 22.2: Head Lift Plastic Surgery—Stage 1

Photo 22.3: Head Lift Plastic Surgery—Stage 2

Photo 22.4: Head Lift Plastic Surgery—Stage 3

my vacation was over (if you can call it a vacation). But, I had used my time wisely to continue maximizing my appearance and transition services.

My self-confidence continued to grow and co-worker's acceptance of Rhonda continued to go well, as I started the 96/97 school year, conducting staff development services with my teachers, meeting with business/industry advisory groups, parents/student orientation meetings, like our new Fire and Rescue Services Program, and putting into place new technical programs with schools and staff with whom I had not previously worked.

I wanted to request and schedule my major surgery with Dr. Eugene Schrang, by September, 1996. I had come to a point where my success at work, my life routine, and my recent letters of support from Dr. Evans, Dr. Lehne, and Patti Cummings would provide the necessary documentation for approval of my SRS surgery. Since Dr. Schrang performs over 300 sex reassignment surgeries each year, I knew I had to finalize my case and schedule my selected date months in advance. Having only lived as a full-time female for eight to nine months, I was on the fast track for approval, since I had to demonstrate that I have lived successfully as a female for at least one year before a doctor would approve and perform the operation. My surgery was now scheduled for Tuesday, December 10, 1996, and I anxiously awaited this final step and confirmation of my womanhood and transition year goals.

Over the fall months, I didn't have much time for a social life, but received nice compliments when I did. For example, I attended a girlfriend's 50th birthday party in late November, wearing my green sequined evening dress. I received a lot of compliments, as many of my friends were surprised at how I look in an evening attire setting.

Rhonda's Last Days at the Log Home

When I sold my home in early August, I had agreed to rent
Jana and her husband's home, a house switch, so they could
qualify for the mortgage until their house sold. Thus, I could

get the equity I needed from the sale to pay off my mounting debts, $50,000 and growing. This meant I would pack, sell items, and physically move in early August and repack and move again once their house sold. I needed to move to the Towson, Maryland, area in an apartment setting before my major surgery and recovery in December. For the time being, I temporarily lived out of boxes, hoping for a quick sale and final move. Fortunately, my step of faith worked out, as Jana and her husband were able to sell and settle on the little house I was now living in at the end of October, just six weeks before my December AVA trip and scheduled surgery.

So, in early November, I gave away and downsized my possessions one more time and moved into a two-bedroom apartment in a complex, Deertree Apartments in Cockeysville, just seven miles from my office. My brother and a few friends from work helped me move, or should I say, squeeze, all my furniture and personal items into this smaller living space. We made it, but in reality, the spare bedroom became one big storage closet. At least I was physically in a setting I could control, a place close enough to work and friends so that I could have help after my surgery. However, the satisfaction of just being me or finally female and the progress I was making in everyday life was more fulfilling than Ron could ever imagine.

As I finalized the steps and details necessary for my operation and no-turning-back (as if I wanted to) physical change, the divorce with Susan needed to be finalized. September of 1996 fulfilled the required year of separation before filing for an uncontested divorce. I had done everything I could to help her rebuild her life and new home back in Pennsylvania. As we tried to finalize the legal obligations on the home financing, which was supposed to be transferred to her name, along with the building lot I had given her, she was dragging her feet in the new loan and mortgage process. Finally, in November she admitted she had new circumstances in her life and wasn't sure if she wanted to stay in or own the home as planned. I was happy she was finding a new life, but we needed to have the loan and lot in one name for the divorce to be finalized. We were still working out these details in early December when I was preparing to leave for the AVA conference in Cincinnati and the surgery with the issue still unresolved and weighing on my mind. Just before I left, she finally admitted she was going to get married and didn't want the home I had worked so hard to establish for her. I was troubled and asked her to let me know what she felt would be fair to settle these new financial obligations, as I left Maryland for the AVA conference on Wednesday, December 4, 1996.

The conference was enjoyable and productive for our entire CTE office team; we conducted an hour-long presentation that year. On Sunday, December 8, as the other staff prepared to fly back to Baltimore, I was at the other end of the terminal, preparing to fly to the little Appleton Airport, eight miles from Neenah, Wisconsin, on a little 20-passenger propeller commuter plane. My scheduled flight was canceled for no reason, and I did not actually arrive at Appleton until 9:00 that evening — unfortunate, since I was trying to allow time to rest up for my big surgery.

As I sat in the Valley Inn Motel in Neenah that night, I was nervous about my pending operation but also glad that I had made it this far. It was a year I would never forget. One thing was for sure. When I returned back to the hotel ten days later, I would not be the same person. The physical pain, the never-ending schedule, the emotional trauma, and the psychological adjustment of my first year in the life as Rhonda were all worth it.

Chapter 23

The Operation: Rhonda's Reality!

On Monday morning, December 9, 1996, I arose early, anticipation running through my veins. I prepared for my first meeting with Dr. Eugene Schrang, M.D., one of the top plastic and cosmetic surgeons in the nation, renowned for his transsexual sex reassignment surgery (SRS). Dr. Schrang is noted as a craftsman, not just a surgeon, in the art of transforming the male anatomy to a fully functional female anatomy.

After a good shower and dressing to look my best for my first meeting with Dr. Schrang, I went down to the hotel restaurant for my "last supper" before entering the hospital. I was strongly advised to travel lightly because I could not lift anything heavier than a gallon of milk for two months after the operation. I wanted some fresh air, and a chance for a walk before being hospitalized for the next eight days, so I decided to carry my personal items the five to six blocks from the Valley Inn Motel, which was very nice, to Dr. Schrang's office and my 1:30 evaluation appointment.

The temperature was cold that day, in the crisp low teens. I followed the signs along the snow-filled streets of the old-fashioned Midwest town of Neenah, Wisconsin. Neenah's claim to fame is its paper mills, which I understand produce many of the country's toiletry and other paper products. In fact, I found out after my operation that, because of this, the transsexual community calls Dr. Schrang's post operative patients "paper dolls." I was greeted warmly by the office staff. I waited with anticipation for Dr. Schrang's evaluation and approval of my surgery. Nothing is automatic, and he reserves the right to accept or reject patients for SRS surgery. He wants to be 100% sure this is the best, and a successful choice, for each patient. Finally around 2:00 pm, I met Dr. Schrang, who was complimentary of my appearance as we talked for a while about my history and why I wanted the surgery. He then gave me a thorough examination, explained the operation, what my next eight days in the hospital and recovery would be like and my follow-up care requirements after I left the hospital. I was relieved when he said he felt I was in good health and an excellent candidate for the surgery.

He explained that I would have two skin graphs to make sure I had adequate depth for my new vagina, that the operation would take three to five hours, and that the cosmetic, stage two labioplasty (to feminize the operation area) could be done three months or longer after the main sex reassignment surgery (SRS) on a return trip. I also asked his opinion of my nose tip from my former face lift. While not a part of the plan, I asked him since I was under anesthesia would he recommend or be able to perform plastic surgery on the tip of my nose to make it curl up more. He looked and said, "Let me think." After studying my face and checking his schedule, he told me he could do it for $2000 more if he started the operation one hour earlier than planned. I seized the moment, wrote a check from my credit card account, and left his office around 4:30 for the hospital.

The Theda Clark Regional Medical Center is one of the finest hospitals in the country with state of the art facilities and equipment, which was important in my surgery plans. I wanted the best care and operative conditions possible. After all, this was the first time in my life I would have surgery and actually stay in the hospital.

Since the hospital was a stone's throw from Dr. Schrang's office, I walked over and checked myself in for my blood test, room assignment, and preoperative procedures. By 5:00 pm, I was unpacking my clothes and changing into a hospital gown for the first time with no time to spare. They drew my blood and asked me to take the next three hours to drink a strong, lemonade-flavored liquid to clean out my digestive track. The problem was that I had to drink a glass every ten minutes and finish the entire gallon jug by 8:00 pm. This was hard, because I had to force it down, without throwing up. Finally, I started going to the bathroom. After this, I had 30 minutes to drink three shot glasses of another stronger diuretic, very bitter, which finished the job. By 10:00 pm, I visited the toilet for the last time and took a mild sleeping pill. I had my picture taken by the 3rd floor Christmas tree to remember that first night, which was not very pleasant.

At 5:00 am, they woke me to give me a pill, which was supposed to make me groggy. I was wheeled into the operating room. The pill worked so fast on me that I was out half-way down the hall; I didn't remember a thing until I woke up in my room at 1:30 that afternoon. I was operated on in the morning and my roommate, a much younger SRS patient from Baltimore whom I had met before, was operated on in the afternoon. I now would stay in the bed, flat on my back, only moving my upper arms and head for the next six days as my body began to heal.

I took along paperwork from the office to use my time productively, but found that other than eating and a little television, there was little energy left for anything else. The days flew by. I slept most of the time, as my body needed the rest, recovering from the operation and the entire year.

On the seventh day, Dr. Schrang came in and removed some of the bandages and allowed me to get out of bed for the bathroom and shower. Still in discomfort and weak, it

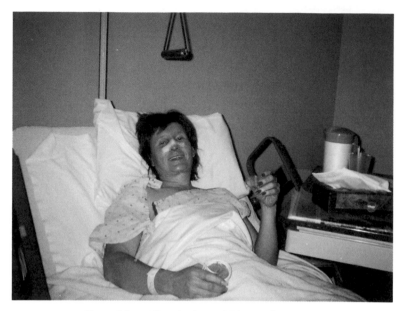

Day After Genital and Nose Surgery

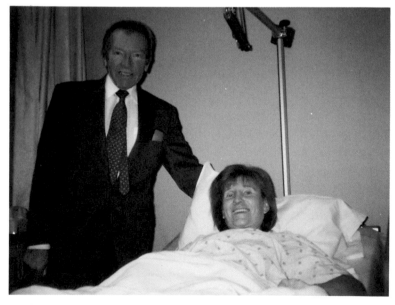

Dr. Schrang Congratulates Rhonda during Recovery Stages

took all my strength and the nurse's help to get my land legs back. I waddled to the bathroom at about 4:00 pm. That evening after supper, I tried taking a shower and walked down the hall to a shower room. I tried to stand up alone for my shower, I was so exhausted and weak that I threw up my entire supper and had to buzz the nurses to be practically carried back to my bed.

By noon on day eight, Dr. Schrang came back in and asked how I was doing. He said I looked great. I was glad at least he felt that way. He proceeded like a magician to pull the endless scarf-life packing from my new vagina. This felt better until he said he was going to show me how I would perform my follow-up therapy for the next year. He showed me what they call a plastic type dilator, about 10 inches long and 1" in diameter, which he liberally lubricated and gently but quickly slid into my newly-formed vagina before I knew what hit me. I was now learning a new definition for the word pain. He pulled it out and asked me to try it. I did. He then explained that in order for my body to get used to my new feminine anatomy, I had to religiously do this procedure six to seven times a day for 30 to 45 minutes at a time over the next two months. After that, I could taper off to fewer times each day. After six months I would only perform my therapy two or three times a day until the following December, 1997. If I did not do as I was told, my body could reject the operation, and I would be back for surgery again. Not this girl. He said I was doing great, and I could leave the hospital that afternoon at 4:30.

Eugene A. Schrang, M.D., S.C. has strong views and discusses transition in the following manner:

My role as a surgeon in the life of the transgendered patient is to simply change male genital anatomy into that which closely resembles and functions as female anatomy. That this can be done at all is quite phenomenal in and of

The Operation: Rhonda's Reality!

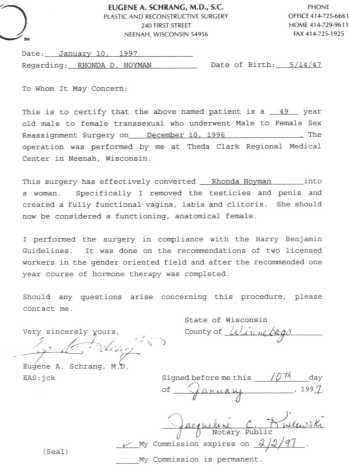

EUGENE A. SCHRANG, M.D., S.C.
PLASTIC AND RECONSTRUCTIVE SURGERY
240 FIRST STREET
NEENAH, WISCONSIN 54956

PHONE
OFFICE 414-725-6661
HOME 414-729-9611
FAX 414-725-1925

Date: __January 10, 1997__

Regarding: __RHONDA D. HOYMAN__   Date of Birth: __5/14/47__

To Whom It May Concern:

This is to certify that the above named patient is a __49__ year old male to female transsexual who underwent Male to Female Sex Reassignment Surgery on __December 10, 1996__. The operation was performed by me at Theda Clark Regional Medical Center in Neenah, Wisconsin.

This surgery has effectively converted __Rhonda Hoyman__ into a woman. Specifically I removed the testicles and penis and created a fully functional vagina, labia and clitoris. She should now be considered a functioning, anatomical female.

I performed the surgery in compliance with the Harry Benjamin Guidelines. It was done on the recommendations of two licensed workers in the gender oriented field and after the recommended one year course of hormone therapy was completed.

Should any questions arise concerning this procedure, please contact me.

Very sincerely yours,

Eugene A. Schrang, M.D.
EAS:jck

State of Wisconsin
County of __Winnebago__

Signed before me this __10th__ day of __January__, 199 7

Jacqueline C. Kwlewski
Notary Public

(Seal)

✓ My Commission expires on __2/2/97__.

____ My Commission is permanent.

Certification of Female Gender

itself but what is even more remarkable is that the operation has been developed to such a high degree of sophistication. In most cases the final result, after SRS and Labioplasty, so

254

resembles the genetic female that neither casual observers nor examining doctors can determine that the operations were ever done. What is even more exciting is the fact that the patient can function as a genetic female enjoying effortless, trouble-free sexual intercourse in addition to experiencing intense orgasmic sensations both of which are so important to a satisfying relationship. Imagine my gratification when I do this for numerous individuals almost daily?

I see in the future another very important development and that is: early recognition and treatment of Gender Dysphoria. If this situation could be recognized early so that patients could receive surgery in their teens or early twenties, we would avoid not only years of frustration by long periods of time allowing testosterone to burn male characteristics into their bodies which can never be erased.

I hope to see the fulfillment of these two goals: superb surgery done at an early age resulting in happy patients living long, satisfying, productive lives in the physical gender of their choice.

Still barely able to walk, but a lot better than the day before, at 3:30 I dressed in my green pants suit, put on make-up for the first time in eight days and packed my bags. I was wheeled out to the Valley Inn Motel van, which took me back to a room I had reserved for the next day and a half before my flight home on Thursday, December 19th. I must say, the nurses and medical professionals at Theda Clark Hospital and the entire staff at the Valley Inn Motel treated me like family and went out of their way to take care of my every need. I have never had such loving care and attention, and this quality service made my trip possible, since I was all alone in a new town for a major operation. Words are not enough to show my appreciation.

I now had to perform and master my therapy from that evening on, and I don't think I had a full night's sleep until sometime in March, as I stuck to my therapy schedule, which was quite painful those first few months until the stitches and my vagina started to heal. The best way to describe the therapy might be by comparing it to an open wound — it feels better after you put ointment on it and cover it with a bandage. Only in this case, just when it stops hurting and you feel better, you have to take off the bandage every four hours, wipe off the ointment, irritate the wound and cover it back up. Just as the pain starts to go away, you do it again. Needless to say, you take it day by day and learn the hospital stay was a piece of cake compared to the recovery process.

On the morning of the 19th, I was determined to look good as I went downstairs for a regular breakfast between therapy sessions. So, I put on my favorite green suit and even had my picture taken in the beautiful motel Christmas lobby, after a great breakfast. I think the picture turned out pretty, considering the day before I was still lying in the hospital bed. That evening, I didn't feel great, but I called Susan to finalize the divorce settlement on the house as negotiations were getting down to the wire before the end of the year. She wanted money in return for the lot, because she was going to move in June after her girls finished school. Even though I had been paying the mortgage construction loan payments in lieu of the alimony, I agreed to pay her for the lot, so she could leave the marriage with something to show for it. I would give her $12,000 for the lot and let her stay in the house until June, at which time I could rent or sell the house to get my investment back. I would have to borrow the $12,000 to settle the divorce. A final signing date had already been arranged when I came back from my surgery on December 24th at my lawyer's office in Frederick.

Things seemed to be taking some unusual turns. The necessity of calling Susan and my lawyer to set up a legal

December 15, 1994, Ron at Opryland, Nashville, TN

December 19, 1996, Rhonda's Day After Release from Hospital

promissory note for her approval from the Appleton, Cincinnati, and Baltimore BWI airports on the way back from my surgery on Thursday, December 19 was very stressful in my weakened state. I had to have wheel chair service to make my connections on the way back from the airlines, and Dr. Gettle was nice enough to meet me and drove a mentally, emotionally, and physically exhausted Rhonda back to her apartment for a long weekend of rest. It was good to be home, healing and at last physically whole. I even had an official letter from Dr. Schrang, saying I had completed the operation and was now physically a woman. This is the letter I then used to get my birth certificate, social security card, and Maryland legal court order changing to my legal status as Rhonda Hoyman, born May 14, 1947, female. I couldn't drive for at least six weeks and, for that matter, I learned just sitting in a car (even with an air cushion) for an hour's trip was difficult for me. Other remembrances from my recovery include a strange reaction during the first month, as I mentally adjusted to my new feminine anatomy. For example, when I was in the bathroom, I would reach down to hold or wash my penis.

Finally, though, the divorce seemed to be almost settled. My friend, Jana came down from Frederick and took me back for my electrolysis appointment the afternoon of Monday, December 23rd (I was a glutton for punishment) and I spent a restful night back in my old (now Jana's) log home, as I prepared to sign my divorce papers on the morning of the 24th.

Unfortunately, just ten minutes before we were supposed to sign the final papers (I was sitting in my lawyer's office in a great deal of discomfort), we received a call from Susan's lawyer, saying he wanted a signed cashier's check for $12,000 faxed to him before he would let her sign the divorce papers. I was crushed and very upset that our agreement had been broken by an unscrupulous lawyer. But, I mustered up enough strength to postpone the signing for three hours and Jana drove me to my Frederick bank the day before Christmas, and I arranged to borrow $12,000 more from my credit card company, which approved a cashier's check I could take back to my lawyers.

Lora L. Grams (employed by the bank) said about that time:

When Ron first came in my work place, I believe it was his first outing dressed as a female. He explained to me his situation. I never told him this, but at first I personally had a difficult time dealing with my feelings; religion verses sexual preference. When I went to Sunday School, I had mentioned how my week had gone and I prayed about it. I was wrong to have those feelings and I'm sorry. Who am I to judge; God loves us all! Later when I got to know Rhonda, a friendship developed. Eventually, after Rhonda's operation, I felt I could ask her anything. I'm really happy for her. I wrote this poem, but never mailed it. Here it is:

I look in the mirror and what do I see?
A beautiful woman, looking at me.
I asked myself, how can this be?
Born a man, I'm finally free!

My lawyer faxed a copy of the check to the Pennsylvania lawyer, even though he'd had a legal promissory note from me a week earlier. We completed the final divorce papers at 2:00 pm over the phone. I was pleased it worked out and the matter was settled. I was so emotionally and physically exhausted from the unexpected complications and my trip, that Jana took me straight back to my apartment, and I literally crawled to my bed and did not get out of it, except for food and the bathroom, for two straight days. I had never been that weak in my entire life, much weaker than when I'd gotten out of the hospital only a week earlier in Wisconsin. I canceled all other plans and outings I had hoped to make after Christmas; I did not leave the house until three weeks later and didn't go back to work until the first week in February. I did shuffle work back and forth and complete phone calls and daily paperwork from January on, but my therapy and recovery period took a good six weeks before I could go from my apartment on my own.

During my recovery, I talked to my family by phone, received food and help from Patty Cummings, Shirley Gordon, Karl Gettle and other friends from work who treated me with kindness and tender loving care. Ms. Cummings also continued to provide counseling services to me in my home. I would even go so far as to say this was the time when my work with her made the most difference in clarifying my feelings and psychological needs.

Always having a soft spot in my heart for teddy bears, I had asked and received a variety of bears instead of flowers in order to remember the kindness and love everyone showed me. I now have a special display and collection of the bears in my family room.

. In late December, I called to track down the legal documents office address for Southwestern Pennsylvania and mailed in my request to have my birth certificate changed with Dr. Schrang's letter. I was pleased to have my new birth certificate as Rhonda Dale Hoyman, female, born on May 14,1947, by the first week of February. I also received the same kind of response and turn around from the Federal Government in correcting my official name and sex while maintaining my same social security number. I had to have my lawyer file an appeal to amend my name change court order to also approve my legal female status in Maryland so I could change my driver's license to show "F" in the sex category. Ironically, the court approved order is dated February 14, 1997.

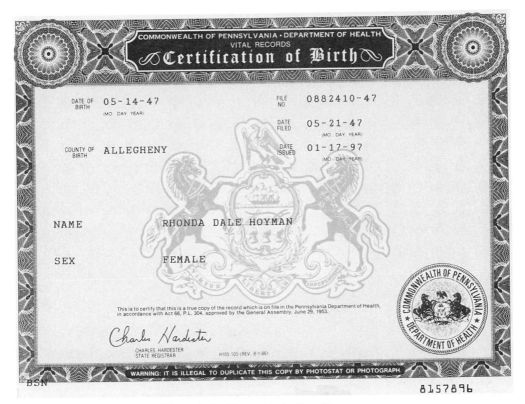

Rhonda's New Birth Certificate

On December 31, 1996, I received my formal divorce decree. I could start 1997 a single woman, making my new year a happy one even though I could not go out to celebrate. During the first part of January, I was busy just keeping up with the essentials: eating, sleeping (at least four hours at night), warm baths, performing therapy. I documented each session on a calendar. I was more emotional in my weakened physical state. For the first time in my life, I could allow myself to cry, express a desire for physical touch (even hugging my big teddy bear), and a deeper sense of happiness and inner joy. I was learning to live in and experience the moment, being mindful of the present like I never could before.

On Tuesday, January 14, three weeks from my trip to Frederick, my friend, Linda Fisher, drove me for a nail appointment and to see Penny for my hair color and to get my other hairpiece refastened. It was a feel-good trip back to real life. I also needed help doing simple physical tasks, pushing a vacuum cleaner, lifting things. By the middle of the month, I was also working full-time on memos, high school program reports , and putting in a full day of work from home. My job never stopped and even though I was weak and could not go out, I tried to keep up with the most important needs and issues. On Monday, February 3, I started back to work in the office and traveling to schools when needed.

I also tried to resume my regular speech therapy, electrolysis, and other transition medical services. I knew I was feeling better when I began to shop at my favorite clothing store, Dress Barn. I checked out the winter sales and took my new purchases to my seamstress, Barbara Allen, to have the hemlines shortened.

On Friday, February 21, I drove down to the Washington area MAGIC transgender group for the first time since my surgery to give a positive report and share my operation experiences and recovery with those who were interested. I wanted to return the help others had given me, as I led one of the break-out sessions for about 15 that night. I didn't need a group for my main support, but many transgender or transsexual persons participate in groups to help find support and resource information.

On Sunday, February 23, I hosted my first event, and I had a Pampered Chef party with eight of my personal and work friends. I learned about and bought some quality cooking items for my new kitchen set-up and plans to be a better cook. This was another big step in establishing my life and acceptance as just one of the other women; I tried to blend in.

By the first of March, I was starting to regain some of my normal strength and endurance. I drove home to my family in Pennsylvania for the first time since my operation, a chance to visit Mom, Walter, my brother, and sisters — a belated Christmas visit. I stayed an extra day to settle some credit union business, and I started back Monday just as an unexpected snow storm hit the Western Pennsylvania mountains. I was driving my little 1991 Mustang convertible, taking it slow at 35 MPH in the fresh three-inch snow. Suddenly my car hit a slick spot, turned completely around, and screeched to a stop just inches from a roadside guard rail. Thankfully, no one was coming the other way; I turned back around and crawled along at 20 MPH. I got over the mountains and onto clear roads. For whatever reason, I believe God was watching over me then and many other times since. I have had close calls on the road. I sure didn't need an accident so soon after my operation; I had too much to live for now.

After all, I had just spent a small fortune on my transition expenses.

10 Major Personal Transition Expenses

1	Plastic Surgery Complete Face Lift 3 separate operations	$20,000
2	Sex Change Surgery Breast Enhancement Surgery 2 separate operations in Neenah, WI	$19,700
3	Counseling Services 2 main counselors & 2 minor referrals	$6,000
4	Foot Surgery 2 operations	$500
5	Speech Therapy	$3,000
6	Electrolysis Face and chest area	$19,000
7	Endocrinologist Services Hormone Therapy and Prosthesis Ongoing for life	$800
8	Specialty Hair Services Wig and hairpieces	$3,000
9	Legal Fees Court name change and sex change	$1,000
10	Wardrobe and Jewelry	$7,000
	TOTAL COST	**$80,000**

Chapter 24

Fine Tuning Life and the First 50 Years

Having completed my operation, initial recovery, and most of my transition services, I started to become known as a person who could provide advice and support to other transsexuals who were just beginning their trials and tribulations of transition. For example, I drove to Harper's Ferry, West Virginia, to meet, inform, and support another transsexual, Tamlyn, who was a new patient of Lelia, my electrolysist.

Tamlyn Gayle Boswell says:

Rhonda set a pace and an example of perseverence and professionalism that helped me achieve my life long goal to become myself!

I also agreed to a special meeting in Shady Grove, Md., on Thursday, March 13th, with Ms. Walters, a production director from NBC's *Dateline*, who was looking for a male to female transsexual to follow for a transsexual life story. We hit it off right away but I was too far into my new life to be the focus of the story. However, Ms. Walters asked me to find and screen a candidate for the story, someone I would mentor through the transition. Katherine, the person I recommended, is well on her way to a successful transition, and we talk weekly.

The other event was when I was driving back to Towson from my meeting in Shady Grove, Maryland. A trucker spotted me, as I entered Route 70, just outside of Frederick.

He must have liked what he saw, because he intentionally slowed down, then sped up, using a spot light as I passed him at least ten times within a 45 miles stretch to the Baltimore beltway. I was flattered that he liked my legs so much, but I did not want to get into a cat and mouse game with a truck driver at 10:00 in the evening. Now, if I could only get a nice single guy to have the same impression...

The first three months of 1997 had flown by quickly, and my healing from my SRS surgery seemed to be complete; I was still following my therapy plan around four times a day now. I prepared to travel back to Neenah, Wisconsin, for phase two. I scheduled the cosmetic labioplasty surgery (to feminize the SRS operation area) and also decided to have Dr. Schrang complete a saline breast enhancement. You could say I was having a two-for-one or "Blue Light Special." Dr. Schrang agreed that the implants would round off my figure and be complimentary but not too large.

He chose a #300 saline implant, but what did that mean? He said that after 1 1/2 to 2 years on hormone therapy, a transsexual usually develops most of her breast size and I was now a size 34B. After the implants and final growth, I would be a size 38C, or what I like to call a couple of 38 specials!

Not wanting to interrupt my work schedule, I took advantage of an early Easter Holiday spring break and flew back to Appleton Airport early Saturday morning, March 22nd, to save on airfare rates. This gave me the time to spend a Saturday afternoon shopping in downtown Neenah. I also took advantage of some good sales, as I purchased a few special pins, my first Selby pumps and flats, which are so cute, and one-of-a-kind, acorn-shaped earrings and a grape cluster necklace—my "grape nuts" look. This will always be a keepsake from my visits to Neenah.

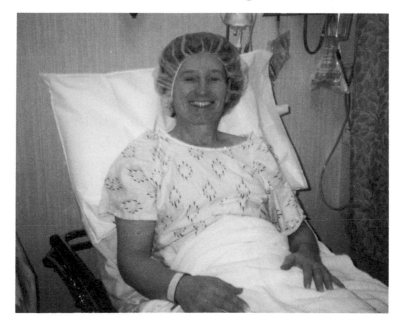

Photo 24.1: Late March 1997, Phase 2—
Cosmetic Genital Surgery & Breast Enhancement

At Home Easter, 1997

After my morning flight, I crashed early that night, so I could enjoy a lovely Palm Sunday worship service at the First Presbyterian Church of Neenah, just a few blocks from my hotel. This service was also special because the congregation participated by reading a Palm Sunday story (by gender), and I felt good reading with the other ladies for the first time as my true self—One of the little things that mean so much as I affirm my womanhood. Just like, it felt good (but different) when I put my hand over my heart during the 4th of July tribute to the flag, especially since my breast enhancement surgery.

A welcome restful Sunday helped me prepare for my early 6:30 am, March 24th arrival date at the Theda Clark Outpatient Surgical Center. As I breathed in the freshness of the crisp air, I tried to calm my nervous anticipation of this final step to my complete physical transformation. The efficient and courteous staff at Theda Clark were wonderful, again; and I checked in, went to pre-op for blood work, and got into my surgical gown. Right on schedule, they wheeled me into the operating room at 7:30. Thankfully, there were no preoperative knock-out pills this time. I looked around the sterile environment from the operating room table before the anesthesiologist put me under for my mammoplasty and labioplasty. After the two hour operation, I woke up in the recovery room around 11:30.

The nurses helped me back into my favorite green pants suit again. They sat me up in a chair for some juice and two pieces of toast with grape jelly. By 2:30 pm, the Valley Inn van picked me up, and took me to Dr. Schrang's office for a brief post-operative report and recovery instructions before arriving back at the hotel by 4:00 pm. They helped me to my room, and I set up my bed with my suitcase on one side and propped up pillows, so I would not roll over on my heavily bandaged breasts. I was relieved that my labioplasty operation did not make my continued vaginal therapy sore again, but having the saline breast implants placed under my own breast muscle tissue made up for the lack of pain in the other area. It hurt to move my arms, and I was in slow motion changing into my nightgown and travel clothes the next morning. I tried but hardly slept that night before an early rise to catch a plane back to Baltimore at 11:20 am, just 24 hours after surgery. By 4:40 pm, I arrived back in Baltimore at BWI airport, and Dr. Gettle was nice enough to provide wheel chair service and a ride back to my apartment, not far from his home. I was tired and sore but also relieved that I was back home safely.

On Wednesday, March 26th, I even stayed awake most of the day writing some important memos for work and checking my technical program materials order catalog for distribution. The rest of the week I gingerly moved around the apartment, as my breasts were very sore, tried to rest, and start my 1996 tax preparation.

On Saturday, March 29th, I went outside for the first time as my friend, Patti Cummings, took me to the local Animal Rights Defenders shelter to see if they had a kitten I could adopt. Now that I had moved to the Baltimore area and completed my surgery trips, I felt I could be home enough to get a new pet. I was surprised to find they didn't have any kittens, so I visited the cat adoption room. As I looked around, there was a smaller black cat; she came over and rubbed her head against my leg, so I said, "You win!" and brought her home. Since she was black and followed me all around the apartment; I decided to call her Shadow. It was nice to have a pet again.

On Tuesday, April 1st, my friend, Linda, drove me to Dr. Converse's office, my facial plastic surgeon, who agreed to provide follow-up care to my breast enhancement surgery and take off the travel tape Dr Schrang had put on. This was a painful process, but I was glad to have Dr. Converse monitor my progress as I had to now wear a special bra until my healing was complete.

Wednesday, April 2nd, and only a week since my recovery period began, I went back to work and driving on a limited basis. The labioplasty was bruised, and took a good month before the soreness from the mammoplasty went away.

Work continued to go well. I continued to notice that Ron was becoming a distant memory in many minds. I was again hosting an ABC construction program group from Kansas, Missouri, and Texas. I received the respect and consideration any other woman would receive from people. It was nice to take the visiting group to Phillip's Seafood, a restaurant at the Baltimore Inner Harbor and sit at a table with the other ladies, an equal.

With my 50th birthday just a month away, I visited the large Anderson Pontiac dealer to check out the new Grand Prix, which I loved. I met a nice salesman with whom I felt comfortable. He showed me a bright red Grand Prix with sport wheels, and I fell in love. I wanted red to match my new sporty look and personality. I wanted a car which made a statement. I added an automatic sunroof and CD player and negotiated a good trade-in for my Mustang, a nice car but too small for my needs. I felt good about the deal and my 50th birthday present — a month early. I was learning that life was too short not to go for the gusto, and Rhonda was going to build excitement into her life — as the Pontiac saying goes. I was becoming a woman on the move, finally putting her needs first. I felt great.

On Tuesday evening, April 22nd, I drove to Frederick to attend a large Youth for Christ banquet, an organization I had always supported. This was my first time attending the event as Rhonda. Since I now had a stronger Christian life than ever, I continued supporting this ministry. This eve-

A Car to Match Rhonda's New Personality

ning I would see many of my old church friends as Rhonda for the first time. I wanted to be considerate of their feelings but also say a friendly hello. The people I sat with at my table were nice and accepting of me, as was my former pastor. I was surprised that many of my old friends looked or turned away when I went to greet them. Since I didn't want to make them uncomfortable, I backed off from saying hello to those who seemed to be avoiding the Rhonda they used to know as Ron.

I left that night glad that I had attended, but also realized that many old friends let their personal prejudice, their so-called Christian beliefs, stand in the way of showing me common courtesy — the very essence of love and friendship, something I had always shown them. Maybe some day they will really understand, but I had to learn to give people space and time. I refused to let anyone's lack of acceptance or friendship make me feel less than a total woman. God made me, too, after all. (Even if I did change a few things).

After attending the Maryland Women's Expo on Sunday, May 4th, which I really enjoyed (I purchased jewelry), I made an initial contact with the Together Dating Service. On Tuesday evening, May 6th, I talked with a lady who was open and honest with me, as I was with her. A girl doesn't know what's possible until she tries, and I wanted to know if their service could really help me find some eligible men to date. I had used this same service as Ron many years earlier back in Frederick. In fact, I had even talked to a Together representative just a few months earlier by phone. Being up front, I told the gentleman my qualifications and interests, and of my recent life change. I asked him if their service could help me. He said he would have to check and call me back, and he did a few days later to say he could not help me under the circumstances. I accepted his answer but also said from my former experiences (with ten different women to whom they had introduced to Ron) that I now had better looks, figure, personality, and potential than nine of those ten.

One special lady I met at that time is a person I'm still glad to call my friend. So, as I told this to the Timonium office representative, she agreed that I had the looks, personality, and intelligence men were looking for (especially for almost being 50); unfortunately, the male clients they served would reject me because of my transition past, which they would have to be told about up front. Besides, she admitted, most of the men were looking for women 15 years younger than they, and they wanted Barbie dolls. I appreciated her honesty, and I agreed that with men that egotistical, I would not want to date them anyway. She wished me luck, as we both agreed it was not worth the time or money to use a dating service. You can't blame me for trying, and at least I knew I would have to follow other methods to meet men who wanted a serious relationship. Since I loved myself for the first time, I knew I could love a man, if only he could get over my past, something I could not control.

On Sunday, May 11th, I made a great investment in fine-tuning my plans. I hired Nancy Ruth Goldblatt, an image consultant, whom I had met at a recent Women's conference, to come to my apartment to critically advise and work with me. Things seemed to be going well, but I wanted to learn to make them even better. After working with Nancy for three hours that afternoon, I realized they could. She gave me some good tips on using a special brush and eye shadow to highlight my eyes with brown, not black, as my base color for my brows and eye liner, to use brown mascara and other make up tips. This would complement my red hair color. She suggested I switch to a chestnut brown purse and shoes for my standard look. Again, I was using black. She advised me on clothing selection, complementing colors, patterns, prints, and styles. Based on her recommendations, I ditched a quarter of my wardrobe. I figured why ask a professional for advice, if I wasn't going to use it. Finally, we talked about jewelry styles, pin location on clothes, the best type of earrings for me. I found I could wear larger or longer ones than I was used to. Nancy's advice was well worth the money. If I don't feel like my look is at least an eight out of ten, I don't go out the door. Presentation is important to any woman, especially a transsexual. I'm not a real casual dresser, and Nancy says my look can be called classic/romantic, and I agree with her.

Nancy Ruth Goldblatt recalls:

I met Rhonda during her "fine tuning year." I showed her how to choose flattering accessories, colors and clothing styles. She was like a sponge, quickly absorbing all of the new information! While searching for the right eyebrow pencil color, I commented, "this is a lot of work." Rhonda replied, " love every minute of it."

Wanting to make the most of my jewelry selection and quality, I approached my former friends Bert and Virginia, the owner's of Gold Thumb jewelry store in Frederick, MD. They knew Ron and while it was a surprise for them to get introduced to and serve Rhonda, their jewelry creations complement Rhonda's presentation.

You could say a lot of water had gone over the dam that last year-and-a-half, as I celebrated my 50th, or in reality my 1st birthday as a completely whole Rhonda on May 14, 1997. That day, my friend, Karl Gettle, treated me to lunch, and my floriculture teacher at Hereford High gave me a nice flower arrangement, as I spent a quiet evening at home, opening my cards, resting and counting my blessings. I could not have been happier or have asked for a better "Big 50," which the office staff plastered all over my desk with lots of well wishes for another 50 years.

Most of my transition services and operations were behind me, I still had good health, love and support of my family, friends, co-workers, and self confidence. My transition made me better looking, stronger and happier than I could ever have dreamed possible. I had lost more than twenty pounds (from a size 14 to a size 10) and I had a good figure and looks for a woman my age — a totally reconstructed body from head to toe. Most importantly, I was glad to be me. I loved myself (the person I saw in the mirror each day) for the first time in my life. As I jokingly say to my friends when they compliment me on my appearance, I wear

50th Birthday on-the-Job

a size 10 dress and size 10 shoe — that must mean I'm a perfect 10.

Rhonda at 50—Watch out World

My heart feels like a perfect 10 many days, and I'm thankful for all of God's blessings. I don't know what the next 50 years will bring, but I'm looking forward to each of them. Besides, after all I have gone through, I feel the second 50 have to be better than the first. I sure don't plan on acting my age any time soon, for age is a state of mind, and this 50-year old woman feels more like a 25-year old, with a lot of catching up to do. Watch out world!

Chapter 25

The Dating Game: Life Moves On!

I started off my 50th year with a weekend I will never forget. On Friday, May 16, 1997, I took the initiative and called a nice man I had met during dinner with some friends a few weeks earlier. That was not a planned match-making evening, but George happened to be there, and we sort of hit it off in our informal conversation. We discussed the possibility of going to the play, "Singing in the Rain," which I was interested in attending at the Baltimore Lyric Theater. I began the call saying, "If I'm not being too forward, would you like to go to the play with me?" He said he would, but asked if he could call me back the next morning to discuss the actual time we could go since he was having dinner, and I told him that would be fine. I feel calling a man was a bold step for a woman, especially me, but I had to start somewhere.

I waited with anticipation Saturday morning wondering when or if he would really call me back. The phone rang around 9:30 am. We had a nice, 30-minute talk, and he asked if I would like to go out that evening to Annapolis around 6:30 pm. I told him I was free (even though I was supposed to go out with my girlfriend, Lauren, to check out the hot spots at Fells Point). I figured a real date had to come first.

When I hung up, I was like a school girl all excited about my first date. I asked George what I should wear, and he said he would be dressed casually. I planned on a nice casual dress, figuring we would be going out for dinner. Patti

Rhonda—Stepping Out on Her 1st Date

Cummings, my counselor and best girlfriend, called to see what was up and said, "How exciting!" She agreed to come over around 2:00 pm to help with my dress selection. Well, we had the bed covered with clothes as I modeled a few, and finally settled on my navy dress with a bright peach-colored top, and a nice open neckline. At 4:30 pm, I said I had to get my shower and give myself time for my make-up, so Patti left, and I went to work on myself, doing the beauty routine. I just finished up around 6:25 pm, with no time to spare.

George called about 6:35, saying he was at my apartment complex, but couldn't find my apartment number, so I gave him directions and stood outside until he saw me. I invited him in and showed him around the apartment. As we were about to leave, he said, "Don't be nervous." I didn't really think I was, but he held my hand and gave me a kiss-right on the lips to my surprise! I said, "I'll get lipstick on you!" He said he didn't care. We left the apartment. He opened the door to his red, two-door compact car — the perfect gentleman.

On the way down to Annapolis, we chatted about our jobs, what we liked, some of our childhood experiences. We arrived in Annapolis on a cool, pleasant May evening and parked the car. He open my door and offered to carry my sweater, but I said, "No thanks."

We held hands off and on, walking through the downtown area of restaurants and quaint little shops. Looking for a nice place for dinner, we decided to try the old Victorian house, which was remodeled into a nice restaurant. The hostess said she had a cancellation and seated us at a candlelight table for two, near the front window. George pulled my chair out for me, and we both checked out the menu. We ordered a shrimp cocktail and selected the same meal, filet mignon. We seemed to have a lot in common with food and other interests. We chatted and enjoyed a very nice dinner and rather romantic time together.

What I found interesting was that in our conversation, he made comments about society's expectations on men and his viewpoints of them (not knowing of my major transition in life). I thanked him for the nice meal and realized for the first time that I was on the non-paying side. It felt good to be treated like a lady and have an affirmation of my femininity.

We held hands as we walked down the rather narrow, cobblestone streets past the old shops, inns, and stores. We made our way to the pier, which overlooked Annapolis Harbor, when George stopped and looked as if he were about to kiss me again. I didn't want to encourage anymore physical advances since I hadn't had a chance to explain my history, so I looked away and we moved on. We took a small diversion from the crowds and headed up a narrow side street, talking about how we wanted to have more personal time in our lives and how we could plan more activities together. He said he wanted to be with a woman who didn't have children or ties that would inhibit having good personal time in the future.

We headed back to the car. Once again, he opened my door, and I slid into the front seat. I can only assume he felt this was his best opportunity to make-out. Right after he got into the car, he reached over and gently put his hand over my shoulder and pulled me towards him. He then turned and kissed me. I didn't mind, but to my surprise, he began French kissing me for what seemed to be a long time. Not wanting to be unresponsive, I returned the French kiss, and he made the comment that I was a good kisser. I told him I was rather new at this, but it felt good to be loved. As he continued to kiss me, he then began to slide his hand along my left leg, slightly moving up the edge of my dress. I didn't want to go too far, but at least I now had all the right parts to fulfill any man's dreams. I sure would not have wanted this experience before completing my operations. To my relief, he moved his hand from my leg before I had to, and immediately went for my right breast. I was glad I had the mammoplasty! Make-out session over, George pulled out of the parking garage with a smile on his face.

I was still surprised. I did enjoy having a man be so interested and affectionate but it was so soon, and I didn't really know how much to do or not to do on the first date. After all, we were two mature adults, but my first experience on the female side. As a man Ron had been married three times but could count his former make-out experiences in single digits.

As we left the parking lot, I could sense George's continued physical attraction. He said, "I bet you look good in a bathing suit!" I told him I wasn't bad. He also said, "I noticed your nice legs when we met before." I said, thank you — I was proud of them.

That night, I gained a new appreciation for the term "parking," only in my case it was "parking garage." Driving home, we held hands, and he lightly rubbed my leg. George talked about going out to other activities. Maybe I'm too vain, but I think he saw me as his dream girl, Ms. Right. His interest did flatter me, and the relationship had some potential to me also.

He walked me to the door, and I invited him in, because I did not want the night to end without telling him of my transition. I did not want him to have false hopes or thoughts of a possible relationship without my being totally honest. He had to know about my past. As I went to the restroom, he sat on the couch. When I came out he said, "I just wanted to smooch some more." I said, "George, I don't mind showing someone affection, but before we do, there's something I want to tell you." I sat down beside him. I searched for the right words and felt a little nervous getting started. George said, "It's okay, just tell me."

I looked at him and said, "This is hard to explain briefly. If you have any questions, I will be glad to answer them after I tell you. Two years ago, I finally began a process to become my true self and begin a major life transition from male to female life. I have always felt I was a woman and have completed all the operations and everything to the point that other than not being able to have children, there is no difference, physically, between me and any other woman. I wanted to tell you this because I respect your feelings and wanted to be totally honest so we could trust each other. I did not want to continue any more physical contact until I told you about my transition history."

He looked at me, totally surprised. "Does this mean you had a penis?"

I told him it didn't mean anything to me, but that yes I had at one time had a penis. He stood up and said he had to go. I offered to explain more. He said, "No, that's okay." As we walked towards the door, he was nice enough to say he hoped he hadn't hurt my feelings, and I told him that I hoped I hadn't hurt his feelings. He was still willing to be friends but nothing else. He said, "Okay, I just hope you don't get AIDS."

At that point, I knew he really didn't understand the situation. "I'm not a loose woman, and you are the one who initiated the physical contact. I explained that I had had so many medical tests recently that I was safer from AIDS than any woman he could go out with. We both said goodnight to each other and he left.

I accepted what happened, and I knew there was no potential with the relationship, but I was not going to mislead anyone. I felt I just wanted one date to get to know each other before trying to explain the past. A few days later, my friend, the one who had us both over for dinner, told me that George called him that next morning after our date and said, "I was up all night thinking I would get AIDS," because of his French kissing and experiences with me.

George asked my friend if he knew of my past and my friend told him yes. He explained that I was a woman all my life who had struggled with this medical condition. My friend's level of respect and acceptance surprised George. He also reassured George that I was a trustworthy person who had recent operations and medical care and that I didn't have AIDS. This reassured George, and he felt a lot better. I appreciated my friends' willingness to explain things to George. I would have been glad to answer any questions George had, but he was not ready to hear any of this from me.

There is no easy answer to dating for me or for the men I go out with. I don't want to mislead any man, but I also want them to get a chance to know and appreciate me as the woman I really am.

My second date resulted from the October 22nd *City Paper* story. Charles called, and we talked a number of times on the phone before actually going out. My former male life was a non- issue with him. We agreed to meet at a nice Italian restaurant in downtown Baltimore, in an area called Little Italy. I arrived first and was seated just before Charles arrived at 7:00 p.m., Tuesday, November 4, 1997. I already knew he was a year older than I, a few inches shorter, was balding, and owned his own business. While maybe not my initial dream man, I was not going to rule out a man because of preconceived notions or without getting to know him personally.

We had a friendly greeting and nice dinner, as we got over the first impressions and talked about personal information and interests. Basically, we sized each other up. During our conversation, I could see he was definitely interested in me. He asked me to go out on future dates and even an upcoming

Thanksgiving Day dinner. I felt he was a sincere, trustworthy man, but yet there wasn't the chemistry or mutual, interpersonal compatibility. With the evening still early, being only 8:30 at the end of dinner, he asked if he could take me for a ride to see his place of business and the Inner Harbor before we call it a night. Being cautious, I asked him if I could trust him to treat me like a lady and he said, "Yes, if I can't help you, I will never hurt you." I appreciated his honesty and said okay. As we walked to his car, he opened the door for me, and I got in, hoping I had made the right decision. I probably should not have been, but I was surprised when he reached over, put his arm around me, and not only gave me a kiss, but went into the French kissing and move for the leg (parking garage routine again). Now knowing the routine, I pulled back and said, "Let's slow down on the physical affection. You said I could trust you."

Fortunately, he was a man of his word and honored my request, as we started off for about a 45 minute drive around the Baltimore area before he took me back to my car. He asked me to go to dinner and a movie Saturday night, and I said I would have to check my schedule. He could give me a call. He did call the next night, but I was out late for a meeting and decided it was not best to generate more interest by dating him further and did not call back. Again, he showed respect for me and did not call me again, which I appreciated. From all indications, this could have developed into a serious relationship, but I did not want to have a man in my life if it was not going to be right for both of us.

The third date came about when I met a man while tagging along with my friend Kathrine, on Sunday evening January 11, 1998. She had participated in a special event in the Washington, D.C. area and stopped by a few bars on the way home to unwind. Since I do not drink, I sat there, and sipped a 7-up. John came up and we started talking.

After talking a while, he said he would like to take me out, even after I had earlier described my transition and previous dating experiences. John was a tall man whom I knew was a few years younger than me and lived in the Maryland suburbs just outside Washington, a good 65 miles from my home. He called me about a week after our meeting, and we got to know each other better before going out to a nice Chinese restaurant. With heavy rains and bad traffic, I hung in there at the restaurant for about 30 minutes waiting for John to show from his long drive. After apologizing for his lateness, we had a nice dinner, discussion about our personal interests, families, and current work lives. He said he realized I was a Type A personality, who was trying to manage a busy job and start a quality personal life. He indicated a strong interest in the physical aspects of a relationship, but I said I was not a "7-11" date. He asked what I meant, and I told him that I was not a quick, one-stop girl; I wanted to have a meaningful respect and friendship before becoming physically involved with a man. As we left the restaurant, it was going on 10:00 pm, and I thanked him for a nice dinner and for coming all the way up to meet me. Since my house was only ten minutes away, I offered to let him see where I lived if he wanted to. He said he'd better not because if he stopped, he would not want to go home until the morning. Since we both knew what that meant, I thanked him for his honesty. I would never see him again. It was nice to know my past was not an issue with him and that he was physically attracted to me, but I was not willing to have a one-dimensional relationship.

I spent the rest of my winter and spring personal time writing this book. I have not gone out or put myself in many circles which would cultivate other dates or relationships, which I want to start again this summer. Time and circumstances will only tell if I ever get to meet Mr. Right. I know

I don't have all the answers, but I also know and believe I could be a good partner, lover, and wife, since I now love myself enough to return that love to a significant other. I believe I can live up to the one line I like to share with guys, "I am a religious girl (meaning church and Christian values are a part of my life) and that's to a man's advantage." Why? "Because the man who hooks up with me will think he died and went to heaven!"

Wanting to find a new church home, I started visiting a few Sunday morning church services in the summer of 1997. On May 25th, I attended the Towson Presbyterian Church and really felt at home from the start. The congregation welcomed me warmly, and the spiritual feeling which comes from the vaulted ceilings and organ music in this large, stone building. Reverend Toole, the senior pastor, has a concrete, common sense message, which I like, and other church staff and members made me feel like I had gone back to my earlier roots in the Presbyterian faith in which my mother nurtured me.

One Sunday in October of 1997, I became a new member of this large congregation. I didn't want others to learn about my past transition (like the *City Paper* article), so I told Reverend Toole of my former male life and struggles. I promised not to make it an issue with other church members. I am part of one of the women's circles, and Reverend Toole has accepted me with true Christian love and respect, saying that I was a lovely woman, and he is glad to have me a member of their congregation. I did ask that if some day I were to get married, would he perform the wedding ceremony. He said that he would love to.

In June and July, I spent some weekends traveling back home to Greensburg to fix up and sell the modular home I had previously built to help Susan until she moved on with her new life. My brother Bill was a big help in this process,

Ready for Church—Long and Lacy

and fortunately, I was able to find a buyer and sold the house in the early fall to bring closure to that part of my past. This major project had been a bigger issue and thorn in my side than I had ever planned during my transition.

On Saturday, June 7, Dr. and Mrs. Berger, the former superintendent of Frederick and Baltimore County Schools threw a 50th birthday party for another close personal friend and me, at their new residence in Baltimore. To prepare for the occasion, I even built a new cupola to cover their patio area the weekend before the party. I appreciated their friendship and all the other friends and fellow Baltimore County educators who came to our big 50th celebration.

On Tuesday, June 24, I visited my secretary's home to bring home a new kitten and playmate for my other black cat, Shadow. Not being home a lot, I felt it best to have two cats, as I had in the past to be company for each other as well as for me. Since the kitten with some Siamese markings was gray in color, I decided to play off Shadow's name and call him Cloud. It took a few weeks of adjustment time, but now they are best buddies. I have also learned women prefer to have cats as pets more so than men.

On Friday, July 11, 1997, I took Jana's 85-year-old grandmother to her new residence in Daytona Beach, Florida. She was moving from Frederick to a veteran's nursing home. Since her granddaughter, Jana, and her husband had purchased my home the previous year, I had gotten very close to her grandmother as well. She asked if I would move her to a place where she would spend the rest of her life. Although my personal time was still limited, I could not turn down her request and in only three day's time, I drove her the 1000 miles to Daytona Beach, set her up in her new room, and drove back to my apartment in Baltimore by Sunday evening at 8:00 pm. I even squeezed in a two-hour shopping spree at a southern Georgia outlet mall on Saturday evening and bought some great Western wear and red

Handy Woman Rhonda Builds Cupola

cowgirl boots. My stamina and my new Grand Prix got a real workout that weekend, and although fast, it was my first real personal out- of-state trip as Rhonda in my new interactions with the world beyond Baltimore.

I hadn't planned on purchasing a home right away, but I needed the tax break that home ownership provided and stability. I looked around and quickly found a home I felt would meet all my needs in late July. Reaching a contract agreement right after I returned from my Florida trip, I purchased a semi-detached, or what some may call two-story, colonial style, duplex in a quiet, family-oriented community, just a few miles from my office. With all my personal expenses, the only way I could afford the home was to

Rhonda Expands Her Wardrobe

reactivate my G.I. Bill, VA Home Ownership Certificate, which was still in Ron's name. Another step in retracing the past. I had to make three visits to the VA headquarters in

Baltimore before they finally reactivated my eligibility as Rhonda versus Ron (they were very nice about the whole matter). This allowed me to make settlement on and purchase my new home at the end of August. I actually moved over Labor Day.

I spent the next four months painting, wallpapering, and remodeling all of the interior rooms of the three-floor, 2100+ square foot home to my feminine, Williamsburg style. The home is a real benefit to my life style, including the huge walk-in closet (I converted one of the small bedrooms), two working fireplaces, a make-up center in my bedroom, and a warm, country-style, paneled basement. Life was taking shape better and faster than I could have hoped from my initial transition.

In late September, 1997, Suzanne Gibson and I were notified that the personal article she had written about me and submitted to Baltimore's largest free paper, *The City Paper* was accepted as the cover story and feature article for the October 22, 1997, weekly edition. I had a full day of photo shoots one Saturday. There I was in my purple suit in a construction setting for the cover of a very public publication! I was pleased with the article Suzanne wrote and the 99.9% positive feedback and reactions I received from taking the chance of going public with my transition story. Many people have told me it really helped them understand why I made the switch to female life and my true identity.

I was still doing my dilator therapy and on Christmas Eve, 1997, I decided to complete this just before turning in for the night. I was so tired that I fell asleep before removing the dilator. The next morning I had a new and unwanted body part! With the lubricant gel now dried to an adhesive quality, I could not seem to twist, turn, or gently budge the dilator out of my vagina. To resolve my dilemma, I cautiously waddled to the bathroom, drew a warm tub full of water

Photo 25.5: Rhonda's New Casual Life

which I felt would easily resolve the problem. However, to my surprise, a simple soaking would not dissolve the gel. I had to slowly pull back and separate this unwanted therapy device from my body. It took 30 minutes before I was once again a safe and sound woman. I was relieved this ordeal was over and vowed never to place anything into my body when I was too tired to control the outcome.

Taking advantage of a Holiday membership special, I joined the Social and Tennis part of the Valley Country Club, which is located just a few blocks down the street in my community. This enabled me to make some new friends in the area, as well as actively work on my goal of establishing a personal life and finding a more physical and pleasurable activity. I'm learning to play tennis, how to hold the racket, all the right moves, etc. In mid-April, 1998, I started participating in the Sunday afternoon women's tennis practice sessions and expect it will take all summer for me to develop the technique and skills needed to play in real games and be a member of the ladies tennis group next year. For my birthday gift this year, I bought myself a good tennis racket, colorful, of course, some tennis skirts, and a cute little tennis dress to at least look like I know what I'm doing. I plan on playing the game the rest of my life and using it as another permanent step in my life long goals of health, wellness, and personal pleasure. The other ladies I have met have been real nice, and I enjoy being accepted into their group. One thing is for sure, I am still strong enough that I don't have to use two hands on my backhand swing.

Over the past few months, I have also joined and participated in area-wide Presbyterian Singles Group activities from time to time, and still plan on doing so in the future to make new friends and improve my social life. I have been accepted in the group with no question to my femininity. Whether a singles group, biking outing, tennis club, dancing

Ron at Work (May 1995)

event or any other social group, I plan on participating in many events and activities. I never have let my hair down and allowed myself some plain old fun. Fun and relaxation are words I am still learning.

There are still people who haven't yet met the new and improved version of me. Thus, life continues to bring new reactions and friendships. One event (two years from now) that I'm looking forward to is my 35th high school reunion in the summer of 2000. I think I'll definitely win the "most changed" award!

As I close this chapter and my story, I hope in some small way my message will not only help you understand why I did what I did. The real answer came only when I allowed Rhonda the chance to be her true and total self. I still have a lot to learn and will make mistakes until the day God takes me to be with Him. But, words can not be spoken to express

RHonda Stepping Out in Her Killer Suit—51st Birthday

the inner joy and peace I find each day when I wake up and look in the mirror. My prayer for you is that you will take the time to search for your dreams, to take the steps, little

Rhonda Looking Forward to Winter

or large, painful or easy, to find your true happiness. Just as I did, only you can make this happen, may you not just live but experience life to its fullest.

I challenge you to search your heart and strive to make your dreams come true. That is why I recommend you develop you own personal, pro-active improvement plan. I have paid for the right to have Christine Larson's "Promise Yourself" message as the last page in this book. Read it over and over again, select your favorite promises, and then start to make your dreams a reality. It was not too late for me, and it's not too late for you. One day of pure and total happiness is worth a lifetime of frustration and unfulfillment.

Mindfulness Counseling by Patty Cummings

On December 10, 1996, Rhonda underwent male to female sex reassignment surgery. This surgical procedure transformed Ron into a woman. After the testicles and penis were removed, a fully functional vagina, labia and clitoris were surgically created. Her surgery was in accordance with the Harry Benjamin Guidelines; therefore, Rhonda was then considered a functioning female.

Rhonda was glowing as if she had just given birth to herself, and indeed she had. Her surgery was the culminating event that supported Rhonda's transformation. Ron had sought treatment with me in July of 1995. At that time he presented with a sense of hopelessness, helplessness, sadness and fear that he would forever remain a female trapped in a male body. His chronic and persistent discomfort with having to function in the male role yielded symptoms of depression, chronic low self-esteem, irrational guilt, pervasive sadness, worry, and suicidal ideation without a plan. However, he had mentioned that his tendency to speed would make it easy for him to kill himself in a car accident, and yet he did not want to die. The mounting pain of repression grew. He was fighting to preserve the life of his true self: Rhonda. A goal in therapy was to have the opportunity to explore his "female" side. After the initial session he came to his appointments dressed as female. He wanted to interact as Rhonda. He had expressed frustration with previous attempts in therapy that was focused on "curing him" of his distorted belief patterns. He presented with a strong and persistent cross-gender identification. He had cross-dressed since early childhood, and had always had cross-gender interests. During this initial session he was preoccupied with the desire to live as a woman, to adopt the social female role, and to ultimately acquire the physical appearance of a female. He had a desire to live and be treated as a female. Ron has consciously chosen therapy as a venue for having the opportunity to explore his feelings and to have support as he proceeded with his transformation. He had never doubted his gender orientation. He had spent the better part of his life denying his own pain and putting other people's needs first. He was always available to do for others. This created a purpose for living, and it allowed him to feel good about himself. He was, however, wasting valuable healing energy keeping his feelings repressed. He was tired of living a life that outwardly conformed to society's expectations. He had been married three times, and was now in couple counseling as the third marriage began to crumble. He appeared to be at a major crossroad in his life, facing not only developmental challenges of mid- life, but making major decisions about following through with sex reassignment surgery, rhinoplasty with a full face lift, speech therapy, electrolysis, foot surgery, and hormone therapy that would enable him to live more fully as a female. He said he was attracted to men out of the female identity, and yearned to be in a loving relationship with a man after he had experienced his transformation. Ron primarily coped by being a work-aholic and rationalizing. He feared he would be rejected by family, friends, and co-workers when he made his transformation.

And so his journey in therapy began. Trust was a major factor in the relationship because of his prior counseling experiences that had rejected his true identity and needs; however, once that was established, Ron began to engage more deeply in the therapeutic process. Gradually, his fears began to dissipate. Work-aholicism was a way of living that had supported his denial of feelings, and it was rewarded in the world of work, consequently, he developed a strong work ethic. He had developed a pattern of avoidance in order to survive. It was a challenge for him to access feelings because his mind was always racing with new ideas of what he could be doing. I introduced him to the idea of living in the present because he had a need to be future oriented. It often prevented him from being fully present, and to feel pain. His need to be positive also prevented him from feeling pain. He was well defended. The main focus of his therapy was the clinical application of mindfulness. Mindfulness is present moment awareness. He also took an eight-week class I was teaching in Mindfulness-based Stress Reduction in Mind-Body Medicine. As he began to regularly practice living more in the present, he began to gain more insight into his resistance to feeling.

It wasn't until shortly after her sex reassignment surgery that she was able to access some deeply repressed grief over having spent two thirds of her life in "hiding." The physical pain of recovery was something she had not anticipated. The resulting stress during this early phase of her physical recovery rendered her vulnerable to experiencing deep emotional pain. Her ability to rationalize her pain had greatly decompensated, and she was feeling raw and vulnerable. She was open and the emotions began flowing for the first time in her life. Her mindfulness practice supported her ability to remain centered in the awareness of her body-mind system. As she allowed the pain of the inner child to be more fully experienced, she began to open to her innate sense of joy and acceptance of self. She, for the first time in her life felt whole, complete and very much connected to herself in ways that she in the past could only imagine.

She continues to live more fully in the present, feeling all that life has to offer, both the bitter and the sweet. She is now more generous and giving to herself and of herself. She continues to do for others, but no longer out of the need to not do for herself. She has learned and practices the art of self-healing. She has become a role model to those who are inspired by her courage and her encouragement. She is not just a physical female. She is in process of becoming more spiritually, emotionally, and mentally integrated as a total human being, and is now prospering in all ways.

Patty Cummings, M.S.W., L.C.S.W.,—C.
With a private practice in psychotherapy
specializing in the clinical application of mindfulness

Rhonda's Signature Choices

Song: Accentuate the Positive
Car: 1997 Pontiac Grand Prix (Red)
Color: Emerald or any shade of green
                 (Birthstone)
Candy: York Peppermint Patty (Get the
                 Sensation!)
Drink: Diet Dr. Pepper
Snack: Popcorn
Movie: *The Sound of Music* (Climb every
                 mountain, follow every
                 dream)
Role Model: Ann Margaret
Word: Pro-Active
Clothing Style: Classic/Romantic
Thought: Attitude is Everything
Greeting: Have a dazzling day!
Expression: Smile, Smile, Smile
Vacation: A mountain retreat
Play: Les Miserables
Flower: Rose

RHONDA

R   *Responsibility*...doing the right thing because IT'S THE RIGHT THING TO DO!

H   *Hope* . . . the magic ingredient that sparks you into POSITIVE ACTION!

O   *Optimism* . . . know that you can...because YOU CAN DO IT!

N   *Negatives* . . . avoid them, keep them out of your environment, especially negative people.

D   *Discipline* . . . it pays off in results, you must have it TO ACHIEVE!

A   *Attitude* . . . the foundations, the Mark of You . . . keep yours POSITIVE!

PERSONAL NAME HISTORY

Rhonda is of Celtic origin. It is believed to have evolved as a Scottish feminine form of Ronald. Rhonda is found almost exclusively in the English-speaking World.

Rhonda's Top 10 Tips!

While some of the following tips may not apply to you, especially the guys, the following life improvement steps have, and continue to make, a difference in Rhonda's life, and many of them may also work for you.

Tip #1
Attitude is everything. Be pro-active instead of reactive to life. Unlock your potential and choose what is best for you.
Tip #2
Don't take no for an answer: always have a Plan B. Take pride in everything you do in life, and do it to the best of your ability.
Tip #3
Quit using soap on your face. Start using a skin care cleansing system and moisturizer every day.
Tip #4
Try to match your nail color with the lipstick shade you most often wear, and when possible, coordinate in threes, like your shoes, belt and purse. The key word is: accessorize, accessorize, accessorize.
Tip #5
Presentation is everything. Don't walk out the door unless you're at least an eight out of ten on your own personal scale. Remember the old saying: If it looks like a duck and walks like a duck, then it's a duck; and you can be a pretty duck.
Tip #6
The best way to remove unwanted body hair (other than electrolysis) without making it grow back stronger, is to remove the surface hair with a small pair of scissors, or better yet a small rechargeable electric hair trimmer.

Tip #7

Don't operate or push yourself at 100% all the time, otherwise you have no time or energy reserves when you really need them.

Tip #8

Make a five year pro-active personal improvement plan, setting meaningful goals for improving your life one year at a time.

Tip #9

Taking a herbal-based vitamin supplement and a natural vegetable/fruit-based supplement system like Juice Plus is the key to increasing energy and maximizing your physical health and wellness. It will pay off now and in the future.

Tip #10

Dream it, believe it, and live it. If you only had one more year, month, week, or day to live, how would you spend it or what would you do differently?

5 Year Pro-Active Personal Improvement Plan

The Choices We Make Dictate The Life We Lead.
—*To thine own self be true.*

_____

Your Name

Year One Goal:

Accomplishments:

Year Two Goal:

Accomplishments:

Year Three Goal:

Accomplishments:

Year Four Goal:

Accomplishments:

Year Five Goal:

Accomplishments:

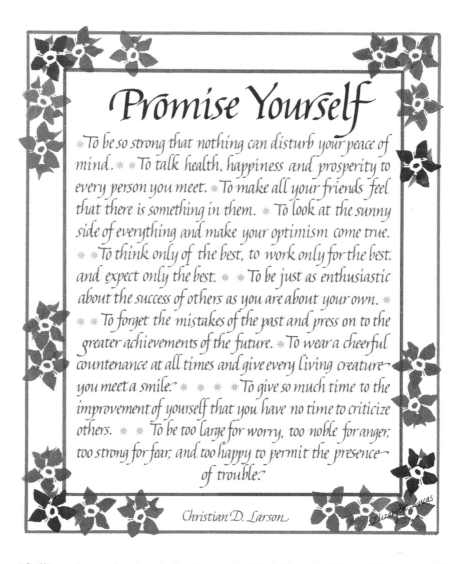

Promise Yourself

* To be so strong that nothing can disturb your peace of mind. * * To talk health, happiness and prosperity to every person you meet. * To make all your friends feel that there is something in them. * To look at the sunny side of everything and make your optimism come true. * * To think only of the best, to work only for the best, and expect only the best. * * To be just as enthusiastic about the success of others as you are about your own. * * * To forget the mistakes of the past and press on to the greater achievements of the future. * To wear a cheerful countenance at all times and give every living creature you meet a smile. * * * * To give so much time to the improvement of yourself that you have no time to criticize others. * * To be too large for worry, too noble for anger, too strong for fear, and too happy to permit the presence of trouble.

Christian D. Larson

"Calligraphy and artwork for the card titled *Promise Yourself* is used with written permission from Elizabeth Lucas Designs, P.O. Box 15276, Long Beach, CA 90815."

ORDER FORM

PEARCE PUBLISHERS, INC.
P.O. Box 4923
Timonium, MD 21094
toll free: 1-800-662-2354

Ship to:	Bill to: (if different than shipping)
Name	Name
Address	Address
City St. Zip	City St. Zip
Day Phone ( )	Day Phone ( )

Quantity	Title/Author	Price Each	Total Price
	Rhonda: The Woman in Me	$28.57	

Did you remember to ?

✓ Print your Name, Address, Zip code & phone #

✓ Enclose payment or charge account number

✓ Signature for charge order

Subtotal	
Sales Tax	
S & H	
Total	

Enclose your money order or personal check or fill in charge card information below.

☐ Money Order   ☐ Personal Check

☐ MasterCard   ☐ Visa

Exp. Date

Account #

Signature

Shipping Schedule
All orders shipped UPS.
No P.O. Boxes.
USA shipments only.

Cost	S & H
up to $30	$3.95
$31 - $90	$6.50
over $90	call

✉ **Mail order to:** Pearce Publishers, Inc.
P.O Box 4923, Timonium, MD 21094 ☎ 1-800-662-2354

tear here

ORDER FORM

PEARCE PUBLISHERS, INC.
P.O. Box 4923
Timonium, MD 21094
toll free: 1-800-662-2354

Ship to:	Bill to: (if different than shipping)
Name	Name
Address	Address
City St. Zip	City St. Zip
Day Phone ( )	Day Phone ( )

Quantity	Title/Author	Price Each	Total Price
	Rhonda: The Woman in Me	$28.57	

Did you remember to ?

Subtotal	
✓ Print your Name, Address, Zip code & phone # Sales Tax	
✓ Enclose payment or charge account number S & H	
✓ Signature for charge order Total	

Enclose your money order or personal check or fill in charge card information below.

☐ Money Order   ☐ Personal Check

☐ MasterCard   ☐ Visa

Exp. Date

Account #

Signature

Shipping Schedule
All orders shipped UPS.
No P.O. Boxes.
USA shipments only.

Cost	S & H
up to $30	$3.95
$31 - $90	$6.50
over $90	call

✉ **Mail order to:** Pearce Publishers, Inc.
P.O Box 4923, Timonium, MD 21094 ☎ 1-800-662-2354

tear here